WEST COAST

the
Okanagan
Valley 156

Lake
Tahoe
116

Napa
Valley
100

Sacramento
110

SAN FRANCISCO
84

Santa
Cruz 74

Carmel 70

BIG SUR 64

Mammoth
lakes 58

Death
Valley
52

Santa Barbara 38

Palm Springs
48

LOS ANGELES 10

San Diego 44

The New York Times

36

HOURS

EDITED BY BARBARA IRELAND

The New York Times

36
HOURS
USA & CANADA
WEST COAST

TASCHEN

Contents

Foreword

This book is for curious travelers with weekends to spend and the Pacific Ocean on their horizon. Adapted from the weekly 36 Hours column in The New York Times, it lays out 38 Friday-to-Sunday trips in the Pacific coast regions of the United States and Canada, from Alaska and British Columbia to the Hawaiian Islands. Each of these itineraries makes the most of just a weekend, bringing what otherwise might be a daunting destination down to an embraceable two-night size.

What will it be? A city experience? Try Los Angeles, the megacity with splashy shopping and night life, hidden walking trails, and surprising under-the-radar restaurants. And it's only a hop to movie-mad Hollywood, the sprawling gardens of Pasadena, celebrity turf in Malibu, and the egalitarian, palm-lined beach at Santa Monica. Or you might try Seattle, where salmon is on the menu, outdoorsy spirit is in the air, and repurposed buildings burst with Pacific Rim-influenced restaurants, contemporary art galleries, and quirky shops.

For urban sophistication in a breathtaking setting of saltwater bayside and hills, spend your weekend in San Francisco or Vancouver. Or for a tropical redefinition of a cityscape, fly out across the Pacific to Honolulu, where you can find Waikiki Beach at the end of the street.

Inland and away from the famed big cities, there's much more: skiing at Mammoth Lakes or Whistler; hauntingly beautiful desert at Death Valley; gold-rush history and riverside biking in Sacramento; wine-touring in the Napa, Sonoma, and Okanagan valleys.

The Pacific states are justly famous, too, for astonishing natural splendor. Surf breaks against majestic cliffs and rocks at Big Sur and on the Oregon Coast. The Sierras tower over the clear alpine Lake Tahoe, and Mount Hood looms over Portland. Volcanoes spit out lava on the Big Island of Hawaii, and the ice of the Mendenhall Glacier creeps down toward Juneau.

Everywhere, there's plenty to do. You can relax on a beach or bask in a spa, hike to a redwood grove, watch for whales, jog to the Golden Gate Bridge. You might tour a museum designed by a world-famous architect or see a first-class performance in a theater or concert hall. Sample the food: Hawaiian mahi-mahi, Alaskan halibut, Julia Child's favorite Santa Barbara tacos.

The 36 Hours column in The New York Times, the travel feature that gave birth to this book, has been inspiring trips, wish lists, and clip-and-saves for more than a decade. Created as a guide to that staple of crammed 21st-century schedules, the weekend getaway, 36 Hours guides readers to an experience that both identifies the high points of the destination and teases out its particular character. From the beginning, it has been a hit with readers.

In late 2011, The New York Times and TASCHEN published The New York Times 36 Hours: 150 Weekends in the U.S.A. & Canada, which gathered together 150 North American 36 Hours itineraries in one volume. In 2012, the decision was made to offer this trove of travel guidance in another format: as five regional books, each easily portable and specifically focused, to meet the needs of a traveler who wants to concentrate on one area of North America at a time. This book is one of the five; the others are devoted to the Northeast, the Midwest and Great Lakes, the Southeast, and the Southwest and Rocky Mountains.

The work of hundreds of writers, photographers, graphic artists, designers, and editors, combining their creativity over many years, has gone into 36 Hours and into this book. In their different ways and with their disparate contributions, all of these talented people invite you now to explore the beauty, variety, and adventure to be found near the Pacific coasts, one weekend at a time.

PAGE 2 Alexander Calder's red steel *Eagle*, at the Olympic Sculpture Park, upstages Seattle's iconic Space Needle.

PAGE 4 Ready for ballooning in the Napa Valley.

OPPOSITE Kachemak Bay in Homer, Alaska.

— BARBARA IRELAND, EDITOR

Tips for Using This Book

Plotting the Course: Travelers don't make their way through a region or a country alphabetically, and this book doesn't proceed that way, either. It begins in a major city emblematic of the region and winds from place to place the way a touring adventurer on a car trip might. An alphabetical index appears at the end of the book.

On the Ground: Every *36 Hours* follows a workable numbered itinerary, which is both outlined in the text and shown with corresponding numbers on a detailed destination map. The itinerary is practical: it really is possible to get from one place to the next easily and in the allotted time, although of course many travelers will prefer to take things at their own pace and perhaps take some of their own detours. Astute readers will notice that the "36" in *36 Hours* is elastic, and the traveler's agenda probably will be, too.

The Not So Obvious: The itineraries do not all follow exactly the same pattern. A restaurant for Saturday breakfast may or may not be recommended; after-dinner night life may be included or may not. The destination dictates, and so, to some extent, does the personality of the author who researched and wrote the article. In large cities, where it is impossible to see everything in a weekend, the emphasis is on the less expected discovery over the big, highly promoted attraction that is already well known.

Seasons: The time of year to visit is left up to the traveler, but in general, the big cities are good anytime; towns where snow falls are usually best visited in warm months, unless they are ski destinations; and summer heat is more or less endurable depending on the traveler's own tolerance. The most tourist-oriented areas are often seasonal—some of the sites featured in vacation towns may be closed out of season.

Your Own Agenda: This book is not a conventional guidebook. A *36 Hours* is meant to give a well-informed inside view of each place it covers, a selective summary that lets the traveler get to the heart of things in minimal time. Travelers who have more days to spend may want to use a *36 Hours* as a kind of nugget, supplementing it with the more comprehensive information available on bookstore shelves or on the locally sponsored Internet sites where towns and regions offer exhaustive lists of their attractions. Or, two or three of these itineraries can easily be strung together to make up a longer trip.

Updates: While all the stories in this volume were updated and fact-checked for publication in fall 2011, it is inevitable that some of the featured businesses and destinations will change in time. If you spot any errors in your travels, please feel free to send corrections or updates via email to 36hoursamerica@taschen.com. Please include "36 Hours Correction" and the page number in the subject line of your email to assure that it gets to the right person for future updates.

OPPOSITE The Kapuaiwa Coconut Grove in Molokai, Hawaii, planted in the 1860s by King Kamehameha V.

THE BASICS	PRICES	Restaurants, dinner without wine:
		Budget, under $15: $
A brief informational box for the destination, called "The Basics," appears with each *36 Hours* article in this book. The box provides some orientation on transportation for that location, including whether a traveler arriving by plane should rent a car to follow the itinerary. "The Basics" also recommends three reliable hotels or other lodgings.	Since hotel and restaurant prices change quickly, this book uses a system of symbols, based on 2011 United States dollars.	Moderate, $16 to $24: $$
		Expensive, $25 to $49: $$$
		Very Expensive, $50 and up: $$$$
	Hotel room, standard double:	**Restaurants, full breakfast,**
	Budget, under $100 per night: $	**or lunch entree:**
	Moderate, $100 to $199: $$	Budget, under $8: $
	Expensive, $200 to $299: $$$	Moderate, $8 to $14: $$
	Luxury, $300 and above: $$$$	Expensive, $15 to $24: $$$
		Very Expensive, $25 and up: $$$$

Los Angeles

Angelenos like to challenge visitors by quipping, "It's a great place to live but I wouldn't want to visit here." Granted, it's tough to decide what to see and do in a city that encompasses 470 square miles. Fortunately, there is always an under-the-radar restaurant, a funky theater, or a splashy store to discover. And you never have to leave the iconic landmarks behind.
— BY LOUISE TUTELIAN

FRIDAY

1 *Stop and Shop* 4 p.m.

The hilly Los Feliz area, just northeast of Hollywood, is an old neighborhood reborn with a hip veneer. A walk along North Vermont Avenue turns up an intriguing trove of vintage clothes, handmade jewelry, antique textiles, books, and much more. **New High (M)Art** (1720 North Vermont Avenue; 323-638-0271; newhighmart.com), an industrial-style space filled with world music and the faint perfume of incense, stocks an eclectic mix. For sale one afternoon were a vintage French army camo jacket and a necklace made from hand-painted leather flags. **Skylight Books** (1818 North Vermont Avenue; 323-660-1175; skylightbooks.com) caters to the many artists, writers, musicians, and actors in the neighborhood — and anyone else who loves a carefully curated arts bookstore. Browse the stacks and you'll see a monograph on Richard Meier next to a tome on *Mad* magazine posters. And don't step on Franny, the resident cat.

2 *Friendly Fare* 6 p.m.

Little Dom's (2128 Hillhurst Avenue; 323-661-0055; littledoms.com; $$-$$$) is the best of homey and hip, a bar/bistro with an inventive menu. The fare is mostly Italian-American, but since executive chef Brandon Boudet hails from New Orleans, there's a dash of the South as well. Pappardelle with house-made sausage? No problem. But Boudet also serves up a succulent fried oyster sandwich with hot sauce mayo, y'all.

OPPOSITE For a lovely walk in west Los Angeles that visitors hardly ever take, stroll among the Venice canals.

RIGHT At the Griffith Park Observatory, stargazers line up for a peek at celestial sights like the rings of Saturn.

3 *Bright Lights, Big City* 8 p.m.

Get the big picture at the **Griffith Park Observatory** (2800 East Observatory Avenue; 213-473-0800; griffithobservatory.org), with its view of the entire Los Angeles basin. Visitors line up for a peek into a massive Zeiss telescope with a 12-inch reflector that reveals celestial sights like the rings of Saturn. The Samuel Oschin Planetarium shows employ laser digital projection and state-of-the-art sound. A show about the brilliant aurora borealis — accompanied by Wagner's *Ride of the Valkyries* — is a cosmic experience.

4 *Alive and Swingin'* 10 p.m.

Featured in the movie *Swingers*, with Vince Vaughn and Jon Favreau, the **Dresden** (1760 North Vermont Avenue; 323-665-4294; thedresden.com/lounge.html) is a welcome throwback to an earlier era, with its upscale 1960s rec room décor and stellar bartenders. You're here to see Marty and Elayne, jazz musicians who also perform pop, standards, and the occasional show tune, with a changing array of guest artists, on Friday and Saturday nights in the lounge. The crowd is a cocktail shaker of twenty-somethings on dates, middle-aged couples with friends, and college kids. Somehow, it all goes down very smoothly.

SATURDAY

5 *From Canyon to Canyon* 10 a.m.

Joni Mitchell doesn't live here anymore, but Laurel Canyon retains its '70s image as a

self-contained artistic enclave (albeit a more expensive one now). Its social hub is the **Canyon Country Store** (2108 Laurel Canyon Boulevard; 323-654-8091), a grocery/deli/liquor store marked by a flower power-style sign that pays homage to its hippie roots. Sip organic oak-roasted espresso at the Canyon Coffee Cart, buy a picnic lunch and head for the high road — Mulholland Drive. The serpentine road follows the ridgeline of the Santa Monica Mountains, and every curve delivers a spectacular vista of the San Fernando Valley and beyond. Drop down into **Franklin Canyon Park** (2600 Franklin Canyon Drive;

310-858-7272; lamountains.com/parks), 605 acres of chaparral, grasslands, and oak woodlands with miles of hiking grounds. Heavenly Pond is a particularly appealing picnic spot.

6 *The Hills of Beverly* 1 p.m.
    The stores range from Gap to Gucci, but you don't need deep pockets to enjoy Beverly Hills. **Prada** (343 North Rodeo Drive; 310-278-8661), designed by Rem Koolhaas, delivers a jolt of architectural electricity. The 50-foot entrance is wide open to the street, with no door (and no name, either). A staircase peopled with mannequins ascends mysteriously. On the top level, faux security scanners double as video monitors and luggage-carousel-style shelves hold merchandise. At the **Paley Center for Media** (465 North Beverly Drive; 310-786-1091; paleycenter.org/visit-visitla), enter your own private TVland. At the center's library, anyone can screen segments of classic TV and radio shows, from *The Three Stooges* to *Seinfeld* as well as documentaries and specials. When it's time to cool your heels, head for the **Beverly Canon**

ABOVE Skylight Books in Los Feliz, just northeast of Hollywood, caters to writers, artists, musicians, and actors.

LEFT The crowd at the Dresden, where Marty and Elayne perform on weekends, is a cocktail shaker of 20-somethings on dates, clumps of middle-aged friends, and college kids.

Gardens (241 North Canon Drive), a public park masquerading as a private Italian-style garden. Adjacent to the Montage Hotel, the Gardens have plenty of benches, tables, and chairs, and a large Baroque fountain adding a splashing soundtrack.

7 *Full Exposure* 4 p.m.

The incongruous setting of corporate high-rises is home to the under-appreciated **Annenberg Space for Photography** (2000 Avenue of the Stars; 310-403-3000; annenbergspaceforphotography.org), an oasis of images. One enthralling group show was by nature photographers shooting under Arctic oceans, on a volcano, and deep within Florida swamps. Another featured photographs by Herb Ritts, Mary Ellen Mark, Chuck Close, and other documentarians of beauty and style. The space itself is open and airy, with an iris-like design on the ceiling to represent the aperture of a lens.

8 *Unleashed* 6 p.m.

Don't knock it till you've tried it. Only a restaurant unequivocally named **Animal** (435 North Fairfax Avenue; 323-782-9225; animalrestaurant.com; $$-$$$) can sell diners on dishes like pig ear with chili, lime, and a fried egg, or rabbit legs with mustard and bacon. Or something else if inspiration strikes: the menu doesn't get printed until a half-hour before opening. The place is nondescript with no name on the storefront (it's four doors up from Canter's Deli), but once you've tried the fat pork-belly sliders with crunchy slaw on a buttery brioche bun, you'll beat a path there again.

9 *The Silent Treatment* 8 p.m.

Dedicated to finding, screening, and conserving unusual films (can you say, *"Killer Klowns from Outer Space"*?), the 120-seat **Silent Movie Theater** (611 North Fairfax Avenue; 434-655-2510; cinefamily.org) is like a quirky film class held in a club. Where else can you claim a well-worn couch and pour a cocktail from a punch bowl while waiting for show time? Insider tip: Regulars bring their own bottles of wine.

SUNDAY

10 *Breakfast by the Beach* 10 a.m.

Berries and Brussels sprouts abound at the **Santa Monica Farmer's Market** (2640 Main Street; Santa Monica; 310-458-8712; smgov.net) but there are also 10 stands where local restaurateurs sell dishes prepared on the spot. Among the best are Arcadie's sweet or savory crepes, Carbon Grill's hefty burritos, and the Victorian's custom omelets.

ABOVE Basking poolside at the eco-chic Palomar boutique hotel on Wilshire Boulevard, near the University of California at Los Angeles.

A live band might be playing any genre from jazz to zydeco. Finish up with a scone from the Rockenwagner bakery stand and munch it on the beach, only a block away.

11 *Secret Gardens* 1 p.m.

One of the loveliest walks in west Los Angeles is one visitors hardly ever take: a stroll among the **Venice canals**. The developer Abbott Kinney dug miles of canals in 1905 to create his vision of a

Venice in America. The decades took their toll, but the remaining canals were drained and refurbished in 1993. The surrounding neighborhood is now on the National Register of Historic Places. Charming footpaths crisscross the canals as ducks splash underneath. On the banks, mansions stand next to small bungalows. Residents pull kayaks and canoes up to their homes. It's quiet, serene, and hidden. Hollywood? Where's that?

ABOVE Spindly palms and an evening sky in Los Feliz.

OPPOSITE Within its expanse of 470 square miles, Los Angeles has room for places that can feel remote, like this trail in the Santa Monica Mountains.

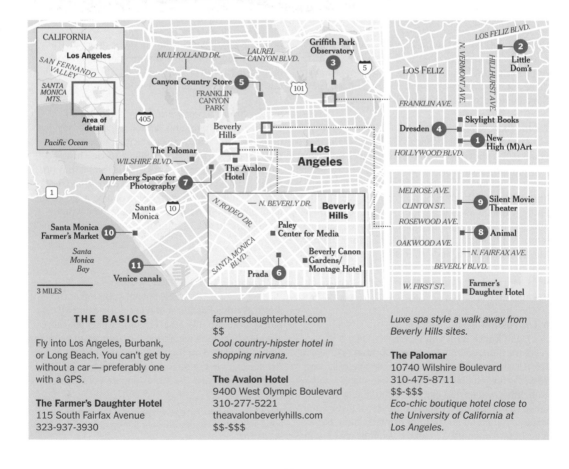

THE BASICS

Fly into Los Angeles, Burbank, or Long Beach. You can't get by without a car — preferably one with a GPS.

The Farmer's Daughter Hotel
115 South Fairfax Avenue
323-937-3930

farmersdaughterhotel.com
$$
Cool country-hipster hotel in shopping nirvana.

The Avalon Hotel
9400 West Olympic Boulevard
310-277-5221
theavalonbeverlyhills.com
$$-$$$

Luxe spa style a walk away from Beverly Hills sites.

The Palomar
10740 Wilshire Boulevard
310-475-8711
$$-$$$
Eco-chic boutique hotel close to the University of California at Los Angeles.

Downtown Los Angeles

The sprawl, the scale, all that freeway time—for many, Los Angeles is an acquired taste. But not downtown. New York-like in its density and mishmash, the long-blighted center has become an accessible, pedestrian-friendly destination in recent years; Angelenos walk around en masse, using their actual legs. The immense L.A. Live entertainment complex is largely responsible for this comeback, but the studiously vintage bars and imaginative restaurants that seem to open every other day are also part of the revival. Skid Row and the drifts of homeless camps haven't vanished altogether, and the grittiness still varies by block. But this part of town is alive again, in ways that make sense even to an outsider.
— BY CHRIS COLIN

FRIDAY

1 *Do the Crawl* 4 p.m.

The Downtown Art Walk — a party-in-the-streets bonanza that draws thousands of revelers the second Thursday of every month — is one way to experience the area's robust art scene. But you can do your own art walk anytime, and you should. Lured by low rents, a number of impressive galleries have found a home here, many of them on Chung King Road, a pedestrian alley strung with lanterns in Chinatown. For starters: **The Box** (No. 977; 213-625-1747; theboxla.com), **Jancar Gallery** (No. 961; 213-625-2522; jancargallery.com), **Charlie James Gallery** (975 Chung King Road; 213-687-0844; cjamesgallery.com), and **Sabina Lee Gallery**

(No. 971; 213-620-9404; sabinaleegallery.com). The shows are intimate and occasionally provocative, featuring a broad array of contemporary artists: William Powhida, Orly Cogan, and others. Most galleries stay open till 6 p.m.; Jancar closes at 5 on Fridays.

2 *The City at Its Brightest* 7:30 p.m.

Whether you're catching a Lakers game, touring the Grammy Museum, or attending a concert at the Nokia Theater, there is always something splashy to do at the 27-acre, $2.5 billion sports and entertainment behemoth that is **L.A. Live** (800 West Olympic Boulevard; 213-763-5483; lalive.com). Just strolling the Tokyo-ish Nokia Plaza — 20,000 square feet of LED signage — is diverting. An array of restaurants and bars is clustered at the periphery, but many visitors prefer just to stroll around this giant pedestrian zone, trying to take it all in.

3 *A Late, Great Bite* 10 p.m.

The Gorbals (501 South Spring Street; 213-488-3408; thegorbalsla.com; $$) is one of the more fantastic — and odd — downtown dining options. The chef and owner, a previous *Top Chef* winner, is part Scottish and part Israeli, and his hybrid concoctions are terrific. On one visit, banh mi poutine merged Quebec and Vietnam in ways criminally neglected until now. Bacon-wrapped matzo balls, anyone? The restaurant is tucked into the lobby of the old Alexandria Hotel, a well-worn but charming landmark where Bogart, Chaplin, and Garbo once roamed the halls.

SATURDAY

4 *On the Nickel* 9 a.m.

The maple bacon doughnut is a stand-out on the breakfast menu at the new but ageless **Nickel Diner** (524 South Main Street; 213-623-8301; nickeldiner.com; $). The rest is mostly well-executed diner food. What's

OPPOSITE Broadway in downtown Los Angeles, a pedestrian-friendly destination rebounding from 20th-century decline.

LEFT Fabric in the Fashion District, a 100-block mix of wholesale-only shops and designer retail discounts.

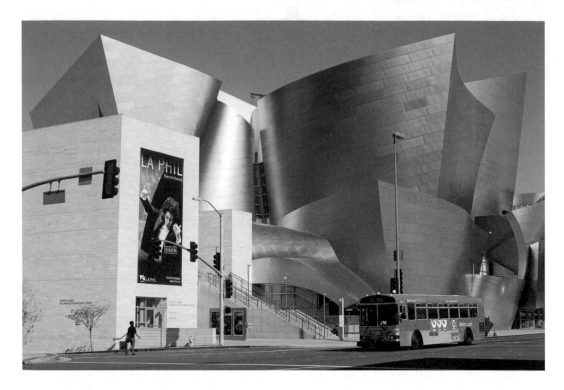

remarkable is the location—until recently, this block was one of Skid Row's most notorious. It's a testament to downtown's revival that the intersection of Main and Fifth (hence "Nickel") is now home to a place where people line up for tables.

5 *Nice Threads* 10:30 a.m.

The 100-block **Fashion District** mixes high and low seamlessly. Though many shops sell wholesale only, you can still find a wide selection of deeply discounted designer clothes, fabric, and accessories. The jumbled shops and warehouses at Ninth and Los Angeles Streets are a good place to start (feel free to bargain). And don't miss the rowdier **Santee Alley** (thesanteealley.com), where cheap meets weird in a thoroughly Los Angeles way. In this chaotic open-air bazaar, energetic vendors hawk the impressive (perfect knock-off handbags) and the odd (toy frogs emblazoned with gang insignias). For a more organized Fashion District expedition, Christine

ABOVE Find the outdoor stairway on Frank Gehry's Walt Disney Concert Hall and climb its curves to a rooftop garden.

OPPOSITE ABOVE Drinks at Seven Grand, one of the retro bars inspired by downtown's colorful history.

OPPOSITE BELOW The Nickel Diner, a busy spot in a revived area that not so long ago was part of Skid Row.

Silvestri of Urban Shopping Adventures (213-683-9715; urbanshoppingadventures.com) leads three-hour romps, tailored to your particular agenda and with an insider's radar for the best finds. The tours cost $36 a person, with a minimum of two people.

6 *Accessible Architecture* 1 p.m.

The arrival of the conductor Gustavo Dudamel at the Los Angeles Philharmonic has brought new crowds to the symphony, but the **Walt Disney Concert Hall** (111 South Grand Avenue; 323-850-2000; laphil.com) —Frank Gehry's deconstructivist celebration of all that is big, curvy, and shiny—deserves a visit even without a ticket. Bring a picnic and wind your way along the semi-hidden outer staircase up to an excellent city vista and rooftop garden oasis. Free guided tours and self-guided audio tours are available most days. Check first (musiccenter.org/visit/tours.html) for schedules.

7 *Lazy Bones* 7 p.m.

Since 2010, **Lazy Ox Canteen** (241 South San Pedro Street; 213-626-5299; lazyoxcanteen.com; $$-$$$) in Little Tokyo has been the kind of tucked-away gastropub people love to insist is the city's best. Casual and buzzing, the bistro has a long menu featuring adventurous delicacies, from trotters to crispy pigs' ears to lamb neck hash. It's hard to pin the cuisine to a specific origin, but a penchant for bold, meat-centric comfort food is evident. Get several small plates.

8 *Pick a Show, Any Show* 8:30 p.m.

If you're downtown for a performance, chances are it's a sprawling affair at L.A. Live. But a handful of smaller settings offer funkier alternatives. The **Redcat Theater** (631 West Second Street; 213-237-2800; redcat.org) plays host to all manner of experimental performances — one Saturday in winter featured theater, dance, puppetry, and live music from a Slovene-Latvian art collaboration. **Club Mayan** (1038 South Hill Street; 213-746-4287; clubmayan.com), an ornate old dance club most nights, occasionally hosts mad events like Lucha VaVoom, which combines burlesque and Mexican wrestling. And the **Smell** (247 South Main Street; thesmell.org), a likably grimy, volunteer-run space, hosts very small bands circled by swaying teenagers.

9 *Drink as if It's Illegal* 10:30 p.m.

Was Los Angeles a hoot during Prohibition? No need to guess, thanks to a slew of meticulously old-timey new bars that exploit the wonderful history of old Los Angeles. From upscale speakeasy (the **Varnish**; 118 East Sixth Street; 213-622-9999; thevarnishbar.com) to converted power plant-chic (the **Edison**; 108 West Second Street; 213-613-0000; edisondowntown.com) to an old bank vault (the **Crocker Club**; 453 South Spring Street; 213-239-9099; crockerclub.com), these spiffy places do set decoration as only Los Angeles can. And fussily delicious artisanal cocktails are as plentiful as you'd imagine. The well-scrubbed will also enjoy the swanky **Seven Grand** (515 West Seventh Street; 213-614-0737; sevengrand.la), while the well-scuffed may feel more at home at **La Cita Bar** (336 South Hill Street; 213-687-7111; lacitabar.com).

SUNDAY

10 *Diamond in the Rough* 9 a.m.

The **Bamboo Plaza** isn't as elegant as its name, but on the second floor of this run-down little Chinatown mall is the **Empress Pavilion** (988 North Hill Street,

ABOVE If an art piece is much older than the first baby boomer, you're not likely to find it in the Museum of Contemporary Art, which is rich in works by Rothko, Oldenburg, Lichtenstein, and Rauschenberg.

OPPOSITE Skyscrapers aglow in the downtown heart of sprawling Los Angeles.

suite 201; 213-617-9898; empresspavilion.com; $$), a dim sum mecca that's lured Angelenos since well before the downtown revival. The vast dining room holds all the appeal of a hotel conference room, but that only underscores the focus on the shrimp har gow, the pork buns, and dozens of other specialties. There will be crowds.

11 *Big Art* 11 a.m.

That rare breed who has gone from gallery owner to director of a significant art institution, Jeffrey Deitch has thrilled (and vexed) critics since taking over the esteemed **Museum of Contemporary Art**. Come see for yourself what he's done with the place, and its renowned collection, including works by Rothko, Oldenburg, Lichtenstein, and Rauschenberg. The museum is spread over three locations; downtown is the main one (250 South Grand Avenue; 213-626-6222; moca.org).

THE BASICS

Flights to Los Angeles are easy to book from anywhere. Walking works better than it used to, but you may still want a car.

Ritz-Carlton
900 West Olympic Boulevard
213-743-8800
lalive.com/stay/ritzcarlton
$$$$
Half of a gleaming new two-hotel complex rising above L.A. Live.

JW Marriott
900 West Olympic Boulevard
213-765-8600
lalive.com/stay/jwmarriott
$$
The other half of the same hotel complex.

Figueroa Hotel
939 South Figueroa Street
213-627-8971
figueroahotel.com
$$
Moroccan-themed.

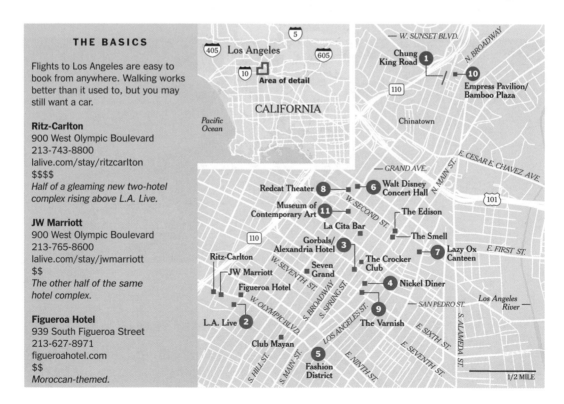

Hollywood

Hollywood is one of those rare places that live up to their stereotypes, right down to the sign. But with minimal effort, it can offer a whole lot more. This pedestrian-friendly district represents both Los Angeles's past, with icons like the Capitol Records building, and the city's future — multi-ethnic, vertical, dense. A recent renaissance means there are now million-dollar condos, trendy restaurants, celebrity watering holes, and a world-class movie theater. But there are still tattoo parlors, sex shops, and homelessness. Tying it all together is the Hollywood Walk of Fame, where it is hard not to be at least momentarily tickled (Hello, Mister Rogers) or merely confused (Who the heck was that?). It remains a place that only Los Angeles could produce.

— BY JENNIFER STEINHAUER

FRIDAY

1 *Costume Change* 4 p.m.

Before you unpack your bags, prepare to fill them up. Hollywood is awash in vintage clothing stores, many of them filled with remnants from television and movie sets past. **Golyester** (136 South La Brea Avenue; 323-931-1339) has amazingly preserved purses, negligees ($278 was the price for one two-piece Christian Dior number), evening gowns (including, on one visit, a white leather dress with fur trim) and more. Of special interest are the shoes — finds like gold sling-backs, emerald stilettos, or elegant Herbert Levine pumps. Down the street is **The Way We Wore** (334 South La Brea Avenue; 323-937-0878; thewaywewore.com) with more vintage treasures. Between them is **Cafe Midi** (148 South La Brea Avenue; 323-939-9860; cafemidi.com), where you can have a cappuccino and take in the Moroccan ceramic bowls and candles in the adjacent store.

2 *Planet Thai* 7:30 p.m.

There are upscale bistros and giant tuna rolls aplenty in the neighborhood, but Los Angelenos love Hollywood for Thai food. Reasonable minds can quibble over the best, which tends to be high on authentic flair, low on atmosphere, and budget-priced. Good examples are the **Sapp Coffee Shop** (5183 Hollywood Boulevard; 323-665-1035) and **Ruen Pair** (5257 Hollywood Boulevard; 323-466-0153). For a slightly more upscale ambience, check out **Bulan Thai Vegetarian Kitchen** (7168 Melrose Avenue; 323-857-1882; bulanthai.com), a chic spot that's hot with the yoga crowd. Look for menu items like busabu pumpkin, jungle curry, and tum kha.

3 *The New Rat Pack* 10 p.m.

O.K., it might feel like you're traipsing through a cliché, but check out **Teddy's** (7000 Hollywood Boulevard; 323-466-7000; hollywoodroosevelt.com) anyway. Located inside the Hollywood Roosevelt Hotel, the lounge long had a reputation for being as loud and exclusive as possible. These days it has a slightly more diplomatic, if not exactly proletarian, door policy. Celebrity sightings are still common, and the slightly sinister look of the place makes for good sipping.

SATURDAY

4 *Is That TomKat?* 8:30 a.m.

Los Angeles is a morning town, so get going at **Square One Dining** (4854 Fountain Avenue; 323-661-1109; squareonedining.com; $$), a cheerful local spot that focuses on farmers' market produce. Order some French toast with banana citrus caramel or the transporting pressed egg sandwich with tomato

OPPOSITE Amoeba Music on Sunset Boulevard, where new and used CDs and DVDs are found by the mile and you might catch a live performance.

BELOW Across the city to the Hollywood sign.

and arugula. Stare at the Scientology headquarters across the street, among the more relevant fixtures in Hollywood, and try and see who is going in and coming out of its parking structure.

5 *Open House* 11 a.m.

Many a native Angeleno knows not of **Barnsdall Art Park** (4800 Hollywood Boulevard; 323-644-6269; barnsdallartpark.com), a public space donated to the city by the eccentric Aline Barnsdall in 1927. Beyond having one of the best views of the Hollywood sign and grass upon which to sit (a rare thing in Los Angeles), the site is home to the **Los Angeles Municipal Art Gallery**, a theater, and the **Hollyhock House** (323-644-6269; hollyhockhouse.net), Frank Lloyd Wright's first Los Angeles project. Tours of the house begin at 12:30 p.m. Wednesday through Sunday.

6 *Food (and Music) for the Soul* 2 p.m.

You thought you went to Hollywood to eat raw food? That's West Hollywood. Before your afternoon walking tour, load up on carbs at **Roscoe's House of Chicken and Waffles** (1514 North Gower Street; 323-466-7453; roscoeschickenandwaffles.com; $-$$). The beloved soul food chain is known for its half chicken smothered with gravy and served with two waffles. From Roscoe's, it's a fast walk to **Amoeba Records** (6400 Sunset Boulevard; 323-245-6400; amoeba.com), one of the last great independent record stores in the country, where new and used CDs and DVDs are found by the mile. There are also live in-store performances (with a special emphasis on up-and-coming Los Angeles bands).

7 *High-Tech Movie* 5 p.m.

Keep walking. Now you are headed to the **ArcLight Cinema** (6360 West Sunset Boulevard; 323-464-1478; arclightcinemas.com), which has one of the best projection and sound systems in the country, plus comfy chairs. Catch the latest popcorn flick, obscure retrospective, or independent picture with every serious cinema buff in town.

8 *Peru in Hollywood* 8 p.m.

Turn the corner on North Vine, and end up in a tiny spot where the spare décor is made up of small replicas of Lima's famous balcones, or balconies. Known for its ceviches, **Los Balcones del Peru** (1360 North Vine Street; 323-871-9600; $) is a charming restaurant, next to a psychic and across from a KFC, where families, couples, and guys who prefer a place on one of the tiger-patterned bar stools all feed. Start with chicha morada (a fruit drink made with corn water), then hit the lomo saltado, or beef sautéed with onions, or tacu tacu con mariscos, which is refried Peruvian beans with shrimp.

9 *Dark Nights* 11 p.m.

End the evening at the **Woods** (1533 North La Brea Avenue; 323-876-6612; vintagebargroup.com/thewoods.html), which, as the name implies, has an outdoorsy theme. The sleek bar has lots of cedar and elk antler chandeliers hanging from the star-encrusted ceiling. As you scope out the young crowd and peruse the juke box, have one of the signature mint juleps or a seasonal drink like the pumpkin pie shot.

SUNDAY

10 *Celebrity Dog Walkers* 9:30 a.m.

Two blocks north of Hollywood Boulevard is one of the most scenic, unusual urban parks in the country, **Runyon Canyon**. The 130-acre park offers steep, invigorating hikes with views of the San Fernando Valley, the Pacific, Catalina Island (on clear days), and the Griffith Observatory. The area

is popular with dog owners (including celebrities), who take advantage of the leash-free policy. Mixed in among the wild chaparral are the crumbling estates of Carman Runyon, a coal magnate who used the property for hunting, and George Huntington Hartford II, heir to the A&P fortune. Parking can be tricky, so enter from the north, off Mulholland. You'll find a parking lot and start the hike going downhill.

11 *Walk This Way* Noon

You can't leave Hollywood without strolling down Hollywood Boulevard on the **Hollywood Walk of Fame** (hollywoodchamber.net). Take in the hundreds of stars embedded in the sidewalks, just to see how many you recognize. While so doing, stop at **Lucky Devil's** (6613 Hollywood Boulevard;

323-465-8259; luckydevils-la.com) for a caramel pecan sundae waffle. It will make you remember Hollywood with fondness.

OPPOSITE ABOVE The retro exterior of the Cinerama Dome at the ArcLight Cinema complex, built in 1963.

OPPOSITE BELOW Between shows at the ArcLight Cinema.

ABOVE Roscoe's House of Chicken and Waffles keeps its soul-food promise: gravy and waffles come with the chicken.

THE BASICS

Fly into Los Angeles, Long Beach, Ontario, or Burbank.

You can get by without a car.

The Hollywood Roosevelt
7000 Hollywood Boulevard
800-950-7667
hollywoodroosevelt.com
$$$
Can be loud, but historic as a favorite of stars in Hollywood's early days. All the night life you'll ever want.

Hollywood Hills Hotel
1999 North Sycamore Avenue
323-874-5089
hollywoodhillshotel.com
$$
A neighborhood bargain.

The Redbury @ Hollywood and Vine
1717 Vine Street
323-962-1717
theredbury.com
$$$-$$$$
Chic new boutique hotel at a famous corner.

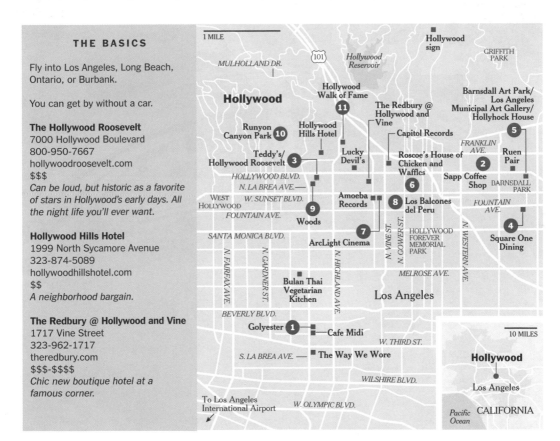

Pasadena

Nestled in the San Gabriel Valley just 10 miles northeast of Los Angeles, Pasadena harbors a distinct, if at times chauvinistic, sense of individual self. Its old-money past continues to flourish in the form of grand mansions and a vast array of museums and gardens, many underwritten by prominent local families. And newer money has helped transform Old Pasadena, in decline for many years, into an energetic shopping and dining destination, with quirky shops and new restaurants. But it is the expansive outdoors, mountain views, and fine climate (except in August, when you could fry a hot dog at the Rose Bowl) that still make Pasadena, the famed City of Roses, a shining jewel of Southern California and an enduring object of jealousy. — BY JENNIFER STEINHAUER

FRIDAY

1 *Dream House* 3 p.m.

Real estate envy is an epidemic in Pasadena, and few homes are more desirable than the **Gamble House** (4 Westmoreland Place; 626-793-3334; gamblehouse.org). While the tour guides can reinforce a certain preciousness, there is no denying the allure of this Craftsman-style home, constructed in 1908 for David and Mary Gamble of the Procter & Gamble Company by the architects Charles Sumner Greene and Henry Mather Greene. To protect the floors, flat shoes are required for the tour, which lasts for an hour. But they'll give you a pair of slippers if you're wearing your Jimmy Choos.

2 *Rose Bowl* 4:30 p.m.

Well, you're here, so why not see where it all happens each winter? You can tool around the Rose Bowl grounds, jog, enjoy the gardens, and imagine you are a rose queen—or one of the many whose efforts add up to the 80,000 hours needed to put together the **Tournament of Roses** (391 South Orange Grove Boulevard; 626-449-4100; tournamentofroses.com).

3 *Burritoville* 6:30 p.m.

There's a depressing number of fast-food restaurants in town, serving the same grub found in any American mall. But one standout is **El Toreo Cafe** (21 South Fair Oaks Avenue; 626-793-2577; $), a hole-in-the-wall that serves terrific and inexpensive

Mexican food. Try the carnitas burritos and chile verde, with large helpings and authentic flair.

4 *Retail Hop* 8:30 p.m.

Many stores in Old Pasadena stay open late. Skip the chains-o-plenty and make your way down Colorado Boulevard, the central corridor, and its side streets. Among the finds: **Distant Lands Travel Bookstore and Outfitters** (20 South Raymond Avenue; 626-449-3220; distantlands.com), which sells travel paraphernalia like Africa maps and packing kits; **Elisa B.** (12 Douglas Alley; 626-792-4746; elisab.com), where the sales staff will get you out of your mom jeans; and **Lula Mae** (100 North Fair Oaks Avenue; 626-304-9996; lulamae.com) for candles and weird gifts like bride-and-groom maracas. End the evening by having some peanut butter or malaga gelato at **Tutti Gelati** (62 West Union Street; 626-440-9800; tuttigelati.com).

SATURDAY

5 *Morning Sweets* 9 a.m.

All good vacation days begin with hot chocolate, so follow the California Institute of Technology students to

OPPOSITE The Japanese garden at the Huntington Library, Art Collections, and Botanical Gardens.

BELOW Changing shoes outside the Rose Bowl.

Euro Pane (950 East Colorado Boulevard; 626-577-1828) and order a hot cup of the chocolaty goodness, along with fresh breads and flaky croissants, which are first-rate. A counter filled with children's books helps keep the young ones entertained.

6 *Fun Under the Sun* 10 a.m.

While children's museums often induce an instant throbbing in the temple — and an urge to reach for a hand sanitizer — a happy exception is **Kidspace Children's Museum** (480 North Arroyo Boulevard; 626-449-9144; kidspacemuseum.org), an active museum where adults can chill with a book under the sun while the kids ride tricycles, check out the dig site, and climb around the mini-model of the city's Arroyo Seco canyon, where it actually "rains" from time to time. The Splash Dance Fountain is a winner.

7 *Order the Obvious* 1 p.m.

No day in Pasadena should pass without a stop at **Pie 'n Burger** (913 East California Boulevard; 626-795-1123; pienburger.com; $), a local institution since 1963. Go ahead and have a chicken pot pie, which is beyond decent, or some pancakes if you're feeling all vegan about it, but honestly, the burger is the way to go. It is a juicy concoction served up in old-school paper liners, with the requisite Thousand Island dressing on the bun. Finish the whole thing

off with a sublime slice of banana cream or cherry pie. Just don't tarry — there are bound to be large groups of folks waiting to get their hands on burgers, too.

8 *Master Class* 3 p.m.

Even if you're feeling a bit tired, there is something oddly relaxing about the **Norton Simon Museum of Art** (411 West Colorado Boulevard; 626-449-6840; nortonsimon.org). There's Degas's *Little Dancer Aged 14*, Van Gogh's *Portrait of a Peasant*, Diego Rivera's *The Flower Vendor*. Natural light streams in from skylights, and a sensible layout makes this a pleasant place to while away the afternoon — not to mention examining the star collection of Western paintings and sculpture from the 14th to 20th centuries. Don't skip the South Asian art downstairs, especially the Buddha Shakyamuni, which sits majestically outdoors. The guided audio tours are quite good.

9 *Solid Italian* 7 p.m.

After a day of cultural and sun soaking, nestle into **Gale's Restaurant** (452 South Fair Oaks Avenue; 626-432-6705; galesrestaurant.com; $$$). A totally local spot, it offers remarkably solid fare just down the road from all the hubbub. Couples, families, and friends who seem to have just finished a day outdoors snuggle amid the brick walls and small wooden tables, drinking wine from slightly cheesy Brighton goblets. Start it off with some warm roasted olives or a steamed artichoke and then move on to the country-style Tuscan steak or caprese salad. For dessert skip the leaden cheesecake and go instead for the poppy seed cake, which is uncommonly tasty.

SUNDAY

10 *Garden Party* 10:30 a.m.

An entire day barely covers a corner of the **Huntington Library, Art Collections, and Botanical Gardens** (1151 Oxford Road, San Marino; 626-405-2100; huntington.org). There are 120 acres of gardens, an enormous library of rare manuscripts and books,

and three permanent art galleries featuring British and French artists of the 18th and 19th centuries. Here is a good plan for a morning: Take a quick run through the exhibit of American silver. Ooh and ahh. Then pick one of the gardens to tour. The Desert garden, with its bizarre-looking cactuses and lunarlike landscapes, is a winner, though the Japanese and Jungle gardens are close rivals. Top it off at the Children's garden, where interactive exhibits can get kids dirty, which pleases everyone but the one stuck changing all the wet shirts. Stay for tea; there's no dress code in the tea room.

OPPOSITE The Gamble House, designed by Charles Sumner Greene and Henry Mather Greene for members of a founding family of Procter & Gamble.

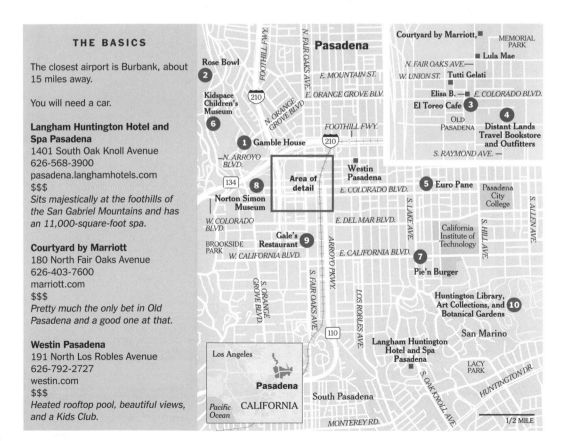

THE BASICS

The closest airport is Burbank, about 15 miles away.

You will need a car.

Langham Huntington Hotel and Spa Pasadena
1401 South Oak Knoll Avenue
626-568-3900
pasadena.langhamhotels.com
$$$
Sits majestically at the foothills of the San Gabriel Mountains and has an 11,000-square-foot spa.

Courtyard by Marriott
180 North Fair Oaks Avenue
626-403-7600
marriott.com
$$$
Pretty much the only bet in Old Pasadena and a good one at that.

Westin Pasadena
191 North Los Robles Avenue
626-792-2727
westin.com
$$$
Heated rooftop pool, beautiful views, and a Kids Club.

Santa Monica

When Los Angelenos think of the perfect beach town, they think of Santa Monica. With its classic amusement pier, glittering bay, and surfers bobbing on swells, it certainly looks the part. But take a short walk inland, and there's a town asserting its unique identity: eight square miles and about 100,000 people surrounded by districts of the City of Los Angeles, but stubbornly remaining a separate city. Within its borders, a well-preserved Mission-style bungalow sits around the corner from a steel performance space by Frank Gehry. Shops sell goods ranging from vintage Parisian wedding gowns to a whimsical map made entirely out of license plates. To make the most of your time here, enjoy the games and famed carousel of the Santa Monica Pier and then step back from the beach to sample the city's variety the way Santa Monicans themselves do.
— BY FRED A. BERNSTEIN AND LOUISE TUTELIAN

FRIDAY

1 First, the Beach 4 p.m.

For a sense of the setting that made Santa Monica, take a stroll in **Palisades Park** (Ocean Avenue at Santa Monica Boulevard; smgov.net/parks),

OPPOSITE Palisades Park, overlooking the Pacific Ocean.

BELOW The Isaac Milbank House, designed by the firm that did Grauman's Chinese Theater, is one of the Craftsman-style houses on Adelaide Drive designated as city landmarks.

an iconic strip of land with manicured lawns and swaying palm trees. Take in the sun and breeze, and wander off on one of the sinuous paths overlooking the beach and Santa Monica pier.

2 Oyster Shack 6 p.m.

You're at the sea, so why not enjoy all that it has to offer? The **Blue Plate Oysterette** (1355 Ocean Avenue; 310-576-3474; blueplatesantamonica.com; $$), one of the dozen or so Santa Monica restaurants that face the ocean, may be the most ocean-y, with its raw bar and daily specials like pan-seared rainbow trout. The casual blue-and-white restaurant, with a tin-pressed ceiling and blackboard menus, draws a chic, flip-flop-wearing crowd.

3 The View That Moves 8 p.m.

At sunset, the most thrilling view in town is at the beach, from the top of the solar-powered, 130-foot-high Pacific Wheel, the Ferris wheel at the **Santa Monica Pier**. Yes, it's touristy, and yes, it might be crowded, but it is, after all, the city's iconic symbol. As you glide upward, watching the entire city of Santa Monica, and far beyond, slide into view, the whole scene will be bathed in the sunset-colored glow. If you prefer a view that's not mobile, head south into Venice to the rooftop lounge of the **Hotel Erwin** (1697 Pacific Avenue; 310-452-1111; hotelerwin.com), where the banquettes seem to hang over the beach. Gaze at a Santa Monica panorama while sipping a pricey but interesting cocktail like the Venice Vixen, made with pear-flavored Grey Goose, St-Germain elderflower liqueur, and Graham Beck sparkling rosé. You can reserve a table through the hotel's Web site.

SATURDAY

4 Duck for Breakfast 8 a.m.

The lines spill out the door, so arrive early at **Huckleberry Bakery and Café** (1014 Wilshire Boulevard; 310-451-2311; huckleberrycafe.com; $$). Breakfast favorites include green eggs and ham, made with pesto and prosciutto, and duck hash with sunny-side-up eggs. The cheerful room — which feels like a large country bakery with pale wood tables and colorful accents — is tended by equally cheerful employees.

5 *Into the Mountains* 9 a.m.

The Backbone Trail, a 69-mile system, roughly follows the crest of the Santa Monica Mountains north from **Will Rogers State Historic Park** just north of Santa Monica (1501 Will Rogers State Park Road, off West Sunset Boulevard, Pacific Palisades; 310-454-8212; nps.gov/samo/planyourvisit/backbonetrail.htm). Hikers can take an easy, sage-scented, two-mile loop from the parking lot at Will Rogers up to Inspiration Point, a sensational overlook of Santa Monica Bay from the Palos Verdes Peninsula to Point Dume in Malibu. Do it on a clear day, and you'll see Catalina Island and the white dots of sails. Behind are the slopes of the Santa Monica Mountains, and in the distance, the high-rises of downtown Los Angeles. Up here, the muted chattering of birds and the hum of insects are the only sounds.

6 *Builders and Shoppers* Noon

Back in northern Santa Monica, natural sights give way to architectural ones. Two houses designated as city landmarks are the Craftsman-style **Isaac Milbank House** (236 Adelaide Drive) — designed by the same firm that did Grauman's Chinese Theater in Hollywood — and the stucco **Worrel House** (710 Adelaide Drive), which was built in the mid-1920s and has been described as a "Pueblo-Revival Maya fantasy." Some of the city's best shopping is nearby on Montana Avenue, known for upscale clothes, home décor, crafts, jewelry, and art. At **Every Picture Tells A Story** (No. 1333; 310-451-2700; everypicture.com), part children's bookstore and part gallery, the specialty is original works by the likes of Maurice Sendak and Dr. Seuss. **Rooms & Gardens** (No. 1311-A; 310-451-5154; roomsandgardens.com) sells furniture, antiques, and accessories like pillows fashioned from an antique Indian sari.

7 *Art at the Trolley Stop* 3 p.m.

The local art scene heated up in 2010 with the arrival of **L&M Arts**, Los Angeles (660 Venice Boulevard, Venice; 310-821-6400; lmgallery.com), a branch of the blue-chip New York gallery. Find its space in a former power station and check what's showing. From there, it's a short drive to **Bergamot Station** (2525 Michigan Avenue; 310-453-7535; bergamotstation.com), a complex of art galleries built on the site of a former trolley-line stop — hence its name. A highlight is the **Santa Monica Museum of Art** (310-586-6488; smmoa.org), a museum with rotating exhibits.

8 *Bistro Evenings* 8 p.m.

There are lots of stylish hotels in Santa Monica, and some of them offer very good food. Case in point is **Fig** (101 Wilshire Boulevard; 310-319-3111; figsantamonica.com; $$$), a contemporary American bistro at the Fairmont Miramar Hotel. The menu features seasonal ingredients and dishes like a halibut "chop" or snap peas with mint. There is seating indoors, in an elegant room with starburst mirrors, as well as on the terrace, with views of the ocean through the lush gardens. The huge Moreton Bay fig tree, from which the restaurant gets its name, will make you feel like climbing.

9 *Disco Nights* 11 p.m.

Santa Monica may be known for sunshine, but there's plenty to do after dark. For a taste of the local night life, head to **Zanzibar** (1301 Fifth Street; 310-451-2221; zanzibarlive.com), a cavernous club that manages to be both cozy and contemporary. It is also the rare venue that seems able to please young and old — you could imagine Joni Mitchell on the dance floor with her grandkids. The D.J.'s play a mix of hip-hop, R&B, and top 40. Even the décor has crossover appeal; hanging from the ceiling are perforated copper lanterns (for a vaguely African feeling) and disco balls.

SUNDAY

10 *No Wet Suit Needed* 10 a.m.

Even in warm weather, the waters of Southern California can be frigid. For a more comfortable swim, duck into the **Annenberg Community Beach House** (415 Pacific Coast Highway; 310-458-4904; annenbergbeachhouse.com), a sleek public facility that opened in 2010. The pool is spectacular, and

you can buy a day pass for a reasonable price. If it's the off-season, head to the public but country-club-stylish **Santa Monica Swim Center** (2225 16th Street; 310-458-8700; smgov.net/aquatics), where the adult and children's pools are kept at 79 and 85 degrees, respectively.

11 *Sunday Retail* Noon
   Amid the sneaker stores and used book shops of artsy Main Street, in the Ocean Park neighborhood, look for the Frank Gehry-designed steel boxes of **Edgemar** (2415-2449 Main Street; edgemarcenter.org), which house retail tenants and a performance space around an open courtyard. Gehry's retail footprint in Santa Monica has shrunk since his **Santa Monica Place**, designed in 1980, was replaced by a new version (395 Santa Monica Place; santamonicaplace.com)

in 2010. The glassy new open-air complex spreads across 500,000 square feet and three stories. The retailers' names may not be surprising, but it's the mall, this is California, and you can count on finding shoppers there.

OPPOSITE Ocean-view dining at Santa Monica Place, a glassy new open-air version of a California shopping mall.

ABOVE At sunset, the best view in town is at the beach, from the top of the solar-powered, 130-foot-high Pacific Wheel, the Ferris wheel at the Santa Monica Pier.

THE BASICS

Santa Monica is about a 20-minute drive from Los Angeles International Airport. There's a terrific bus system (bigbluebus.com), but most visitors find it more convenient to drive.

The Ambrose
1255 20th Street
310-315-1555
ambrosehotel.com
$$$
Feels like a Mission-style hideaway with stained-glass windows.

Hotel Shangri-La
1301 Ocean Avenue
310-394-2791
shangrila-hotel.com
$$$$
A storied, bright-white apparition on bluffs high above the Pacific.

Hotel California
1670 Ocean Avenue
310-393-2363
hotelca.com
$$
Surfer-style hotel with 35 rooms.

Malibu

Locals call it "the Bu" — a laid-back, celebrity-filled strip of a city that sparkles in the collective consciousness as a sun-drenched state of mind. With the busy Pacific Coast Highway running through and no discernible center of town, some of the best of Malibu, which has around 13,000 residents, can disappear in a drive-by. The staggering natural beauty of the sea and mountains is obvious, but pull off the road and stay awhile, and you'll find more: a world-class art museum, local wines, top-notch restaurants, and chic shops.
— BY LOUISE TUTELIAN

FRIDAY

1 *The Wind, the Waves . . .* 5 p.m.

What's so appealing about Malibu's little slice of coast? Visit **Point Dume State Preserve** (Birdview Avenue and Cliffside Drive; 818-880-0363; parks.ca.gov), and you'll see. A modest walk to the top of this coastal bluff rewards you with a sweeping view of the entire Santa Monica Bay, the inland Santa Monica Mountains, and, on a clear day, Catalina Island. A boardwalk just below the summit leads to a platform for watching swooping pelicans and crashing waves. To feel the sand between your toes, drive down Birdview Avenue to Westward Beach Road and park at the very end of the lot on your left. You'll be looking at Westward Beach, a gem that most visitors miss. Strike a yoga pose. Sigh at will.

2 *Chasing the Sunset* 7 p.m.

Little known fact: Most of Malibu faces south, not west. That means sitting down at just any seaside restaurant at dusk won't guarantee seeing a sunset over the water. But the aptly named **Sunset Restaurant** (6800 Westward Beach Road; 310-589-1007; thesunsetrestaurant.com) is a sure bet, with just the right orientation. Claim a white leather banquette, order a carafe of wine and a tasting plate of cheeses, and settle in for the light show.

3 *Shore Dinner* 9 p.m.

If you're going to spot a celebrity, chances are it will be at **Nobu Malibu** (3835 Cross Creek Road, in the Malibu Country Mart; 310-317-9140; nobumatsuhisa.com; $$$), one of the famed chef Nobu Matsuhisa's many restaurants. The sushi is

sublime, and the entrees measure up. Reservations are essential. The front room is convivial but noisy; the subtly lighted back room is quieter.

SATURDAY

4 *Walk the Pier* 9 a.m.

The 780-foot long **Malibu Pier** (23000 Pacific Coast Highway; 888-310-7437; malibupiersportfishing.com) is the most recognizable (and, arguably, only) landmark in town. Take a morning stroll out to the end, chat with the fishermen, and watch surfers paddle out. You'll be walking on a piece of Malibu history. The pier was originally built in 1905 as a loading dock for construction material, and it was a lookout during World War II. It crops up in numerous movies and TV shows.

5 *Ancient Art* 10 a.m.

The **Getty Villa** (17985 Pacific Coast Highway; 310-440-7300; getty.edu) is just over the city's southern border in Pacific Palisades, but no matter: it shouldn't be missed. The museum, built by J. Paul Getty in the 1970s to resemble a first-century Roman country house, contains Greek, Roman, and Etruscan vessels, gems and statuary, some dating back to 6500 B.C. On the second floor is a rare life-size Greek

OPPOSITE Beach and pier at Malibu, the little slice of Pacific coast that celebrities like to call their own.

BELOW Kai Sanson, a surfing instructor, initiates students into the ways of the waves.

bronze, *Statue of a Victorious Youth*, a prize of the museum. In the outside peristyle gardens, watch the sun glint off bronze statues at the 220-foot-long reflecting pool. Admission is free, but parking is limited, so car reservations are required.

6 *Magic Carpet Tile* 1 p.m.

Even many longtime Angelenos don't know about the **Adamson House** (23200 Pacific Coast Highway; 310-456-8432; adamsonhouse.org), a 1930 Spanish Colonial Revival residence that's a showplace of exquisite ceramic tile from Malibu Potteries, which closed in 1932. Overlooking Surfrider Beach with a view of Malibu Pier, the house belonged to a member of the Rindge family, last owners of the Malibu Spanish land grant. Take a tour and watch for the Persian "carpet" constructed entirely from intricately patterned pieces of tile. Other highlights: a stunning star-shaped fountain and a bathroom tiled top to bottom in an ocean pattern, with ceramic galleons poised in perpetuity on pointy whitecaps in a sea of blue.

7 *Vino on the Green* 4 p.m.

The drive to **Malibu Wines** (31740 Mulholland Highway; 818-865-0605; malibuwines.com) along the serpentine roads of the Santa Monica Mountains is almost as much fun as tipping a glass once you get there. Set on a serene green lawn, the tasting room is really a covered outdoor stone and wood counter. Sidle up and choose a flight of four styles. Or buy a bottle and lounge at one of the tables. (Tip: Regulars request the horseshoes or bocce ball set at the counter.) And don't miss the collection of vintage pickup trucks spread around the property.

8 *Farm to Table* 7 p.m.

Terra (21337 Pacific Coast Highway; 310-456-1221; terrarestaurantla.com; $$$), in the building that was once the original Malibu jail, is an intimate gathering place serving organic meats and nonfarmed fish, with most produce grown in its own gardens. Choose from the menu of the season; past diners have been

delighted to find dishes like oven-roasted organic baby beets or pounded filet mignon with Terra Farms arugula. In warm weather, French doors open to a spacious patio decorated with thousands of fragments of broken Malibu Potteries tile, the better to ward off evil spirits.

SUNDAY

9 *Ride the Surf* 10 a.m.

Surf shops offering lessons and board rentals line the Pacific Coast Highway (P.C.H. in local lingo), but Kai Sanson of **Zuma Surf and Swim Training** (949-742-1086; zsstraining.com) takes his fun seriously. Sanson, a Malibu native, will size you up with a glance and gear the instruction to your skills. Lessons for two are $90 a person. His tales of growing up in Malibu are free. Locals also give high marks to **Malibu Makos Surf Club** (310-317-1229; malibumakos.com).

10 *Brunch in Style (or Not)* Noon

Put on your oversize sunglasses if you're going to **Geoffrey's Malibu** (27400 Pacific Coast Highway; 310-457-1519; geoffreysmalibu.com; $$$). Geoffrey's (pronounced Joffreys) is the hot meeting spot for the

ABOVE A beach view from the bluff at Point Dume. Sweeping vistas here take in Santa Monica Bay, the Santa Monica Mountains, and, on a clear day, Catalina Island.

BELOW Tasting the reds at Malibu Wines.

well-heeled with a hankering for a shiitake mushroom omelet or lobster Cobb salad. Its Richard Neutra-designed building overlooks the Pacific, and every table has an ocean view. If you just want to kick back with *The Malibu Times*, head to **Coogie's Beach Café** (23750 Pacific Coast Highway in the Malibu Colony Plaza; 310-317-1444; coogies.malibu.menuclub.com; $$) and carbo-load with Coogie's French Toast: bagels dipped in egg whites with cinnamon sugar and served with peanut butter and bananas.

11 *Shop Like a Star* 2 p.m.

Whether it's diamonds or designer jeans you're after, the open-air **Malibu Country Mart** (3835 Cross Creek Road; malibucountrymart.com) is the place

to cruise for them. Its more than 50 retail stores and restaurants include Ralph Lauren, Juicy Couture, and Malibu Rock Star jewelry. In an adjacent space is luxe **Malibu Lumber Yard** shopping complex (themalibulumberyard.com), with stores like Alice + Olivia and Tory Burch.

ABOVE The Getty Villa museum, built by J. Paul Getty to resemble a first-century Roman country house.

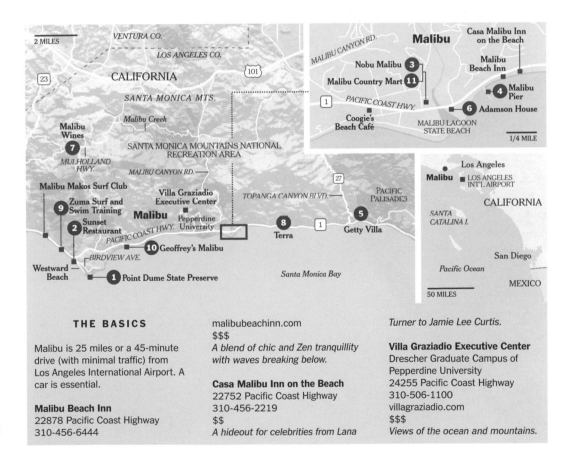

THE BASICS

Malibu is 25 miles or a 45-minute drive (with minimal traffic) from Los Angeles International Airport. A car is essential.

Malibu Beach Inn
22878 Pacific Coast Highway
310-456-6444

malibubeachinn.com
$$$
A blend of chic and Zen tranquillity with waves breaking below.

Casa Malibu Inn on the Beach
22752 Pacific Coast Highway
310-456-2219
$$
A hideout for celebrities from Lana

Turner to Jamie Lee Curtis.

Villa Graziadio Executive Center
Drescher Graduate Campus of Pepperdine University
24255 Pacific Coast Highway
310-506-1100
villagraziadio.com
$$$
Views of the ocean and mountains.

Santa Barbara

Santa Barbara may be tiny—its 90,000 residents could be seated in the Los Angeles Coliseum—but it packs Oprah-like cachet. Indeed, the queen of daytime TV and other A-listers have made this former outpost of Spain's American dominions their second home. Posh hotels, seven-figure mansions, and trendy boutiques have opened along the so-called American Riviera, catering to members of the Hollywood set who drive up every weekend to frolic among the languorous palms and suntanned celebrities. But don't let the crush of Ferraris and Prada fool you. With its perpetually blue skies and taco stands, Santa Barbara remains a laid-back town where the star attraction is still the beach.
— BY FINN-OLAF JONES

FRIDAY

1 *Lingering Glow* 5 p.m.
Santa Barbara's main beaches face southeast, but you can still catch the Pacific sunset by driving along Cliff Drive until it takes you to secluded **Hendry's Beach**. Hemmed by vertiginous cliffs that turn deep orange as the sun sets, the beach is popular with locals, surfers, and dolphins. Order a rum punch at the **Boathouse at Hendry's Beach** (2981 Cliff Drive; 805-898-2628; boathousesb.com), where you can still feel the warmth of the sun (or is it the fire pit?) long after it has set.

2 *Making Friends* 8 p.m.
Fresh California cuisine is the rule in this region of outstanding vineyards, luscious orchards, and right-off-the-boat seafood. Some of the freshest is at **Brophy Brothers Restaurant and Clam Bar** (119 Harbor Way; 805-966-4418; brophybros.com; $$$), which overlooks the harbor. Sit at the long communal table and strike up a conversation with your new friends. The night I was there, I was offered a job by a local developer. While I didn't take the job, I did sample the clam chowder ("The best in town," I was told about five times), followed by a terrific grilled swordfish

OPPOSITE A Santa Barbara sunset at Hendry's Beach.

RIGHT La Super Rica, pronounced by Julia Child to be the best of several good places in Santa Barbara to get a fresh and authentic homemade taco.

with artichoke sauce. Hmmm, what was that starting salary again?

SATURDAY

3 *Bike to Brunch* 10 a.m.
Rent a bike at **Wheel Fun Rentals** (23 East Cabrillo Boulevard; 805-966-2282; wheelfunrentals.com) and roll along the ocean to the **East Beach Grill** (1118 East Cabrillo Boulevard; 805-965-8805; $), a greasy but bright breakfast institution popular with surfers, cyclists, and skaters, who swear by its banana wheat germ pancakes with eggs and bacon.

4 *Sacred Mission* 11:30 a.m.
It's hard not to feel awed when driving up the hill to **Mission Santa Barbara** (2201 Laguna Street; 805-682-4713; sbmission.org), a 1786 landmark with ocher-colored columns that is known as the Queen of the 21 original Spanish missions built along the California coastline. Escape the crowds by wandering outside the flower-scented Sacred Garden. If there's a docent around, ask if you can see the glazed terra-cotta sculpture of St. Barbara watching over Mary and Jesus. A masterpiece from 1522, it was discovered three years ago in a storage room that was being cleaned out. It is now installed in an alcove in the garden's private portico.

5 *Taco Heaven* 1 p.m.

Locals argue endlessly about the city's best taco joint. Julia Child threw her weight behind **La Super Rica** (622 North Milpas Street; 805-963-4940; $), ensuring perpetual lines for its homemade tortillas filled with everything from pork and cheese to spicy ground beans. **Lilly's** (310 Chapala Street; 805-966-9180; $), a tiny spot in the center of town run by the ever-welcoming Sepulveda family, serves up tacos filled with anything from pork to beef eye. And **Palapa** (4123 State Street; 805-683-3074; www.palapa.biz; $) adds fresh seafood to the equation in its cheery patio just north of downtown, where the grilled sole tacos are fresh and light. Try all three places and join the debate.

6 *Paper Chase* 3 p.m.

Walt Disney's original will. A letter by Galileo. Lincoln's second Emancipation Proclamation (the 13th Amendment). The **Karpeles Manuscript Library and Museum** (21 West Anapamu Street; 805-962-5322; www.rain.org/karpeles; free) was started by David

Karpeles, a local real estate tycoon, and has one of the world's largest private manuscript collections. If this whets your appetite for collecting, wander seven blocks to **Randall House Rare Books** (835 Laguna Street; 805-963-1909; www.randallhouserarebooks. com), where the ancient tomes and rare documents have included a signed calling card from Robert E. Lee ($4,500) and the first official map of the State of California ($27,500).

7 *Shop Like the Stars* 5 p.m.

The main shopping drag, State Street, is filled with the usual chain stores like Abercrombie & Fitch. The consumerist cognoscenti head for the hills, to the Platinum Card district of **Montecito**,

ABOVE AND OPPOSITE Three views of Mission Santa Barbara, known as the Queen of the 21 original Spanish missions built along the California coast. Escape the crowds by wandering outside in the flower-scented Sacred Garden.

RIGHT A guest room at San Ysidro Ranch, the longtime celebrity hangout where J.F.K. and Jackie honeymooned.

where you'll find local designers and one-off items along the eucalyptus-lined Coast Village Road. Highlights include **Dressed** (No. 1253; 805-565-1253; dressedonline.com), a small boutique that counts Teri Hatcher and Britney Spears among the fans of its resortwear look, which might include an earthy necklace made of bamboo coral ($733) by a local jeweler, Corrina Gordon. Next door, **Angel** (No. 1221; 805-565-1599; wendyfoster.com) sells casual sportswear with a youthful vibe and hot accessories like tie-dyed hair ties. Across the street, **Lewis & Clark** (No. 1286; 805-969-7177) sells funky curios like colorful Guatemalan altar figures (from about $110), a local favorite given the city's Franciscan roots.

8 *Celebrity Dining* 8 p.m.

J.F.K. and Jackie honeymooned there, Hollywood luminaries like Groucho Marx were regulars, and in 2007 the **San Ysidro Ranch** reopened after a $150 million renovation by a new owner, the Beanie Babies creator Ty Warner. Warner added an enormous terrace, a 4,000-bottle wine cellar, and a lot of buzz by redoing the **Stonehouse** restaurant (900 San Ysidro Lane; 800-368-6788; www.sanysidroranch.com/dine1.cfm; $$$$). Expect to see the T-shirt-with-blazer set sitting around an open fire while dining on dishes like warm mushroom salad, juniper-dusted venison loin, and fresh pastries. Take a post-dinner stroll around the terraced gardens where many of the ingredients were grown.

9 *Glamorous State* 11 p.m.

State Street heats up after 11 o'clock as college students and moneyed folk from the glittering hills descend to its bars and nightclubs. **Wildcat Lounge** (15 West Ortega Street; 805-962-7970; www.wildcatlounge.com), a retro bar with red-vinyl banquettes, is the place to mingle with the university crowd and local bohos grooving to house music. Cater-corner is **Tonic** (634 State Street; 805-897-1800; www.tonicsb.com), an airy dance club that draws students in chinos and recent graduates in designer T-shirts to its cabanas. The international set heads to **Eos Lounge** (500 Anacapa Street; 805-564-2410; www.eoslounge.com) to dance to world music in a tree-shaded patio that looks like Mykonos on the Pacific.

SUNDAY

10 *Paging Moby-Dick* 10 a.m.

From December to February, some 30,000 gray whales migrate from Alaska to Baja California through a five-mile gap among the Channel Islands, a cluster of rocky isles 20 or so miles off the coast. Catch the commute — and breaching whales — from the decks of the **Condor Express**, a high-speed catamaran that makes daily whale-watching trips (301 West Cabrillo Boulevard; 805-882-0088; www.condorcruises.com;

$94). Porpoises, sea lions, and the occasional killer whale join in on the fun.

11 *Crimson Tide* 3 p.m.

The vineyards of central California gained prominence from the movie *Sideways*, but few can match the vistas at the **Coastal Winery** (217 Stearns Wharf; 805-966-6624; www.coastalwinery.com). It features an airy tasting room where you can tap your inner Miles Raymond and for $15 compare seven wines, including cabs, pinots, and chards, while marveling at amazing views of the Pacific.

OPPOSITE Mission Santa Barbara dates to 1786.

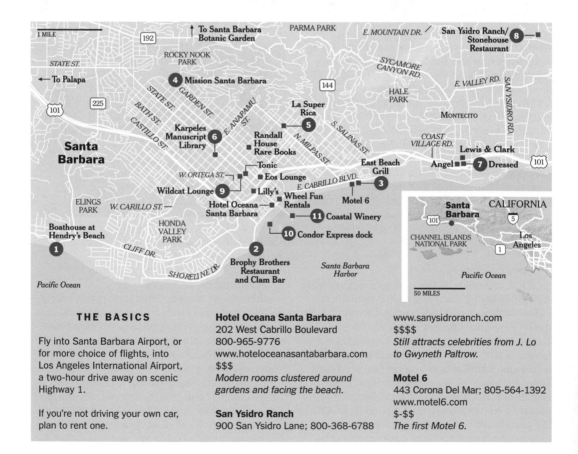

THE BASICS

Fly into Santa Barbara Airport, or for more choice of flights, into Los Angeles International Airport, a two-hour drive away on scenic Highway 1.

If you're not driving your own car, plan to rent one.

Hotel Oceana Santa Barbara
202 West Cabrillo Boulevard
800-965-9776
www.hoteloceanasantabarbara.com
$$$
Modern rooms clustered around gardens and facing the beach.

San Ysidro Ranch
900 San Ysidro Lane; 800-368-6788

www.sanysidroranch.com
$$$$
Still attracts celebrities from J. Lo to Gwyneth Paltrow.

Motel 6
443 Corona Del Mar; 805-564-1392
www.motel6.com
$-$$
The first Motel 6.

San Diego

If San Diego feels half empty, that's because it is. At any given time, swarms of residents have decamped a few miles south to Mexico or a few miles north to upscale resort towns. Also, the Navy is the area's largest employer, so a sizable chunk is presumably floating around on aircraft carriers somewhere. Is it any wonder, then, that the town leans so heavily on big tourist attractions (Shamu, the zoo)? A deeper look, however, will reveal San Diego's personality. A necklace of quirky, sun-kissed neighborhoods rings downtown, from surfer hangouts like Pacific Beach to gentrifying neighborhoods like University Heights. Restaurants are flourishing, too. There is even an emphasis on preserving history, which, for Southern California, is a headline in itself. — BY BROOKS BARNES

FRIDAY

1 *Ease On Down* 5 p.m.

There's no better indoctrination to San Diego's laid-back style than a stroll along the Embarcadero, a two-mile stretch of downtown waterfront where a gentle sea breeze will lull you into a zombie-like state in no time. The decommissioned aircraft carrier *Midway* sits nearby and can be admired from Tuna Harbor Park, a shady nook next to the touristy but tasty **Fish Market** restaurant (750 North Harbor Drive; 619-232-3474; thefishmarket.com; $$). Warning: Skip Seaport Village, a shopping plaza on the boardwalk, unless you're into pushy pedicab drivers and shops that sell obnoxious T-shirts.

2 *Gaslamp Glamour* 7:30 p.m.

Much energy and money have been spent gussying up the Gaslamp Quarter, a 16-block downtown neighborhood that was once an archetype of urban blight. The jumble of frat bars is still rather depressing, but several boutique hotels have opened attractive lounges and restaurants. Avoid the W with its hipper-than-thou staff and head to the sleek but comfy **Andaz San Diego** (formerly called the Ivy; 600 F Street; 619-814-1000; sandiego.andaz.hyatt.com).

OPPOSITE AND RIGHT Eye catchers in a Navy Town: *Unconditional Surrender*, by Seward Johnson, and the decommissioned aircraft carrier *Midway*, now a museum, occupying space along the San Diego Embarcadero.

Hollywood bigwigs roost there when attending Comic-Con, the annual comic-book convention and movie marketing extravaganza in July. The hotel's restaurant, **Quarter Kitchen** ($$$) woos with a sophisticated menu and modern décor.

3 *Culture Clash* 10 p.m.

How adventurous are you feeling? If the answer is not very, then perhaps top off the night with a sashay through the Andaz's multilevel Ivy nightclub. For the stronger at heart, there is the Casbah, as in "Rock the…." Conjuring the 1982 hit from the English punk rockers Clash, the **Casbah** (2501 Kettner Boulevard; 619-232-4355; casbahmusic.com) is a venerable, if a tad dingy, music club where Nirvana, the Smashing Pumpkins, and the Lemonheads cultivated an audience. Don't be frightened by the phone number (listed on the Web site as 232-HELL). The club also features more mainstream acts à la Alanis Morissette.

SATURDAY

4 *Pacific Xanadu* 8:30 a.m.

No visit to San Diego is complete without taking in **Balboa Park** (1549 El Prado; 619-239-0512; balboapark.org), the 1,200-acre public park that is home to the Old Globe theater, a gargantuan outdoor pipe organ, and a half-dozen major museums. A morning walk or jog along the park's central thoroughfare is a perfect way to experience it. If some of those Spanish Baroque Revival buildings look familiar, it's because they starred as Xanadu, the over-the-top estate in *Citizen Kane*.

5 *California Past* 10 a.m.

Tucked in an easy-to-miss enclave just north of downtown, **Old Town** (oldtownsandiego.org) offers a peek into what life was like in San Diego when agave plants still outnumbered people. Start at the **Old Town Mexican Café** (2489 San Diego Avenue; 619-297-4330; oldtownmexcafe.com), where the "tortilla ladies," visible through giant windows, can be seen frantically hand-rolling corn and flour tortillas, some 7,000 on a busy day, the restaurant says. Don't stop to eat: those tortillas are better seen than tasted. Rather, wander into the **Old Town San Diego State Historic Park** (parks.ca.gov/?page_ID=663) to explore exhibits like the 143-year-old Mason Street School, a one-room shack decorated with pictures of schoolmarms past. Shops scattered around the Old Town grounds sell the wares of local crafts makers. Large glazed ceramic tiles (usually between $100 and $200) are big sellers.

6 *Taco Treat* Noon

This is a desert, after all, and the sun can be exhausting. Recharge at **Casa de Reyes** (2754 Calhoun Street; 619-220-5040; fiestadereyes.com; $), a traditional Mexican restaurant at the Fiesta de Reyes. Decorated in a theme reminiscent of Spanish haciendas, this open-air but breezy restaurant provides a festive atmosphere with folkloric dancers and a mariachi band. Try the tacos, preferably stuffed with crispy-edged carnitas.

7 *Beach Bound* 1:30 p.m.

There are dozens of beaches, but none are more authentic than Ocean Beach, a funky surfers' haven that has stayed frozen in time because of strict zoning rules from the 1970s. Wander through the stuffed-to-the-rafters **Ocean Beach Antique Mall** (4926 Newport Avenue; 619-223-6170; antiquesinsandiego.com). The

ABOVE The Pacific from Sunset Cliffs.

RIGHT You could ride, but walking is also a nice way to make your way down the central thoroughfare of Balboa Park.

sidewalk along Newport Avenue, the main drag, is an attraction in itself. As part of a business district improvement effort, the community sells inscribed sidewalk tiles to anybody with $130 and a printable message. The results are oddly touching. ("Jeff Loves Rosie.") O.B. is a locals' favorite, so you might feel conspicuous without a surfboard or bare feet. Just call everyone dude and you'll be fine.

8 *Salty Sea Air* 4 p.m.

Just south of the Ocean Beach Pier is a recently constructed concrete path that leads to one of Southern California's most spectacular stretches of shoreline. **Sunset Cliffs** (sandiego.gov/park-and-recreation/parks/shoreline/sunset.shtml) spans 68 acres. Stretch out on the grass, fly a kite (as many locals do), or explore the bluffs and tidal pools.

9 *Dinner at a Diner* 6:30 p.m.

You've sampled one of San Diego's pricier restaurants; now go the other way and check out one of the diners that locals gush over. **Hash House a Go Go** (3628 Fifth Avenue; 619-298-4646; hashhouseagogo.com; $$) promises "twisted farm food." It's mobbed at breakfast and lunch but more manageable at dinner. Menu items run from ultra-familiar (salmon with garlic potatoes; chicken pot pie) to the wacky (macaroni and cheese with a duck skewer).

10 *The Fox Rocks* 9 p.m.

If the Regal Beagle, the pub from the 1970s TV sitcom *Three's Company*, ever had a twin, the **Red Fox Steak House** (2223 El Cajon Boulevard; 619-297-1313) would be it. Except that the Red Fox is also a piano

bar. Dimly lighted and with red Naugahyde booths, its lounge attracts a diverse crowd from hipsters to elderly couples. Everybody sings along after a couple of drinks. Give the adjacent dining room a peek; the room was originally built in 1642 in England but was dismantled and shipped to California in 1926 by the actress Marion Davies, who used it as part of a summer home.

SUNDAY

11 *If They Build It* 10 a.m.

Tour the hot and dusty San Diego Zoo if you must. The preferable option, especially for families with younger children, is **Legoland** (One Legoland Drive, Carlsbad; 760-918-5346; legoland.com). No lines, immaculate grounds, and a surprising lack of pressure to buy souvenirs. This is an amusement

park? Come before the masses discover it (annual attendance is about a million compared with nearly four million for the zoo). The 128-acre park focuses on interactive educational attractions like the Lost Kingdom Adventure, a ride themed around recovering hidden treasure in 1920s Egypt. For Lego fans — admit it, they're not just for kids — the park features a cavernous store that sells hard-to-find sets as well as little colored bricks in bulk.

ABOVE Strolling the Embarcadero. As the sculpture suggests, fish is often on the menu at the waterfront restaurants.

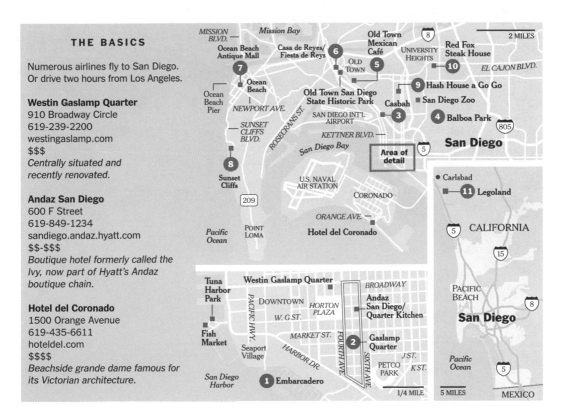

THE BASICS

Numerous airlines fly to San Diego. Or drive two hours from Los Angeles.

Westin Gaslamp Quarter
910 Broadway Circle
619-239-2200
westingaslamp.com
$$$
Centrally situated and recently renovated.

Andaz San Diego
600 F Street
619-849-1234
sandiego.andaz.hyatt.com
$$-$$$
Boutique hotel formerly called the Ivy, now part of Hyatt's Andaz boutique chain.

Hotel del Coronado
1500 Orange Avenue
619-435-6611
hoteldel.com
$$$$
Beachside grande dame famous for its Victorian architecture.

Palm Springs

Palm Springs was once the miles-from-Hollywood getaway that Malibu is now: a place for '60s movers and shakers to eat, drink, and sunbathe poolside while they awaited calls from studio execs. Today, after some hard-earned changes, this California desert town nestled in the Coachella Valley is becoming a destination for laid-back cool once again. The revival of modernism that inspired makeovers of its midcentury hotels, restaurants, and shops brought a revival of style, and the desert sun has never lost its appeal. Now Palm Springs attracts visitors just as happy climbing canyons as sipping cocktails on a lounge chair amid the design and architectural treasures of the past.
— BY ERICA CERULO

FRIDAY

1 *Cruising on Two Wheels* 4 p.m.

Because of its modest size, Palm Springs can easily become familiar over a couple days, or even a few hours. Start your trip with a self-guided bike tour. **Big Wheel Tours** (760-802-2236; bwbtours.com) rents bicycles and can arrange bike and hiking tours. Free maps are available at the **Palm Springs Visitors Center** (777 North Palm Canyon Drive; 760-778-8418; palm-springs.org). To scope out the dramatic terrain and local hot spots, pedal the Downtown Loop, which can be done in less than an hour, or the 10-mile Citywide Loop that takes you past the Moorten Botanical Gardens.

2 *Austria and Beyond* 7 p.m.

At **Johannes** (196 South Indian Canyon Drive; 760-778-0017; johannesrestaurants.com; $$$), the chef Johannes Bacher bills the food as modern Austrian, combining classic Central European special-ties like spaetzle and sauerkraut with decidedly borrowed ingredients and flavors, ranging from polenta to wasabi. But one of the best dishes is also the most traditional: a heaping plate of Wiener schnitzel with parsley potatoes, cucumber salad, and cranberry compote.

OPPOSITE Indian Canyons, a natural oasis on the Agua Caliente Indian Reservation just outside Palm Springs.

RIGHT The Kaufmann House, designed by Richard Neutra.

3 *Partying Poolside* 9:30 p.m.

Back when Frank Sinatra held raucous shindigs at his Twin Palms home, Palm Springs was known for its party scene. These days, the best drinking establishments are in hotels. The white stucco exterior of the **Colony Palms Hotel** (572 North Indian Canyon Drive; 760-969-1800; colonypalmshotel.com) conceals a welcoming hideaway with stone walkways, towering palms, and, when needed, patio heaters. At the buzzing restaurant **Purple Palm**, ask to be seated by the pool and order a plate of Humboldt Fog chèvre, organic honey, and local dates with your drink to top off the night.

SATURDAY

4 *Modernist America* 9:30 a.m.

Along with the moneyed 20th-century tourists came eye-catching buildings: hotels, commercial spaces, and vacation homes. Next to a hopping Starbucks on the main drag sits one of the city's oldest architectural touchstones: a concrete bell tower salvaged from the long-gone Oasis Hotel, which was designed by Lloyd Wright (son of Frank) in 1924. This spot is also where Robert Imber, the often seersucker-clad architectural guru and one-man show behind **PS Modern Tours** (760-318-6118; psmoderntours@aol.com), starts his three-hour excursions, which provide a survey of the city's key structures with a focus on the midcentury sweet spot. Design enthusiasts can catch glimpses of the iconic Albert Frey-designed Tramway Gas Station, Richard Neutra's 1946 Kaufmann Desert House, and the mass-produced but stunning Alexander homes

that your guide identifies by pointing out the four key components — "garage, breezeway, windows, wall" — in their various arrangements. Reserve well in advance.

5 *Chic Cheek* 1 p.m.

The wait for brunch at **Cheeky's** (622 North Palm Canyon Drive; 760-327-7595; cheekysps.com; $$) should be a tip-off: the bright, streamlined space, which feels airlifted from L.A. — in a good way — is popular. The standard eggs and waffles are spiced up with ingredients like beet relish, homemade herbed ricotta, and sour cherry compote.

6 *Used Goods* 3 p.m.

Stroll **Palm Canyon Drive**, a strip that's terrific for high-end vintage shopping, if a little dangerous for those who quickly reach for their credit cards. Among the many stores that focus on better-with-age décor, just a few have mastered the art of curating. At **a La MOD** (768 North Palm Canyon Drive; 760-327-0707; alamod768.com), nearly 70 percent of the merchandise, which is heavy on Lucite and lighting, is sourced locally, according to the shop's owners. Across the street, **Modern Way** (745 North Palm Canyon Drive; 760-320-5455; psmodernway.com) stocks an eclectic collection of larger pieces like Arthur Elrod couches, Verner Panton cone chairs, and Hans Olsen dining sets. For something you can actually take home, head

down to **Bon Vivant** in the **Palm Canyon Galleria** (457 North Palm Canyon Drive, No. 3; 760-534-3197; gmcb.com) where the store's charming proprietors make you feel like a genuine collector for purchasing an $18 engraved brass vase or a $5 tie clip.

7 *Stay Silly* 5 p.m.

At the **Palm Springs Yacht Club**, at the **Parker Palm Springs** hotel (4200 East Palm Canyon Drive; 760-770-5000; theparkerpalmsprings.com), standard spa offerings like deep-tissue rubdowns and wrinkle-fighting facials come with a playful attitude of retro irony. The pampering is real. Expect to pay high-end prices (some treatment packages are well over $300) but go away feeling refreshed and maybe — is it possible? — a little younger.

8 *Friend of the House* 8 p.m.

Most of the favored area restaurants have an old-school vibe: tuxedoed waiters, a headwaiter who has worked there since opening day, and steak-and-lobster specialties. Though **Copley's** (621 North Palm Canyon Drive; 760-327-9555; copleyspalmsprings.com; $$$) might not have the culinary history of nearby Melvyn's Restaurant and Lounge, which opened as an inn in 1935, it has a different sort of storied past — it is housed in what was once Cary Grant's estate. It also has food that incorporates 21st-century flavors (one spring menu included dishes like a duck and artichoke salad with goat cheese, edamame, and litchi).

9 *Toasting Friends* 11 p.m.

The cocktail craze has made its way to the desert, and the guys manning the bar at the cavernous **Amigo Room** at the Ace Hotel (701 East Palm Canyon Drive; 760-325-9900; acehotel.com/palmsprings) are leading

ABOVE Palm trees line a highway entering town.

LEFT Residential architecture of the mid-20th century distinguishes Palm Springs. This example is the Kaufmann House exterior.

the way. In addition to measuring, shaking and pouring classic concoctions like the margarita, they offer more offbeat options like the Figa (fig-infused vodka with Earl Grey and honey tangerine) that reek of late-night innovation. The cool but mellow vibe—supplemented by décor featuring burgundy leather booths and glass tables with inlaid pesos—will keep you ordering.

SUNDAY

10 *Get Close with Cactus* 9 a.m.

Those looking for an early-morning calorie burn might prefer the uphill battles of Gastin or Araby Trail, but a hike through **Tahquitz Canyon** (500 West Mesquite Avenue; 760-416-7044; tahquitzcanyon.com),

part of the natural oasis area called Indian Canyons, offers a leisurely alternative. A small entrance fee gets you access to a 1.8-mile loop and the sights and smells that come with it: desert plants, lizards aplenty and a stunning, 60-foot waterfall. Take a two-hour ranger-led tour or explore the trail at your own pace. You'll see arid desert and cool, palm-lined gorges.

ABOVE Hiking at Tahquitz Canyon.

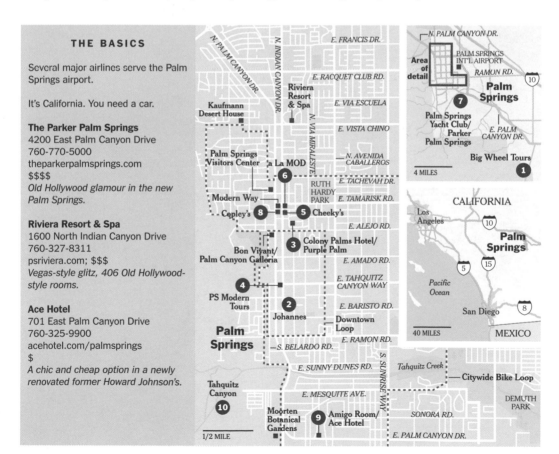

THE BASICS

Several major airlines serve the Palm Springs airport.

It's California. You need a car.

The Parker Palm Springs
4200 East Palm Canyon Drive
760-770-5000
theparkerpalmsprings.com
$$$$
Old Hollywood glamour in the new Palm Springs.

Riviera Resort & Spa
1600 North Indian Canyon Drive
760-327-8311
psriviera.com; $$$
Vegas-style glitz, 406 Old Hollywood-style rooms.

Ace Hotel
701 East Palm Canyon Drive
760-325-9900
acehotel.com/palmsprings
$
A chic and cheap option in a newly renovated former Howard Johnson's.

Death Valley

Although Death Valley remains starkly dramatic, electricity, the automobile, and a reliable water supply have conspired to rob it of its terror. It is not what you would call a "pleasant" place, but it is a spectacularly beautiful one, containing typical and unusual Southwestern features in its manageable sprawl. (Death Valley National Park is nearly as large as Connecticut.) It can be hellishly hot in summer — the record is 134 degrees — and ice closes roads in the winter. But in spring and fall, the weather is cooperative. Drive up from Los Angeles, and you will begin by passing through Antelope Valley — where in early spring psychedelic California poppies may blanket the hills — and from there into the unexciting town of Mojave, once a center for borax shipments coming out of the valley. From this point on, things become really interesting. — BY MARK BITTMAN

FRIDAY

1 *Steep Descent* 5 p.m.

As you drive north up Interstate 395 toward **Death Valley National Park** (nps.gov/deva), you will see the Sierra Nevada and Mount Whitney, at nearly 15,000 feet the tallest peak in the contiguous United States, to the west, and a series of far smaller ranges to the east. But at **Olancha**, as you veer eastward on Highway 190, the landscape suddenly takes on an eerie air. Ahead is a barren, deep-orange mountain range, and to the right and left are salt plains, former lakes that shimmer in the late-afternoon light. This is Saline Valley, and it leads to the Argus Range, where a massive red-rocked canyon gapes below the road. Ahead lies a wide, stark valley, which turns out to be not Death Valley but Panamint Valley, and in any other part of the country it would be striking enough. Here, however, there is still the Panamint Range to cross and, after a climb to 5,000 feet, the steep descent begins; it will end at sea level on the floor of Death Valley.

2 *Overnight Oasis* 8 p.m.

Death Valley bares its geologic soul at every turn, and you will soon discover the kinds of details that make the desert delightful: the toughest plant life in the world, well-camouflaged wildlife, and a stunning array of rocks and minerals. If winter has been "wet" (that is, if rain has fallen at more than the usual

pace of two inches a year), spring brings carpets of wildflowers. Head to **Stovepipe Wells**, one of several oases in the park. You'll find a general store, a ranger station that is sometimes open, and **Stovepipe Wells Village**, a serviceable hotel. Dinner at the **Toll Road Restaurant** (760-786-2387; escapetodeathvalley.com; $$) includes some vegetarian options. Drinks are at the **Badwater Saloon**.

SATURDAY

3 *Multiple Sunrises* 6:30 a.m.

Dawn walks are guaranteed to be cool, and a stroll or hike in a canyon will give you several sunrises as the sun peeks above and dips below the upper reaches of the steep walls. **Mosaic Canyon**, in the foothills of Tucki Mountain, is just up the road and through a long alluvial fan. As in many of the park's canyons, you can drive right to the entrance and within minutes find near-pristine isolation. Here, the passage between the steep walls narrows to just a few feet, and you will immediately be engulfed by formations of mosaic and smooth, swirling, multicolored marble.

4 *Sculpted Sand* 10 a.m.

On the road to **Furnace Creek** are the valley's most accessible sand dunes. These look best (and

OPPOSITE A view of eroded hills from Zabriskie Point in Death Valley National Park.

BELOW A bullet-pocked backcountry road sign.

are at their coolest, of course), when the shadows are still long. For kids, the dunes will be the highlight of the trip, but their texture and beauty will excite everyone. Be prepared to become sandy as you wander barefoot, especially if it is breezy. Carry water. You can visit the original Stovepipe Well near here and, back on the road, you will pass Devil's Cornfield, an expanse of arrowweed whose dried stems at first glance resemble bundles of cornstalks.

5 *A History of Borax* Noon

The **Visitor Center & Museum** at Furnace Creek boasts a super collection of material about the area as well as exhibitions that will answer your rapidly accumulating questions about borax. (Should this not be enough, nearby are a borax museum with an impressive collection of machinery and wagons of 20-mule-team fame, and the semi-preserved Harmony Borax Works. Like it or not, chances are you will leave Death Valley a borax expert.) The human history of the valley is outlined here too, from its original known inhabitants, the Shoshones, to the unfortunate 49ers who stumbled into and named the valley while looking for a shortcut to the gold fields.

6 *The High and the Low* 1 p.m.

Have lunch at the **49'er Café** in the Ranch at Furnace Creek (furnacecreekresort.com; $$), which serves standard fare of salads, burgers, and pasta.

(In general, the food in Death Valley is not as bad as you might fear.) Then get directions for the 45-mile round trip down a dead-end road to the mile-high **Dante's View**, from which you can see both the highest (Mount Whitney) and lowest (Badwater, nearly 300 feet below sea level) points in the Lower 48.

7 *Panoramic Palette* 3 p.m.

Late in the afternoon is the best time to see central Death Valley's best-known and most beautiful spots: **Zabriskie Point** and the **Artist's Drive**. The former, thanks to the fame brought by the film of the same name, has a large parking lot and paved walkway to its top. From here there are panoramic views of the gently rounded golden hills nearby, a relatively friendly landscape compared with the stark, darkly colored Panamints in the background. Just down the road is the car-friendly visual highlight, **Artist's Palette**. These vast, multicolored hills, dominated by pink, green, and lavender, virtually pulsate in the soft light of late afternoon and early evening.

8 *Moonlight* 6 p.m.

Have a drink in the quietly tasteful lobby of the **Inn at Furnace Creek** (furnacecreekresort.com) and then amble down to the **Wrangler Steakhouse** ($$$) at the Furnace Creek Ranch for dinner. Despite the name, steak is not the only option. If you're adventure-some—especially if there is a full moon—this is a

great time to tackle Golden Canyon. Otherwise, you will be tired enough to sleep, and there is plenty to do in the morning.

SUNDAY

9 *Stroll the Canyons* 7 a.m.

Golden Canyon is nestled among the hills seen from Zabriskie Point. Seventy-five years ago it was such a popular destination that a road was built through it. Now it is an easy hike — a stroll, really — that you can enjoy for a quarter of a mile or so, wandering in and out of the lovely side canyons, or take for a mile and a half, until you gain an open

OPPOSITE A campfire glowing against a black desert sky.

ABOVE A scene from Saline Road.

BELOW Hot springs at Saline Valley.

view of the red rocks of the **Red Cathedral** next to the yellow flank of Manley Beacon (you will see the Cathedral almost as soon as you get into the canyon).

10 *Option 1: Easy Exit* 9 a.m.

If you take the southern route out of the park, make a quick stop to gaze again at Artist's Drive, this time from the **Devil's Golf Course**, where the ground is a compacted mass of pure salt and mud. You can walk on it, but be careful: the crystals are sharp enough to cut you if you fall. A few miles down the road is **Badwater**, the lowest point in Death Valley (and the country), a terrifying expanse of salt fields and salt water, and a bitter disappointment to early travelers. Exit the park at Shoshone, and stop for a burger and a

root beer float at the **Crowbar Cafe & Saloon** (Highway 127, Shoshone; 760-852-4123; $$).

11 *Option 2: Rugged Detour* 9 a.m.

If you have time and a four-wheel drive vehicle, you may want to detour to the **Saline Valley Warm Springs**, a countercultural hangout since free spirits planted palms and built soaking tubs on its three levels of natural hot springs in the 1960s. The park took over in the '90s, but the "clothing optional" ethos still

thrives, and a private group (salinepreservation.org) works with the park service. Stock up on fuel and supplies, and then, still just inside the park, turn north off Highway 190 onto a dirt road down into the valley. (It has traditionally been marked by a bullet-perforated "Road Closed" sign left from a long-ago winter.) Wrestle the washboard road for 53 miles. At the end, you'll find a mellow, relaxing scene and friendly people—often including families—bound by a love of the desert and its wide-open spaces.

ABOVE Remains of a tram line that hauled salt.

OPPOSITE The salt flats at Badwater Pool, the lowest point in the United States.

THE BASICS

Drive 200 miles from Los Angeles or 120 miles from Las Vegas.

On main park roads, any car will do. For back-roads adventures, you will need four-wheel drive.

Stovepipe Wells Village
Highway 190
760-786-2387
escapetodeathvalley.com
$$
Low-rise hotel with eye-popping vistas and a stargazing program. South-facing rooms are best.

Inn at Furnace Creek
Highway 190
800-236-7916
furnacecreekresort.com
$$$$
Luxury lodging in a resort with pools, golf, and horseback riding.

Ranch at Furnace Creek
Highway 190
800-236-7916
furnacecreekresort.com
$$
In the same resort, but less expensive.

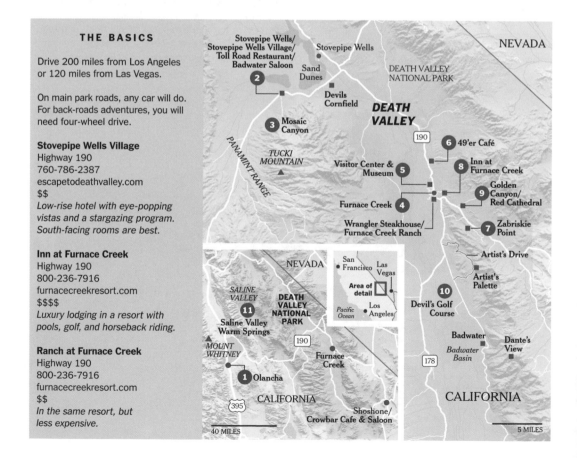

Mammoth Lakes

For over half a century, winter recreation-seekers from Southern California have flocked to this secluded corner of California's Sierra Nevada mountains. It's easy to see why. Despite the 8,000-foot altitude, Mammoth Lakes' sprawl of splashy condos and strip malls has a distinct Los Angeles feeling. But the surrounding frozen lakes and granite peaks, immortalized by the photographer Ansel Adams, are decidedly un-Los Angeles, and can hold their own with any landscape in Colorado or Canada. Now, with more flights to its airport and a flurry of new après-ski offerings, Mammoth is hoping to draw skiers from beyond California.
— BY LIONEL BEEHNER

FRIDAY

1 *Siberian Spa* 4 p.m.

Imagine a vast white expanse of what looks like frozen Siberian tundra, dotted with natural hot springs and surrounded by soaring peaks. **Hilltop Hot Spring** is popular with locals, but you can join in, too. There are no formal signs or footpaths — just follow the S.U.V.'s past the airport five minutes east of Mammoth Lakes and enjoy a steaming soak, free of charge. For more privacy, cross the road to **Wild Willy's**, a more secluded spring, which requires a 20-minute trek and a pair of snowshoes.

2 *By the Fireplace* 7 p.m.

On the other side of town is **Tamarack Lodge and Resort** (163 Twin Lakes Road, off Lake Mary Road; 760-934-2442; tamaracklodge.com). A rustic log cabin with bark-wood ceiling fixtures and 1920s-era fireplace, it also happens to have an impressive wine collection and an excellent chef: Frederic Pierrel. The intimate **Lakefront Restaurant** ($$$) serves up hearty dishes like a combination platter of elk medallions, grilled quail, and pork marinated in wine on a bed of spicy mashed potatoes. Before being seated, have a mulled wine or hot cider by the fire.

SATURDAY

3 *Pancakes and Biscuits* 6:30 a.m.

Before hitting the slopes, fill up on pancakes and black-and-white memorabilia at the **Stove** (644 Old Mammoth Road; 760-934-2821; $$), a cozy spot with long wooden booths and old pictures of cattle ranchers on its walls. For over 40 years, the Stove has served hearty meals like the Sierra Sunrise, a heap of fried potatoes, peppers, onions, and ham topped with eggs and cheese. On your way out, pick up a homemade pie — apple, apricot, cherry. Get there early. The place fills up fast.

4 *Black Tie Skiing* 7:30 a.m.

Experts from **Black Tie Ski Rentals** (760-934-7009; blacktieskis.com) will come to your condo and fit you for skis or snowboards. And if the boots don't feel snug by midday, they will meet you on the slopes and exchange your gear, or switch your snowboard for a pair of skis.

5 *Fresh Tracks* 8 a.m.

With over 3,500 acres of trails, Mammoth has more variable terrain than most mountains (mammothmountain.com). There are three lodges: Eagle, Canyon, and Main. Skiers in search of soft powder and fresh-groomed runs start on Eagle and follow the sun over to Main or the backside of the mountain (to avoid lift lines, reverse the order). Or take the gondola from Main to the summit, 11,053 feet above sea level, where you can find a relaxing spot for hot cocoa. Marvel at the daredevils who ski

OPPOSITE Imagine a vast white expanse dotted with natural hot springs and surrounded by soaring peaks.

BELOW Outside of ski season, there's always fishing in the cold mountain lakes.

off Hangman's Hollow. Or brave the steep and icy chutes of Dave's Run or Scotty's. A safer alternative is Santiago, off the summit's less crowded backside, which offers scattered glades as well as gorgeous views of the Minarets, a majestic series of jagged granite peaks.

6 *South of the Border* Noon

Lunch on Mammoth typically involves Mexican fare. If you can't find the new Roving Mammoth, a bright orange snowcat that doubles as a food cart, serving up burritos — you can even track the snowcat's whereabouts on Twitter — there are pulled-pork nachos at the **Mill Cafe** (760-934-0675; $$), a festive après-ski spot at the base of Chair 2 (in true California fashion, its entrance is scattered with beach chairs). Or, for overflowing plates of nachos and fish tacos, head to the **Yodler** (10001 Minaret Road; 760-934-2571; $$), a Swiss-style chalet off the Main Lodge. **Gomez's** (100 Canyon Boulevard; 760-924-2693; gomezs.com; $), a Mexican place with over 200 tequilas and fittingly mammoth margaritas, relocated to a spot in the middle of the village last year.

7 *Art Park* 1 p.m.

Take Chair 10 up to ski down a few wide-open runs like Easy Rider or Solitude that stay powdery throughout the day. Or try Quicksilver, a well-groomed trail with gently sloped glades and variable terrain.

Snowboarders should head to the new terrain **Art Park**, which made its debut in December and showcases funky artworks affixed to its rails and steel structures. Mammoth also recently opened the Stomping Grounds, a terrain park packed with jumps, jibs and an Acrobag — which resembles a giant blue moon bounce — to practice flips. Nonsnowboarders should take the newly carved Village Ski Back Trail, a scenic path that meanders past pine trees and the backyards of condos, linking the mountain with the village.

8 *Growlers and Pastries* 4 p.m.

Thankfully, après-ski at Mammoth does not involve bad cover bands. If anything, it revolves around its eponymous microbrew. Insiders make their way to a warehouse converted a few years back into a beer-tasting room for the **Mammoth Brewing Company** (94 Berner Street; 760-934-7141; mammothbrewingco.com). Still in ski gear, they

ABOVE Nighttime options have expanded as Mammoth Lakes has grown.

OPPOSITE ABOVE Relaxing in the dining room at the Tamarack Lodge & Resort.

OPPOSITE BELOW A cozy cabin in the snow. Lodging options include condos, cabins, and hotel rooms.

down free samples before filling up their growlers with IPA 395, a local favorite, or grabbing kegs and cases to go. A favorite spot among Mammoth's growing international crowd is **Shea Schat's Bakery** (3305 Main Street; 760-934-6055), which feels, and smells, like the inside of a gingerbread house. The shop serves up steaming hot chocolate and stocks rows of pastries — cinnamon nut bread, ginger cakes, and bread pudding.

9 *Mid-Mountain Dining* 6 p.m.

The swanky restaurant **Parallax** (800-626-6684; mammothmountain.com; $$$$) takes up almost half of the cafeteria at McCoy Station, a midmountain gondola station up from the Main Lodge. Its modern décor and Asian-themed trimmings, including white bark walls, would not look out of place in downtown Manhattan, save, perhaps, for the tacky TV Yule log fireplace. Yet at 9,600 feet, it is reachable by only

snowcat, which picks people up at the **Mammoth Mountain Inn** (10001 Minaret Road; 760-934-2581; mammothmountain.com). Hop aboard a heated snowcat that feels like a spaceship as you gaze up at the stars through its glass roof. Then feast on a satisfying entree — perhaps New Zealand lamb or grilled chicken with risotto. For optimal views, get there as night falls.

10 *Rockies Meets Hollywood* 9 p.m.

Never mind the gondola D.J. booth and vintage lanterns above the bar. **Hyde Lounge** (6201 Minaret Road; 760-934-0669; sbe.com/hydemammoth) lives up to its Sunset Boulevard forefather. There

are bottle-service-only booths, lasers everywhere, and Mammoth's version of a strict door policy (no snowboard gear). The crowd sipping pricey cocktails is a mix of slovenly clad snowboarders and dressed-to-impress partygoers, all crammed within its fire-engine

ABOVE With over 3,500 acres of trails, Mammoth has more variable terrain than most ski mountains.

OPPOSITE A summer view of the wild beauty at Twin Lakes near the village at Mammoth Lakes.

red walls. Warm up with a burning mango, a jalapeño and vodka concoction, and settle in for a night of people watching.

SUNDAY

11 *Olympic Workout* 9 a.m.

In recent years, Mammoth Lakes has become a year-round hub for Olympic and pro athletes attracted to the high altitudes and easygoing ethos. A nice byproduct is the state-of-the-art facilities at the Snowcreek Athletic Club, which resembles a giant barn just outside town. The club recently opened the **Double Eagle Spa** (51 Club Drive; 760-934-8511; snowcreekathleticclub.com), with earthy massage rooms, Vichy showers, and a yoga studio.

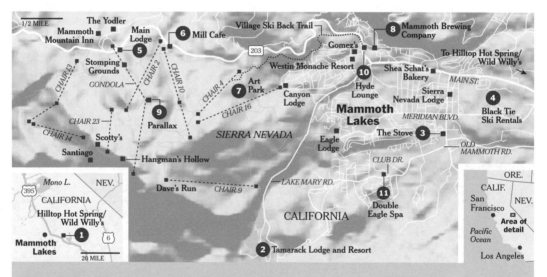

THE BASICS

Fly to Mammoth-Yosemite airport from Los Angeles, San Francisco, or Las Vegas. By car, drive about 300 miles from San Francisco or Las Vegas.

In town, use resort shuttles or drive.

Tamarack Lodge and Resort

163 Twin Lakes Road
760-934-2442
tamaracklodge.com
$$$
Private cabins and studios with all the modern amenities a short drive from town.

Sierra Nevada Lodge
164 Old Mammoth Road
800-824-5132

sierranevadalodge.com
$$
Close to town and family-friendly.

Westin Monache Resort
50 Hillside Drive
760-934-0400
westinmammoth.com
$$$$
Full-service luxury across from the village gondola.

Big Sur

Running southward from Carmel, 150 miles south of San Francisco, to San Simeon, Big Sur's mass of tight mountains pushes brazenly against the Pacific swell. Kelp forests sway at the feet of the rugged sea cliffs. Deep valleys shelter some of California's southernmost redwoods. Writers, artists, dreamers, and hippies have all been drawn here; Henry Miller described it as "a region where one is always conscious of weather, of space, of grandeur and of eloquent silence." Although the rich and famous are now building homes here, the geography prevents sprawl and most development is invisible, preserving the feeling of solitude. Big Sur still rewards serendipity, but this is no place to rely upon it: the few lodgings fill quickly. Make reservations well in advance, allow plenty of time for the drive, and then let the ocean and the mountains take over.

— BY GREGORY DICUM

FRIDAY

1 *View from the Road* 2 p.m.

The only way into and through the Big Sur coast is along winding, breathtaking **California Highway 1**. Its construction here in the 1930s was controversial (sheer cliffs and constant rockfalls attest to the project's audacity), but today it is a testament to the ambition of New Deal public works projects. Though Big Sur is as much an idea as a place, you will know you have arrived when, driving south from Monterey, you cross **Bixby Bridge**. A marvel of concrete spanning a deep coastal gorge, it has appeared in a thousand car commercials, and it's worth a stop if you're into infrastructure: turn out at either end of the span. Other viewpoints abound on the road, so keep your camera at the ready and expect to stop frequently.

2 *Waterside* 5 p.m.

Though the Pacific is everywhere in Big Sur, the enfolding coast guards access like a jealous lover. Beaches nestle in coves backed by fearsome cliffs, and in only a few places is it easy—or even possible—to set foot on them. **Pfeiffer Beach** is one. Take a sharp right turn a quarter-mile south of the Big Sur Ranger Station onto the unmarked Sycamore Canyon Road, and follow it down to a bay sheltered from the ocean's

full force by chunky offshore rocks. The fine tan sand there is streaked with purple minerals. Wander in the warm sun and test a toe in the cold water. On one sunny late afternoon, handfuls of college students basked in sweatshirts and sunglasses like style-conscious sea lions. An arch in the rocks serves as a proscenium for the lowering sun and the backlit orange seawater splashes of gentle swells.

3 *Sunset Sustenance* 7 p.m.

Big Sur has remarkably few dining options for a place so visited. Fortunately, some of them are sublime. **Cielo**, the restaurant at **Ventana Inn** (48123 Highway One; 831-667-4242; ventanainn.com; $$$) takes archly appropriate ingredients—wild Dungeness crab, seasonal local organic vegetables, Sonoma duck, bison from a Wyoming ranch—and turns them into finely wrought California cuisine. Get a table by the big windows, or outside, and enjoy a view of the sun dropping into the rippling waves. Unless it's foggy, of course.

OPPOSITE McWay Falls pours 80 feet onto a perfect, though inaccessible, beach around a blue Pacific cove.

BELOW A yurt at Treebones Resort, a mid-priced lodging option. Land-use restrictions both keep Big Sur beautiful and limit places to stay.

4 *Grandpa's Eggs Benedict* 9 a.m.

One of Big Sur's heartiest breakfasts is at **Deetjen's** (48865 Highway 1; 831-667-2378; deetjens.com; $$), this coast's original roadhouse. The inn dates to the 1930s, when Grandpa Deetjen built a redwood barn here that grew into a cluster of cabins. The restaurant, open to all, has an unpretentious but efficient and friendly feel that seems the epitome of Big Sur at its best. Eggs Benedict are a specialty, but there's a varied menu that also includes smoked salmon and huevos rancheros. If you're lucky, you can eat by the fire, but resist the urge to sit there all day: it's time to work off that breakfast.

5 *The Redwoods Are Waiting* 10 a.m.

State parks are strung up and down the coast. Many offer short hikes to astounding coastal vistas, while others permit access to the rugged mountain wilderness of the interior. At **Pfeiffer Big Sur State Park** (26 miles south of Carmel on Highway 1), trails lead through dense, damp groves of redwoods and oaks to coastal overlooks, a waterfall, and up to open ridges and mountaintops. The three-mile Oak Grove Trail gives hikers a taste of the diversity of Big Sur landscapes and, with luck, the wildlife: Big Sur is one of the places where majestic California condors have been reintroduced following their near-extinction.

6 *Go for the View* 1 p.m.

Nepenthe (48510 Highway 1; 831-667-2345; nepenthebigsur.com; $$–$$$), has long been a favorite tourist aerie. It is worth a visit on sunny days for the magnificent views and cheery crowd,

ABOVE A cabin in a redwood grove at Deetjen's, an inn that dates to the 1930s.

RIGHT At Pfeiffer Big Sur State Park, trails lead through dense redwood groves to open ridges and mountaintops.

OPPOSITE Pfeiffer Beach, one of the few accessible Big Sur beaches. Most are below fearsome cliffs.

although the food is undistinguished. Think of it as the price of admission.

7 *Waterfall to the Sea* 2 p.m.

Julia Pfeiffer Burns State Park (on Highway 1, 831-667-2315; parks.ca.gov, not to be confused with Pfeiffer Big Sur State Park) is an all but requisite stop: from the parking area it's an easy stroll to view McWay Falls. The 80-foot-high cataract pours onto a perfect, though inaccessible, beach around a blue Pacific cove. It's the image most likely to come to mind later as you reminisce about Big Sur.

8 *Enlightenment* 3 p.m.

"There being nothing to improve on in the surroundings," Miller wrote of Big Sur in 1957, "the tendency is to set about improving oneself." He could have been describing the **Esalen Institute** (55000 Highway 1), a sort of New Age Harvard founded in 1962, whose campus tumbles down toward a precipitous cliff above the ocean. Seekers and celebrities come for "energy" and Atlantis, registering for workshops in yoga, meditation, and various kinds of self-realization. Participants stay overnight. To get a taste of the place in a shorter time — and work away any lingering stress that has managed to survive Big Sur so far — book a massage (831-667-3002; esalen.org/info/massage; time slots limited and reservations essential; $165). It's a rare chance to enter the Esalen grounds without booking for a longer stay. You're allowed to arrive an hour early and stay an hour afterward to experience the hot springs.

9 *The Soak* 5:30 p.m.

By now you've emerged refreshed from your bodywork and are soaking (nudity optional, but de rigueur), in the **Esalen Hot Springs Baths** (esalen.org/place/hot_springs.html). Esalen is known for these legendary tubs. Hugging a seaside cliff, the complex of baths momentarily captures natural hot springs before they pour into the Pacific. Board-formed concrete walls, warm and grippy sandstone floors, and floor-to-ceiling windows look out to sea. Outdoor soaking pools and a living roof lend the baths a sense of belonging in the landscape. From the hot water bathers can look down on sea otters lounging in the kelp. If your brief soak isn't enough, sign up to return between 1 a.m. and 3 a.m., when the baths are open to the public for $20. The hours are inconvenient (the nighttime drive over corkscrew Highway 1 will instantly undo the baths' restorative effects), but breakers below shake the cliff and thousands of stars shine out of a black sky, giving the place the feel of a celestial point of embarkation.

10 *Above It All* 8 p.m.

On the ridgeline hundreds of feet above Pfeiffer Beach, the **Post Ranch Inn** perches in unobtrusive luxe, its cottages spread tactfully over rolling acres of grass and woods. But like the rest of Big Sur, the inn has a charm that has as much to do with its attitude as with the landscape—not every thousand-dollar-a-night resort has an in-house shaman. Even if your wallet places you in a different category from the establishment's target clientele, you will find a welcoming spirit at the inn's restaurant, the **Sierra Mar** (831-667-2800; postranchinn.com; $$$$). Seek a table on the outdoor deck and order the four-course prix fixe dinner.

OPPOSITE A hot spring pool at the Esalen Institute, where you can seek enlightenment or just a relaxing massage.

11 *Literary Nexus* 11 a.m.

The **Henry Miller Memorial Library** (Highway 1; 831-667-2574; henrymiller.org) maintains a reference collection of Miller's work, a bookshop, and a big wooden deck where visitors can enjoy coffee and Wi-Fi. Special events include readings, concerts, art shows, performances, and seminars. It's hardly monumental—little more than a house in the woods before a grassy yard strewn with sculptures and bric-a-brac that might be sculptural. Like much of the rest of Big Sur, the library is a casual place where lounging and artistic pursuit go hand in hand.

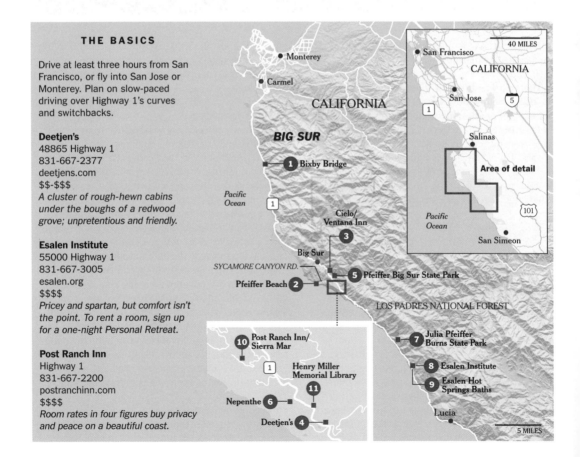

THE BASICS

Drive at least three hours from San Francisco, or fly into San Jose or Monterey. Plan on slow-paced driving over Highway 1's curves and switchbacks.

Deetjen's
48865 Highway 1
831-667-2377
deetjens.com
$$-$$$
A cluster of rough-hewn cabins under the boughs of a redwood grove; unpretentious and friendly.

Esalen Institute
55000 Highway 1
831-667-3005
esalen.org
$$$$
Pricey and spartan, but comfort isn't the point. To rent a room, sign up for a one-night Personal Retreat.

Post Ranch Inn
Highway 1
831-667-2200
postranchinn.com
$$$$
Room rates in four figures buy privacy and peace on a beautiful coast.

Monterey

Carmel

CALIFORNIA

BIG SUR

Pacific
Ocean

1 Bixby Bridge

1

Cielo/
Ventana Inn

3

Big Sur

SYCAMORE CANYON RD.

Pfeiffer Beach 2

5 Pfeiffer Big Sur State Park

40 MILES

San Francisco

CALIFORNIA

San Jose

5

1

Salinas

Area of detail

Pacific
Ocean

101

San Simeon

LOS PADRES NATIONAL FOREST

Post Ranch Inn/
Sierra Mar
10

1

Henry Miller
Memorial Library

11

Nepenthe 6

Deetjen's 4

7 Julia Pfeiffer
Burns State Park

8 Esalen Institute

9 Esalen Hot
Springs Baths

Lucia

5 MILES

Carmel

With its architectural mishmash of storybook English cottages and Swiss Alpine chalets, the small California town of Carmel-by-the-Sea resembles a Disneyland version of Europe. You half expect a bereted Parisian to saunter out of one of the ridiculously cute Euro-themed bistros. But walk a few blocks to Carmel's steep, sandy beach and the view is pure California: a rugged Pacific coastline spangled with rocky outcroppings, ghostly cypress trees, and the electric green slopes of the famed Pebble Beach golf course. The one-square-mile village has no street lights, parking meters, or numbered addresses, but you wouldn't call it low-key. Once a bohemian outpost for people like Jack London, Carmel today is prime real estate, and the surrounding valley is abuzz with top-notch restaurants, boutique wineries, and precious shops. — BY JAIME GROSS

FRIDAY

1 *Cocktails with Clint* 6 p.m.

Carmel has had its share of boldfaced residents, but few more enduring or beloved than Clint Eastwood, who was the town's mayor from 1986 to 1988 and still lives in the area. You might catch a glimpse of him at his restaurant at **Mission Ranch** (26270 Dolores Street; 831-624-6436; missionranchcarmel.com), his 22-acre property just outside of town, where he's been known to eat with his family and greet old-timers at the piano bar. Order a glass of wine and snag a seat on the heated restaurant patio overlooking a striking tableau: sheep meadows, rolling hills, and the shimmering ocean in the distance.

2 *California French* 8 p.m.

For an intimate dinner with plenty of foodie appeal, try Aubergine, the restaurant at the Relais & Châteaux hotel **L'Auberge Carmel** (Seventh Avenue and Monte Verde Street; 831-624-8578; laubergecarmel.com; $$$$). The French-influenced menu reflects the availability of fresh local produce, celebrating the seasons with dishes like roasted lamb with cranberry bean cassoulet.

OPPOSITE The Point Lobos State Reserve.

RIGHT A landscape painter at Bernardus Winery in vineyard country near Carmel-by-the-Sea.

3 *Biking for a View* 8 a.m.

Beat the gawking motorists and entry fee for cars by waking early and biking the **17-Mile Drive**, the jaw-dropping corniche that hugs the rocky coastline between Carmel and Pacific Grove. **Adventures by the Sea** (299 Cannery Row, Monterey; 831-372-1807; adventuresbythesea.com) rents bikes for $7 an hour and is an easy five miles from the drive's most scenic stretches, which are lined with sandy beaches, golf courses, and a 250-year-old cypress tree sprouting from a seaside boulder.

4 *Mission Museum* 11 a.m.

The **San Carlos Borroméo del Rio Carmelo Mission** (3080 Rio Road; 831-624-1271; carmelmission.org) was founded at its present site in 1771 by Father Junipero Serra and was once the headquarters for the entire California mission system. Known more simply as the Carmel Mission, the site includes a poppy-filled garden, an abalone-strewn cemetery, and a stone Basilica with original 18th-century artworks. At the Mission's **Convento Museum**, you can peer into Father Serra's spartan living quarters — with a table, a chair, and a highly uncomfortable-looking wooden bed — and check out his book collection, identified as "California's first library."

5 *In-Town Tastings* 12:30 p.m.

Pick up lunch on a walking tour of some of Carmel's best food shops. Here's a cheat sheet: **Bountiful Basket** (San Carlos Street off Ocean Avenue; 831-625-4457; bountifulbasketcarmel.com)

imports more than 100 olive oils and vinegars from around the world; **Bruno's Market and Deli** (Sixth Avenue and Junipero Avenue; 831-624-3821; brunosmarket.com) has gourmet tri-tip and barbecued chicken sandwiches; and the **Cheese Shop** (Carmel Plaza, Ocean Avenue and Junipero Avenue, lower level; 800-828-9463; thecheeseshopinc.com) stocks picnic fixings, wine, and about 300 cheeses. They'll let you taste as many as you like, or they can assemble a customized cheese plate that you can nibble at the cafe tables out front.

6 *Sip the Valley* 2 p.m.

Thanks to its coastal climate and sandy, loamy soil, Carmel Valley is gaining renown for its wines. Most of the tasting rooms are clustered in Carmel Valley Village, a small town with a handful of restaurants and wineries 12 miles east of Carmel-by-the-Sea. **Bernardus** (5 West Carmel Valley Road; 800-223-2533; bernardus.com), the granddaddy of area wineries, is known for the breadth and quality of its wines. A relative newcomer, **Boekenoogen Wines** (24 West Carmel Valley Road; 831-659-4215; boekenoogenwines.com), is a small family-owned winery with a few varietals. Teetotalers can opt for topical wine treatments at **Bernardus Lodge** (415 Carmel Valley Road; 831-658-3560; bernardus.com), where a spa offers chardonnay facials and grape seed body scrubs.

7 *Stuff for Home* 4 p.m.

Walk off the buzz back in town, where 42 hidden courtyards and alleys shelter a plethora of stylish new galleries and boutiques. **Trouvé** (San Carlos Street and Sixth Avenue; 831-625-9777; trouvehome.com) is a well-curated collection of modern housewares and global antiques. The whimsical **Piccolo** (Dolores Street between Ocean and Seventh Avenues; 831-624-4411; piccolocarmel.com) is packed to the gills with handmade glassware, pottery, stationery, and jewelry. And the working studio and gallery of **Steven Whyte**, a local sculptor (Dolores Street

between Fifth and Sixth Avenues; 831-620-1917; stevenwhytesculptor.com), sells his hyper-realistic cast bronze portraits. Looking for something humbler? The **Carmel Drug Store** (Ocean Avenue and San Carlos Street; 831-624-3819; carmeldrugstore.com) has been selling handmade Swiss combs, grandma colognes, and Coca-Cola in glass bottles since 1910.

8 *Casual Flavors* 8 p.m.

For dinner, make a beeline for one of Carmel's über-charming French or Italian restaurants. **La Bicyclette** (Dolores Street at Seventh Avenue; 831-622-9899; labicycletterestaurant.com; $$$) resembles a rustic village bistro. The compact menu spans Europe with dishes like beef with Gorgonzola-red wine sauce or German sausage with homemade sauerkraut. Also worth a try is **Cantinetta Luca** (Dolores Street between Ocean and Seventh Avenues; 831-625-6500; cantinettaluca.com; $$$), an Italian restaurant popular for its wood-fired

ABOVE The Cheese Shop stocks picnic fixings, wine, and about 300 different cheeses.

BELOW Trouvé, a housewares and antiques shop downtown.

OPPOSITE Cycling on the winding 17-Mile Drive, which hugs the rocky coastline between Carmel and Pacific Grove.

pizzas, homemade pastas, all-Italian wine list, and a dozen types of salume aged on site in a glass-walled curing room.

SUNDAY

9 *Sea Life* 11 a.m.

Legend has it that Robert Louis Stevenson hit on the inspiration for the 1883 novel *Treasure Island* while strolling the beach near Point Lobos. Retrace his steps at **Point Lobos State Reserve** (Route 1, three miles south of Carmel; 831-624-4909; pt-lobos.parks.state.ca.us), a majestic landscape with 14 meandering trails. Don't forget binoculars: you can spot sea otters, seals, and sea lions year-round, and migrating gray whales December through May. Scuba divers take note: 60 percent of the reserve's 554 acres lies underwater, in one of the richest marine habitats in California. Scuba diving, snorkeling, and kayaking reservations can be booked through the park's Web site.

10 *Poodles and Scones* 2 p.m.

In a town known for being dog-friendly, the **Cypress Inn** (Seventh Avenue and Lincoln Street; 831-624-3871; cypress-inn.com) takes the cake with poop bags at the door, bone-shaped biscuits at the front desk, and a *Best-in-Show*-worthy tea service. In addition to serving scones and crustless cucumber sandwiches, the tea service draws a head-spinning parade of Shih Tzus, toy poodles, and other impeccably groomed pups taking tea with their equally well-coiffed owners.

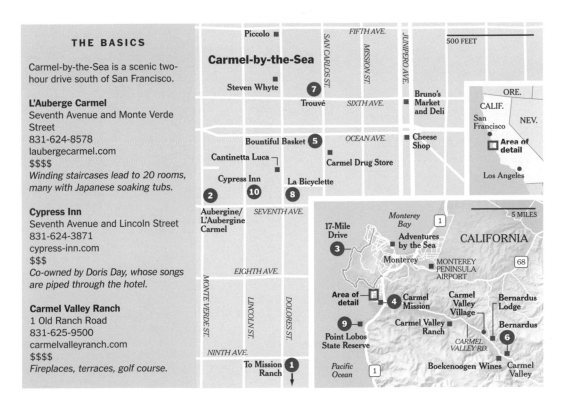

THE BASICS

Carmel-by-the-Sea is a scenic two-hour drive south of San Francisco.

L'Auberge Carmel
Seventh Avenue and Monte Verde Street
831-624-8578
laubergecarmel.com
$$$$
Winding staircases lead to 20 rooms, many with Japanese soaking tubs.

Cypress Inn
Seventh Avenue and Lincoln Street
831-624-3871
cypress-inn.com
$$$
Co-owned by Doris Day, whose songs are piped through the hotel.

Carmel Valley Ranch
1 Old Ranch Road
831-625-9500
carmelvalleyranch.com
$$$$
Fireplaces, terraces, golf course.

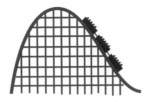

Santa Cruz

Santa Cruz has Mediterranean weather and an artfully skewed sense of reality. Yes, there are world-class surf breaks, sidewalk cafes, and a seaside amusement park, but on the city's streets you will also see jugglers, a saw player, and a street accordionist named the Great Morgani who dresses like an alien robot. This town has a high tolerance for eccentricity. And don't mistake it for a Southern California beach town. There isn't much in the way of glitz, celebrities, or pushy talent agents. Instead, the temperate weather, the Pacific Ocean, and the University of California, Santa Cruz, have attracted a mixture of surfers, street musicians, intellectuals, bookworms, authors, professors, and young professionals, all happy to share the sun and the salt air.
— BY DAN WHITE

FRIDAY

1 *Pacific Cruise* 4 p.m.

Once the domain of seedy bars and bong displays, the southern section of Pacific Avenue is now a more fashionable strip where the city's lust for vintage is on display. **Idle Hands Dry Goods** (803 Pacific Avenue; 831-466-9305; idlehandsdrygoods.com) feels like an updated Rolling Stones track, melding vintage American outlaw looks (cowboy boots, belt buckles) with rock-'n'-roller attitude (graphic T-shirts, Pendleton shirts). **True Love Antiques & Vintage** (805 Pacific Avenue; 714-847-3961) is a wonder cabinet of curios, art, and odd-ends. And on nearby Cedar Street, **MetaVinyl** (320 Cedar Street; 831-466-9027; metavinyl.com) carries new and old LPs, turntable gear, and rare finds like a mint-condition copy of 2 Live Crew's "As Nasty as They Wanna Be."

2 *Haut Kebabs* 7 p.m.

The dining scene in downtown Santa Cruz got a jolt with the arrival of **Laili** (101B Cooper Street; 831-423-4545; lailirestaurant.com; $$), a stylish Afghan restaurant. With its nattily dressed waiters, soaring ceilings and wall-size photo display of precious Afghan jewelry, this is no hole-in-the-wall kebab joint. A cross-section of Santa Cruz can be found on a given night, sampling Persian chive-stuffed Aushak dumplings and the braised lamb shank with kabuli rice and yogurt. Ask for a seat at the communal table, where you can

rub elbows with surfers and techies, and watch a cook in an open kitchen preparing naan dough with a giant rolling pin.

3 *Latin Rhythms* 9 p.m.

The spiciest spot downtown is arguably the weekly salsa dance party at the historic **Palomar Ballroom** (1344 Pacific Avenue; 831-426-1221; palomarballroom.com), where dancers swirl in tight dresses, miniskirts, and high heels. If you know your salsa moves, pay $5 at the door. If you need to brush up, a $10 fee covers a salsa class and the dance party.

4 *Deep Red* Midnight

A crimson glow beckons late-night patrons upstairs to the **Red Restaurant & Bar** (200 Locust Street; 831-425-1913; redsantacruz.com), a curiously dark lounge with hidden nooks that stays open until 2 a.m. Unless you sit by the fire, reading the menu can be a challenge, so try the Winnie, a house-infused rose tea vodka with fresh lemon and simple syrup. Don't confuse this spot with the Red Room, which occupies the floor below and is a rite of passage for college students.

OPPOSITE Sand, surf, and a sunset, all commodities in generous supply in Santa Cruz.

BELOW Even if you're a novice at salsa, consider joining the weekly salsa dance party at the Palomar Ballroom. If you don't know the moves, you can pay $5 extra for a class.

SATURDAY

5 *Warm Brioche* 10 a.m.

Stock up for an outdoor picnic along the scenic coastline. True to its name, the **Buttery** (702 Soquel Avenue; 831-458-3020; butterybakery.com) specializes in butter-rich comfort foods like lemon cheese pockets and blueberry muffins. It also sells French baguettes. Round out your supplies across the street at **Shopper's Corner** (622 Soquel Avenue; 831-423-1398; shopperscorner.com), a local institution with a neon clock, local wines, hard cheeses, and tapenades.

6 *Take a Hike* 11 a.m.

A slow ride on West Cliff Drive offers views of cypress trees, eroded cliffs, and epic surf breaks. Park at the **Wilder Ranch State Park** (1401 Old Coast Road; 831-423-9703; parks.ca.gov), a 7,000-acre park with numerous hiking trails that tunnel through misted forests of alders, Douglas firs, and coastal redwoods. The park is also home to bobcats, feral piglets, and the occasional cougar.

7 *Green Hedonists* 3 p.m.

Once home to a frozen-vegetable processing plant, the **Swift Street Courtyard** (402 Ingalls Street) has been transformed into a kind of epicurean food court. The bittersweet Black IPA is a specialty at **Santa Cruz Mountain Brewing** (Suite 27; 831-425-4900; santacruzmountainbrewing.com), an organic microbrewery with a tiny tap room. If you're hungry, order a platter of fish tacos delivered to the bar from the shop next door, **Kelly's French Bakery** (831-423-9059; kellysfrenchbakery.com). Or, if you want to sample biodynamic wines, head to the tasting room at **Bonny Doon Vineyard** (328 Ingalls Street; 831-425-4518; bonnydoonvineyard.com), where a metal spaceship hovers overhead. A flight may include wines like

ABOVE The Walton Lighthouse near Seabright State Beach.

a white Spanish varietal called albariño or a dry muscat, both made from Monterey County grapes.

8 *Seabright Salumi* 6:30 p.m.

At **La Posta** (538 Seabright Avenue; 831-457-2782; lapostarestaurant.com; $$), the flavors might hail from Italy, but the ingredients are local. This handsome restaurant, which opened a few years ago in a former general store, draws locavores to the hushed neighborhood of Seabright. Examples of its farm-to-table ethos include the ortiche brick-oven pizza with wild nettles foraged at Route 1 Farm in Santa Cruz, and an escarole salad topped with a boiled egg that comes from the chickens out back.

9 *Music Boxes* 8 p.m.

With its large college population, Santa Cruz has long been a hub for indie music. One of the best spots to hear live music is the **Rio Theatre** (831-423-8209; 1205 Soquel Avenue; riotheatre.com), a former movie house from the 1940s that reopened 10 years ago as a concert hall and features acts like Neko Case and Cat Power. Another reliable option is the **Crepe Place** (1134 Soquel Avenue; 831-429-6994; thecrepeplace.com), a small venue housed in a century-old Victorian building, where acts like Erin McKeown and the cult favorite Dan Bern perform under the original stamped-tin ceiling.

SUNDAY

10 *Beach Walk* 10 a.m.

After ordering a butter-slathered hot cinnamon roll at **Linda's Seabreeze Cafe** (542 Seabright

Avenue; 831-427-9713; seabreezecafe.com), walk to nearby **Seabright State Beach** (East Cliff Drive at Seabright Avenue), a long stretch of tan-white sand with a midget lighthouse, a foghorn, and a cave. The **Municipal Wharf** (21 Municipal Wharf; 831-420-6025; santacruzwharf.com), a large pier built in 1914 that draws fishermen and pods of barking sea lions, is nearby. Don't trust your eyes: that set of "islands" is a fog-bound stretch of coastline.

11 *Deep Freeze* 2 p.m.

Two scoops of celery raisin ice cream? You won't find that in the freezer case of the local supermarket, but it is among the eccentric flavors that have been dreamed up at the **Penny Ice Creamery** (913 Cedar

Street; 831-204-2523; thepennyicecreamery.com). The shop changes its menu daily, so you never know whether it will have familiar options like rum raisin and dark chocolate or something wacky like black sesame or mandarin creamsicle.

OPPOSITE BELOW Sea lions under the municipal wharf, which dates back to 1914.

ABOVE Idle Hands Dry Goods on Pacific Avenue.

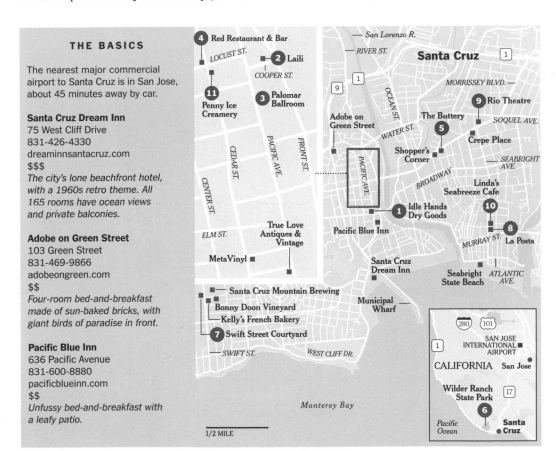

THE BASICS

The nearest major commercial airport to Santa Cruz is in San Jose, about 45 minutes away by car.

Santa Cruz Dream Inn
75 West Cliff Drive
831-426-4330
dreaminnsantacruz.com
$$$
The city's lone beachfront hotel, with a 1960s retro theme. All 165 rooms have ocean views and private balconies.

Adobe on Green Street
103 Green Street
831-469-9866
adobeongreen.com
$$
Four-room bed-and-breakfast made of sun-baked bricks, with giant birds of paradise in front.

Pacific Blue Inn
636 Pacific Avenue
831-600-8880
pacificblueinn.com
$$
Unfussy bed-and-breakfast with a leafy patio.

Red Restaurant & Bar

LOCUST ST.
COOPER ST.
Laili
Palomar Ballroom
Penny Ice Creamery

CEDAR ST.
PACIFIC AVE.
FRONT ST.
CENTER ST.
ELM ST.
True Love Antiques & Vintage
MetaVinyl

Santa Cruz Mountain Brewing
Bonny Doon Vineyard
Kelly's French Bakery
Swift Street Courtyard
SWIFT ST.
WEST CLIFF DR.

San Lorenzo R.
RIVER ST.
Santa Cruz
MORRISSEY BLVD.
OCEAN ST.
Rio Theatre
Adobe on Green Street
WATER ST.
The Buttery
SOQUEL AVE.
Crepe Place
Shopper's Corner
SEABRIGHT AVE.
PACIFIC AVE.
BROADWAY
Linda's Seabreeze Cafe
Idle Hands Dry Goods
Pacific Blue Inn
MURRAY ST.
La Posta
Santa Cruz Dream Inn
Seabright State Beach
ATLANTIC AVE.
Municipal Wharf

Monterey Bay

1/2 MILE

280 101
SAN JOSE INTERNATIONAL AIRPORT
CALIFORNIA   San Jose
Wilder Ranch State Park   17
Santa Cruz
Pacific Ocean

Silicon Valley

Like the high-tech companies that give this hyper-prosperous region its name, Silicon Valley thrives on reinvention. Situated just south of San Francisco Bay, the valley was once home to orchards and vineyards. These days, of course, it bears fruit of a different sort, as the home of tech giants like Apple, Google, and Intel. Buoyed by the resilience of tech companies, the valley's dozen or so cities, which include Mountain View and Palo Alto, continue to evolve from corporate strip malls to urban hubs. The valley now buzzes with cultural spaces, lively restaurants, and the energy of a hyper-educated workforce that has no problem keeping up.
— BY ASHLEE VANCE

FRIDAY

1 *Small Town Downtown* 4 p.m.

San Jose may still call itself the capital of Silicon Valley, but picturesque **Los Gatos** is emerging as its trendier downtown, with historic cottages and upscale boutiques. The chains have begun an invasion, but dozens of independent shops remain, selling fashion, children's clothing, baby duds, shoes, accessories, home decor, and collectors' items. Start your prospecting on North Santa Cruz Avenue at West Main Street and follow your whims as you head north. The people cruising the streets in Los Gatos give off a vibe that matches the bright, charming town, which is full of surprises off the main drag.

2 *Pitch Your Venture* 6 p.m.

Sand Hill Road is one the valley's main arteries, cutting through Palo Alto, Menlo Park, and Stanford University. As the weekend gets under way, follow the stream of Prius hybrids, Mercedes coupes, and the occasional Tesla electric car to **Madera** (2825 Sand Hill Road, Menlo Park; 650-561-1540; maderasandhill.com), at the Rosewood Sand Hill hotel. The indoor-outdoor bar is a hot spot for venture capitalists to unwind and gossip as they survey their domain on a terrace that looks out on the surrounding mountains. Down

a cocktail or three, and find your pluck to pitch that brilliant Web idea you had.

3 *American Fare* 8 p.m.

St. Michael's Alley (140 Homer Avenue, Palo Alto; 650-326-2530; stmikes.com; $$) seized a page straight out of the valley playbook when it reinvented itself and moved to an ambitious new home, a few blocks off crowded University Avenue in Palo Alto, in 2009. Two and a half years in the making, the new incarnation has three elegant dining areas, including a bar anchored by an artful hunk of walnut. The business casual attire matches the informal cuisine, which leans toward Californian and American fare.

4 *Choose Your Libation* 10 p.m.

Shame on Stanford students for allowing such tame bars along their home turf, University Avenue. For a more energized crowd, head to nearby California Avenue. A favorite among Silicon Valley's young titans is **Antonio's Nut House** (321 California Avenue, Palo Alto; 650-321-2550; antoniosnuthouse.com), a low-key neighborhood place where patrons can chuck their peanut shells on the floor, scribble on the walls, and take a photo with a peanut-dispensing gorilla. Down the road is **La Bodeguita del Medio** (463 California Avenue, Palo Alto; 650-326-7762; labodeguita.com), a Cuban-style bar and restaurant that serves tall glasses of rum, along with hand-rolled cigars.

SATURDAY

5 *Ogle Google* 9 a.m.

Unless you're the next Mark Zuckerberg, the high-tech campuses that dot the valley are off-limits.

OPPOSITE A view over the high-tech hotbed of Silicon Valley toward San Francisco Bay, from Thomas Fogarty Winery.

RIGHT Checking out a 1970s-era Microchess game at the Computer History Museum in Mountain View.

But there are ways to sneak a look. For a glimpse of the **Googleplex** (1600 Amphitheatre Parkway, Mountain View), the headquarters-cum-playground of Google, drive north on Shoreline Boulevard until you see a pair of colorful towers rising on your left. There's a small public park next to the entrance that peeks inside the laid-back campus. Grander views can be found through **Airship Ventures** (Building 20, South Akron Road; Moffett Field; 650-969-8100;

ABOVE The garage where Hewlett-Packard began.

BELOW The circuit board of an Apple I, the first Apple computer, at the Computer History Museum.

OPPOSITE ABOVE The Airship Ventures zeppelin.

OPPOSITE BELOW Google's headquarters.

airshipventures.com), a tour company that offers rides aboard a 246-foot-long airship. Plan on shelling out at least $200 for a 30-minute ride, but you'll glide over geek hot spots like Apple's shimmering headquarters and Larry Ellison's 23-acre Japanese-style compound. The airship travels along the West Coast, so check its Web site to be sure it's in town.

6 *Cafeteria Lunch* Noon

Some chefs parlay a reality show into a restaurant. Charlie Ayers used his stint as the top chef of the Googleplex cafeteria — and a few of his Google shares — to open **Calafia Café** (855 El Camino Real, Palo Alto; 650-322-9200; calafiapaloalto.com). It is split down the middle between a sit-down restaurant and to-go counter. The fare is a lunch-style version of Californian comfort food: tacos, salmon, lamb hash, turkey meatloaf, and, of course, a vegetarian menu.

7 *Computers 101* 3 p.m.

The name Silicon Valley may have been coined in the early 1970s, but the tech timeline goes even further back here. For a self-guided tour of computer lore, start at 367 Addison Avenue in Palo Alto, site of the humble wood garage where Bill Hewlett and Dave Packard started their company in 1939. Next, drive by 391 San Antonio Road in Mountain View, a squat, dilapidated produce shop that housed the first true silicon start-up — Shockley Semiconductor

Laboratory — in 1955. Finally, swing by 844 Charleston Road in Palo Alto, an office building where Fairchild Semiconductor invented a commercial version of the integrated circuit in 1959. Much of that history is now lovingly captured at the **Computer History Museum** (1401 North Shoreline Boulevard, Mountain View; 650-810-1010; computerhistory.org), where you'll get a sense of how we got from room-filling mainframes to nanochips.

8 *Vietnamese Plates* 8 p.m.

Thanks to Google and its army of millionaires, Castro Street, the main drag in Mountain View, has undergone a culinary and nightlife revival. Among the bubblier spots is **Xanh** (110 Castro Street, Mountain View; 650-964-1888; xanhrestaurant.com; $$), a sprawling Vietnamese fusion restaurant with a handsome patio and dining rooms bathed in green and blue lights. The playful names on the menu — Duck Duck Good, Truth Serum cocktails — fail to capture the elegance of the dishes, plated in delicate fashion with exotic sauces. On weekends, the bar/lounge turns into a quasi-nightclub, with D.J.'s and more cocktails.

9 *Geek Talk* 10 p.m.

Back in 2010, an Apple software engineer lost an iPhone 4 prototype at **Gourmet Haus Staudt** (2615 Broadway; 650-364-9232; gourmethausstaudt.com), a German beer garden in Redwood City. Images of the prototype were splattered on Gizmodo, foiling the company's well-known obsession with secrecy. The beer garden has since shaken off its notoriety and remains a low-key place for engineers to gab about the newest products of their wizardry.

SUNDAY

10 *Local Harvest* 9 a.m.

Farmers' markets dot the valley on Sundays. One of the most bountiful is the **Mountain View Farmers' Market**, in the parking lot of the town's Caltrain Station (600 West Evelyn; 800-806-3276;

cafarmersmkts.com), where flowers, fruits, and vegetables are sold along with locally raised meats and artisanal cheeses. You can pick up prepared foods to munch on as well, including homemade pork dumplings and fresh samosas.

11 *Up to the Hills* 11 a.m.

It's called a valley for a reason. The Santa Cruz Mountains rise along the valley's western edge and provide a treasure hunt for people willing to explore. Wineries, including the **Thomas Fogarty Winery** (19501 Skyline Boulevard; Woodside; 650-851-6777;

fogartywinery.com) sit atop the mountains, offering unrivaled views of the valley. Hikes abound. The **Windy Hill Open Space Preserve** (openspace.org), a 15-minute drive from Stanford in Portola Valley, has a range of trails that cut through 1,312 acres of grassland ridges and redwood forests. By the end of the hike, you'll be able to spot Stanford, the NASA Ames Research Center, and the mega-mansions like a valley pro.

ABOVE Gourmet Haus Staudt found a place in valley lore when an iPhone prototype was carelessly left behind there.

OPPOSITE The Googleplex, headquarters of Google, spreads out over a campus in Mountain View. Visitors can access the small public park at the entrance

THE BASICS

Fly into San Jose or San Francisco. Rent a car.

Rosewood Sand Hill
2825 Sand Hill Road, Menlo Park
650-561-1500
rosewoodsandhill.com
$$$$
On a 16-acre estate with stunning rose gardens overlooking the hills.

Avatar Hotel
4200 Great America Parkway,
Santa Clara
408-235-8900
avatarhotel.com
$$
Newly remodeled, with Wi-Fi and iPod docks.

Larkspur Landing Sunnyvale
748 North Mathilda Avenue,
Sunnyvale
408-733-1212
larkspurhotels.com
$$
All-suite hotel catering to business travelers.

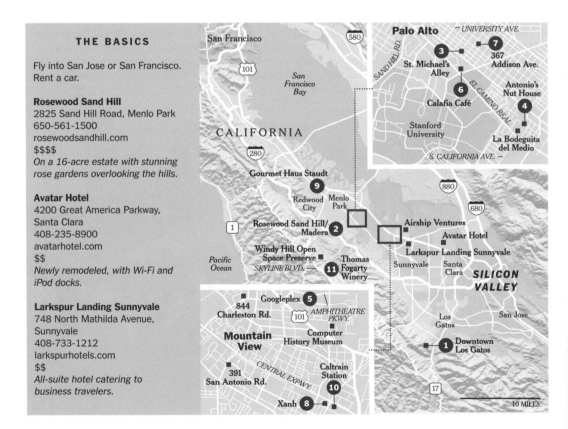

San Francisco

San Francisco typically wows visitors with its heights. The hills sear themselves into memory after a few up-and-down-and-up-again cable car rides or punishing walks. Then there are the hilltop sights: the sweeping vistas and the picturesque Victorians. But surrounding all of that is coastline, miles of peninsula shore along the Pacific Ocean and the expansive natural harbor of San Francisco Bay. Once a working industrial area with pockets of outright blight, much of the city's waterfront has been polished into another of its pleasures. To sample what it offers, start exploring in the east, south of the Bay Bridge, and loop your way west to the Golden Gate and then south to Ocean Beach. In one weekend romp, you'll join San Franciscans in many of the places they love best—and see what remains of their city's maritime heart. —BY JESSE MCKINLEY

FRIDAY

1 *A Ride along the Water* 4 p.m.

China Basin, south of the Bay Bridge, is home to an entirely new neighborhood since big changes began around 2000. The University of California, San Francisco has developed its **Mission Bay Campus**, adding handsome new buildings and public art including two soaring steel towers by Richard Serra, a San Francisco native. And the opening of **AT&T Park**, the baseball field that's home to the San Francisco Giants, brought new energy and new monuments including tributes to greats like Willie Mays and Willie McCovey (the basin is often called McCovey Cove). Rent a bike at the **Bike Hut**, a non-profit outlet at Pier 40 (415-543-4335; thebikehut.org), and pedal the wide promenade along the water.

2 *Embarcadero Imbibing* 5:30 p.m.

Once the home to a raised freeway—demolished after the 1989 Loma Prieta earthquake—and before that a busy wharf area receiving cargo from around the world, the **Embarcadero** is now one of San Francisco's most inviting Friday night spots, filled with workweek-wearied downtown workers ready to relax. Two inviting spots for a drink and appetizers are **Waterbar** (399 Embarcadero; 415-284-9922; waterbarsf.com) and **Epic Roasthouse** (369 Embarcadero; 415-369-9955; epicroasthouse.com). Views of the Bay Bridge are unbeatable at either, but oysters at Waterbar can really set the mood.

3 *Boat to a Bistro* 8 p.m.

Forbes Island (off Pier 39; 415-951-4900; forbesisland.com; $$$) is not an island, but it is an experience. Created from a 700-ton houseboat, it's a floating restaurant complete with an underwater dining room (with portholes), a 40-foot lighthouse, and an outdoor bar within barking distance from local sea lions. Its nautically minded creator and owner, Forbes Thor Kiddoo, pilots the pontoon boat that brings patrons from a nearby pier. The fish chowder is briny and yummy, as is an assortment of turf (including flat steak in a cognac cream sauce) and surf (organic salmon). Kiddoo, a houseboat designer who combines Gilligan's mirth with the Skipper's physique, is a charming host. Don't miss the 360-degree view from the top of the lighthouse; it may be the best—and the most unusual—vantage point in the city.

SATURDAY

4 *Flip, Flop, Fly* 9 a.m.

Yearning for a Saturday-morning workout? Go for a run at **Crissy Field**, once a waterfront airfield and now San Francisco's weekend outdoor gym, with

OPPOSITE On the Embarcadero near the San Francisco Oakland Bay Bridge. Outdoor workouts, often including jogging near the water, are a theme of San Francisco life.

RIGHT The Bay Bridge view from Waterbar.

masses of joggers, walkers, and cyclists cruising its paths. It's part of the **Presidio**, formerly a military complex guarding San Francisco Bay and the strategic strait at its entrance—the Golden Gate. Now it's all part of the Golden Gate National Recreation Area. Activities run from the quirky (crabbing classes at the Civil War-era Fort Point, under the Golden Gate Bridge) to the caffeinated (outdoor coffee at the **Beach Hut**, 1199 East Beach; 415-561-7761). But the bounciest option is the **House of Air** (926 Mason Street; 415-345-9675; houseofairsf.com), a trampoline center in one of the repurposed buildings on the main Presidio post. Flanked by a kids' swimming school and an indoor climbing center, the House of Air also features a dodgeball court, a training center, and an old-fashioned bouncy castle for tots.

5 *Chow Time* Noon

Dining at the Presidio has come a long way since the days of reveille at dawn. Several restaurants now dot the northeastern corner, where much of the Presidio's development has occurred since it was transferred to the National Park Service in the

mid-1990s. One spot that retains the old military feel is the **Presidio Social Club** (563 Ruger Street; 415-885-1888; presidiosocialclub.com; $$$). As unpretentious as an Army grunt, the club offers old-time drinks (the rye-heavy Sazerac, which dates to 1840) and a pleasantly affordable brunch. A dessert of beignets with hot cocoa can fuel you up for your next offensive.

6 *Union Street Stroll* 2 p.m.

Detour off base to Union Street, long a shoppers' favorite for its locally owned boutiques and home furnishings stores. The owner of **Chloe Rose** (No. 1824; 415-932-6089; chloeroseboutique.com), who lives upstairs, has a keen eye for silk dresses, chiffon blouses, and gold jewelry. Nearby are **Sprout San Francisco** (No. 1828; 415-359-9205; sproutsanfrancisco.com), which carries clothing, toys, and other items for children, and more women's wear at **Ambiance** (No. 1864; 415-923-9797; ambiancesf.com) and the nearby **Marmalade** (No. 2059; 415-673-9544; marmaladesf.com). The **San Francisco Surf Company** (No. 2181; 415-440-7873; sfsurfcompany.com), run by a local wave rider, stocks surf wax candles and all manner of aquatic accoutrements.

7 *Nature and Art* 4 p.m.

Take a walk through the hills and woods on the Pacific coast side of the Presidio, where miles of hiking trails lead to scenic overlooks (presidio.gov). You may also find an artwork or two. The Presidio

ABOVE The downtown skyline under a ceiling of clouds. The gold dome crowns the Palace of Fine Arts, built for a 1915 exposition.

LEFT The wind can be biting, but the mood is usually warm as groups gather for impromptu fires on Ocean Beach.

OPPOSITE ABOVE The House of Air, a trampoline center in one of the repurposed buildings of the Presidio.

OPPOSITE BELOW *Spire*, a sculpture by Andy Goldsworthy, at the Presidio. Miles of trails lead to ocean views.

doesn't need much help being beautiful, but that hasn't stopped artists who have placed installations and sculpture on the grounds. One is Andy Goldsworthy, an environmental British sculptor whose ephemeral pieces in the park include *Spire* — a soaring wooden spike — and *Wood Line*, a serpentine forest-floor sculpture made of eucalyptus.

8 *Dinner at the Edge* 8 p.m.

The **Cliff House** (1090 Point Lobos; 415-386-3330; cliffhouse.com) has been serving visitors at the end of the continent since the Civil War. Still perched on the same rocks, facing shark-fin-shaped Seal Rock and the crashing waves below, the Cliff House underwent a major renovation in 2004. The result was a vastly improved dining experience on two levels, each with commanding views of the Pacific. The **Bistro** ($$), upstairs, serves entrees and cocktails under the watchful eyes of celebrity headshots (Judy Garland, for one, on an autographed glamour shot,

sending her "best wishes"). Downstairs is the higher-end **Sutro's** ($$$), where the specialty is seafood dishes like a two-crab sandwich or grilled scallops. Try a Ramos Fizz, a gin cocktail — and purported hangover cure — made with egg whites, half-and-half, and orange juice.

9 *Burning, Man* 10:30 p.m.

Few things say California more than beach bonfires, a proud tradition up and down the coast. In San Francisco, free spirits keep it going at **Ocean Beach**, the wide sand expanse south of Baker Beach (the spot where Burning Man, the now Nevada-based arts fest, was born). While the wind can be biting, the mood at the impromptu fires is usually warm

and public nine-hole, par-3 golf course, a lovely bison enclave, and serene fly-fishing ponds. A good place to convene for any park adventure is the **Park Chalet** (1000 Great Highway; 415-386-8439; parkchalet.com; $$$). In this somewhat hidden spot just off Ocean Beach, kids run free in the wilds of the park and parents enjoy a brunch buffet that advertises "bottomless champagne."

as groups congregate with guitars, pipes, and good vibes. Take a blanket and a pullover and watch the stars, surf, and sparks collide.

SUNDAY

10 *Other Side of the Park* 11 a.m.

The western edge of **Golden Gate Park**, facing Ocean Beach, has a Rodney Dangerfield feel, less known and appreciated than the park's cityside flanks. But its offerings are impressive, including a cheap

ABOVE On the trail that leads from Fort Point, under the Golden Gate Bridge, along the bay to Crissy Field.

OPPOSITE A 21st-century addition, *Cupid's Span*, by Claes Oldenburg and Coosje van Bruggen, frames a view of the Ferry Building clock tower, a more traditional San Francisco landmark.

THE BASICS

Take the BART train from San Francisco International Airport to downtown.

Use taxis and public transportation.

Hotel Vitale
8 Mission Street
415-278-3700
hotelvitale.com
$$$$
Style and luxury on the Embarcadero, across from the landmark Ferry Building.

Harbor Court Hotel
165 Steuart Street
415-882-1300
harborcourthotel.com
$$
Boutique hotel with bay views.

Union Street Inn
2229 Union Street
415-346-0424
unionstreetinn.com
$$$
Quiet and charming bed-and-breakfast.

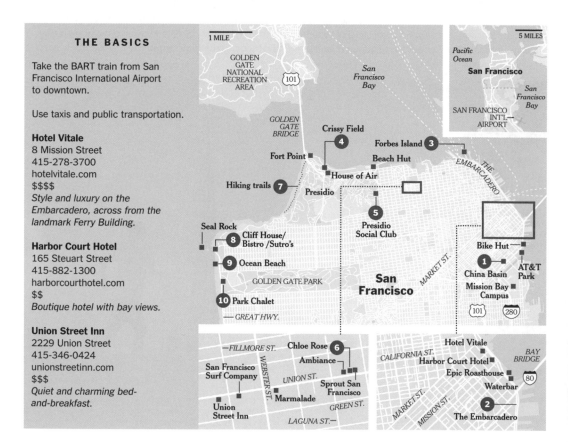

The Mission
San Francisco

For much of the 1990s, San Francisco's Mission District maintained a precarious balance between its colorful Latino roots and a gritty bohemian subculture. Then came the overfed dot-com years. Rising real estate prices threatened the Mission's status not only as a working-class enclave, but also as the city's center of all things edgy and artsy. Sleek bars moved next door to divey taquerias. Boutiquey knick-knack shops came in alongside fusty dollar stores. But prosperity did not sap the district of its cultural eclecticism. With a population that is about half Latino, a third white, and an estimated 11 percent Asian, the Mission still remains a wonderful mishmash. Where else can you find epicurean vegan cafes, feisty nonprofits, and a Central American butcher shop that, for a memorable time, anyway, had women's undergarments in the window?
— BY CHRIS COLIN

FRIDAY

1 *Illicit Doughnuts* 4 p.m.
It's one thing to operate a pirate radio station, with foul-mouthed D.J.'s hopping from rooftop to rooftop to hide the transmitter. But the ever-defiant Pirate Cat Radio, now called the **PCR Collective**, went and opened a cafe (2781 21st Street; 415-341-1199). Now you can stick it to the man over a spot of tea or vegan doughnuts. The grungy décor and sparse offerings are true to pirate form — the fun lies in watching the broadcasts (now confined to the Internet, to appease the FCC) through the smudged window.

2 *Eat with the Fishes* 6:30 p.m.
Don't let the trendiness fool you: the food at **Weird Fish** (2193 Mission Street; 415-863-4744; weirdfishsf.com; $$) is actually terrific. Situated on chaotic Mission Street, this guppy-sized spot serves inspired dishes like sweet-and-spicy rainbow trout, local cod with cauliflower puree and young chestnuts, and something called the Suspicious Fish Dish (varies). There's often a line, but you can wait outside on the street, enjoying that singular pleasure

of sipping wine beside the bus stop that serves as the restaurant's de facto lounge.

3 *Acting Out* 8 p.m.
On a good Friday night, the neighborhood is theatrical in its own right. For more distilled drama, catch a performance at the **Marsh** (1062 Valencia Street; 415-826-5750; themarsh.org), a small theater devoted to small stagings. Award-winning productions have included *Squeezebox* and *Tings Dey Happen*, a one-man show about Nigerian oil politics. Seating is first come, first served, so buy tickets in advance and arrive early.

4 *Hot Diggity* 10 p.m.
It can seem that one hears indie rock or Mexican polka in the Mission, and little else. But **Savanna Jazz** (2937 Mission Street; 415-285-3369; savannajazz.com) has live sets every night but Monday in its cozy, New Orleans-style room. When the last chord is struck and you're still longing for something late-night and local, discover the bacon dog craze on your walk home. Vendors sell them — a food best consumed in the dark — on the sidewalk along Mission.

SATURDAY

5 *Art and Noble Pie* 10 a.m.
You'll never sample all the creative galleries, shops, and restaurants in the Mission. Carve out a few hours for strolling, concentrating on Valencia, Mission, 16th, and 24th Streets. **Aquarius Records** (1055 Valencia Street; 415-647-2272; aquariusrecords.org) is the city's oldest independent record store and a sanctuary for

OPPOSITE San Francisco has a storied mural tradition, and the Mission has a vast, ever-changing collection.

RIGHT Burritos and a skyline view at Dolores Park.

music lovers. For a flavorful snack, take your taste buds to **Mission Cheese** (736 Valencia Street; 415-553-8667; missioncheese.net). The hot pressed sandwiches are good, but for now, just buy a gorgeous loaf of levain—a bread that's a cousin to sourdough—and pair with a selection of artisanal cheeses.

ABOVE At first glance, the Mission District might seem perennially 23, but it has a long history.

BELOW Aquarius Records, a haven for music lovers.

OPPOSITE ABOVE St. Francis Fountain.

OPPOSITE BELOW Mission Dolores.

Galería de la Raza (2857 24th Street; 415-826-8009; galeriadelaraza.org) showcases projects by Chicano and Latino artists and activists. And check out **Creativity Explored** (3245 16th Street; 415-863-2108; creativityexplored.org), a nonprofit studio where developmentally disabled men and women make and sell beautiful art.

6 *Gorging in the Grass* 2 p.m.
  What you've heard about Mission burritos is true: they're big and everyone eats them. Arguing over the best is a popular sport, but you won't go wrong with **Taquería Cancún** (2288 Mission Street; 415-252-9560), a no-frills joint that packs a crowd. Take a Super Veggie up 19th Street to **Dolores Park**, and enjoy the downtown views among the Frisbeeing, smuggled-beer-drinking multitudes. If it's the last Saturday of the month, scout out the **Really Really Free Market** (reallyreallyfree.org), a haphazard and funky exchange that's worth investigating. The prices are really really unbeatable.

7 *Where It All Began* 3 p.m.
  At first glance, the Mission District might seem perennially 23, with a Pabst Blue Ribbon fixed forever in its collective fist. But there's real history in this youthful quarter. Two blocks from Dolores Park is the city's oldest landmark and the district's namesake, **Mission Dolores** (3321 16th Street; 415-621-8203;

missiondolores.org). Founded before San Francisco itself, it remains a hub of cultural and religious life. It's a quick tour, but the bright frescoes and hushed basilica balance the surrounding hoopla with a welcome calm. Hitchcock buffs will recall its cameo in *Vertigo*.

8 *Cocktail Hour* 6 p.m.

San Francisco is a cocktail-before-dinner kind of town—just ask Sam Spade. Among Mission's grooviest bars are the **Latin American Club** (3286 22nd Street; 415-647-2732), **Doc's Clock** (2575 Mission Street; 415-824-3627; docsclock.com), and **Papa Toby's Revolution Cafe** (3248 22nd Street; 415-642-0474). The combination of ambience, music, and robust gawking make these perfect run-ups to dinner.

9 *Dinner and a Movie* 8 p.m.

It may sound gimmicky, but the dinner-and-a-movie at **Foreign Cinema** (2534 Mission Street; 415-648-7600; foreigncinema.com; $$$) is an elegant,

white tablecloth affair. If the weather's nice, snag an outdoor table in the austere, vaguely Soviet cement courtyard. Start with oysters before carving into the likes of bavette steak or delicate tombo tartare with ginger-lime vinaigrette. When the sun sets, a foreign film is projected silently on the far wall with subtitles. Heat lamps keep you toasty and, if you want to follow the dialogue, the waiter will even bring vintage drive-in speakers.

10 *Sweating to the Music* 10:30 p.m.

Hot, sweaty bodies shaking it on a plywood floor in a thimble of a room with holes in the ceiling. If that's your cup of tea—and, in a way, that sums up the Mission perfectly—head over to **Little Baobab** (3388 19th Street; 415-643-3558; littlebaobabsf.com).

The bass thumps and an international crowd sloshes around admirably.

SUNDAY

11 *On the Wall* 11 a.m.

San Francisco has a storied mural tradition, and the **Precita Eyes Mural Arts Center** (2981 24th Street; 415-285-2287; precitaeyes.org) runs casual yet informative tours of the Mission's vast, ever-changing collection. They include scenes of a bloody Honduran massacre and of weeping families pushed out by developers. But perhaps most poignant are the simple portraits of neighborhood figures — the flower seller, the bakery owner, the guy who break-dances. After your tour, stop by **St. Francis Fountain** (2801 24th Street; 415-826-4200; stfrancisfountainsf.com; $) for brunch. Look past the trendy crowd's tattoos and leggings and you'll see a fastidiously preserved ice cream parlor from 90 years ago. They still make a terrific egg cream, and the eggs Florentine aren't bad, either. According to legend, the San Francisco 49ers were founded on the back of a napkin in one of the booths.

ABOVE The food is good at Weird Fish — and that includes the daily Suspicious Fish Dish.

OPPOSITE Dinner and a show at Foreign Cinema.

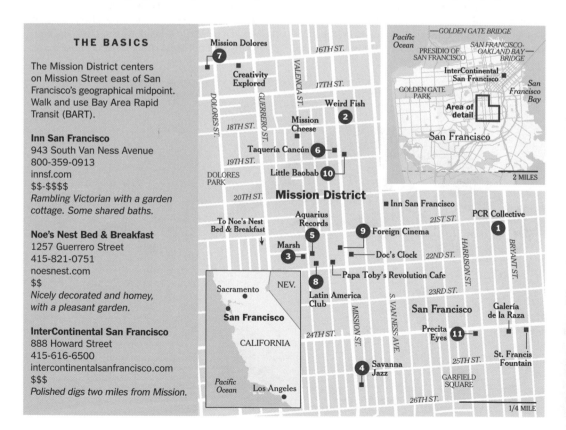

THE BASICS

The Mission District centers on Mission Street east of San Francisco's geographical midpoint. Walk and use Bay Area Rapid Transit (BART).

Inn San Francisco
943 South Van Ness Avenue
800-359-0913
innsf.com
$$-$$$$
Rambling Victorian with a garden cottage. Some shared baths.

Noe's Nest Bed & Breakfast
1257 Guerrero Street
415-821-0751
noesnest.com
$$
Nicely decorated and homey, with a pleasant garden.

InterContinental San Francisco
888 Howard Street
415-616-6500
intercontinentalsanfrancisco.com
$$$
Polished digs two miles from Mission.

Berkeley

Berkeley, California, sticks in the collective memory as a hotbed of '60s radicalism and '70s experimentation. But anyone who thinks that's the whole picture is in for a surprise. From the main gate of the flagship campus of the University of California to revamped sophisticated boutiques, this city overlooking San Francisco Bay offers variety few towns can match. On College Avenue, the main drag, costumed hipsters mix with high-tech geeks in training, and freelance philosophers rub elbows with label-conscious materialists. Not that the spirit of 1969 has completely gone away. Walk down Telegraph Avenue, and along one block you may encounter activists for Free Tibet, patchouli-scented advocates of homeopathic medicine, and crusty purple-haired free-love followers still eager to convert you to their cause.
— BY JOSHUA KURLANTZICK

FRIDAY

1 *Bookmark This* 5 p.m.

Old and new Berkeley, activists and achievers, all head to **Moe's Books** (2476 Telegraph Avenue; 510-849-2087; moesbooks.com). Founded in 1959 and piled high with used books, Moe's is a place to wander for hours, flipping through choices from out-of-print tomes on 1950s African history to kabbalah manuals. The store also hosts frequent readings.

2 *Comfort Soba* 8 p.m.

Berkeley's food scene has blossomed well beyond student hangouts. Consider the local favorite **O Chamé** (1830 Fourth Street; 510-841-8783; $$). Its classy Japanese fusion fare is decidedly un-college-town, but the slightly beaten-up tables and unpretentious crowd make you feel like you're eating in someone's home. And dishes like onion pancakes, soba platters, and grilled eel are as satisfying as Japanese comfort food gets.

3 *Cinema Paradise* 10 p.m.

The **Pacific Film Archive** (2621 Durant Avenue; 510-642-0808; bampfa.berkeley.edu) at the Berkeley Art Museum offers one of the most refreshingly unpredictable moviegoing experiences in the Bay Area. At the archive's theater across the street from the museum, you might find a French New Wave

festival followed by a collection of shorts from West Africa. The archive is particularly strong on Japanese cinema—and grungy-looking grad students.

SATURDAY

4 *Hill Country* 8 a.m.

This is California, so you'll have to get up early to have prime walking paths to yourself. Wander through the main U.C. Berkeley campus, quiet at this time, and into the lush Berkeley hills overlooking the university. You'll pass sprawling mansions that resemble Mexican estates, families walking tiny manicured poodles, and students running off hangovers along the steep hills. It's easy to get lost, so take a map; Berkeley Path Wanderers Association (berkeleypaths.org) offers one of the best. If you want a longer walk, try nearby **Tilden Park**, a 2,000-acre preserve that includes several peaks and numerous trails open for mountain biking. Or head to the **University of California Botanical Garden** (200 Centennial Drive; 510-643-2755; botanicalgarden.berkeley.edu), a home for more than 12,000 species of plants.

5 *Veggie Bounty* Noon

It's tough choosing from the many farmers' markets in the San Francisco Bay Area, but for the real deal, head to the **Berkeley Farmers' Market** (Center Street at Martin Luther King Way). The

OPPOSITE At Moe's Books, the stock spills off the tables and all of Berkeley streams in the door.

BELOW Berkeley Bowl, a fruit-and-vegetable heaven.

Berkeley market is run by actual farmers and has a workingman's vibe. Afterward, stop by the **Berkeley Bowl Marketplace** (2020 Oregon Street; 510-843-6929; berkeleybowl.com) for a comparison. A veritable fruit-and-vegetable heaven, the Bowl offers a staggering array of peaches, apples, and rows of heirloom tomatoes — pudgy, lumpy, flavorful. Grab a roasted chicken and fresh beet salad at the deli counter, and snack on it while arguing with the various activists who congregate outside the Bowl's doors.

6 *Snake Pit* 3:30 p.m.

For a shopping experience not easily duplicated, drop in at the **East Bay Vivarium** (1827-C Fifth Street; 510-841-1400; eastbayvivarium.com), perhaps the city's strangest attraction. But don't come with a fear of snakes: the massive gallery and store, which specializes in reptiles, amphibians, and arachnids, is like a living nightmare. Strolling through, you'll pass gargantuan boas and more scorpion species than you'd ever imagined.

7 *Rock Out* 5 p.m.

The best views of campus aren't from the 10-story Evans Hall, but from **Indian Rock Park**. Wedged in a residential neighborhood along the city's northeast, the park has large rock outcroppings that offer 360-degree views across Berkeley and Oakland, and over the Bay into San Francisco. For more spectacular

sunset views, bring some rope and carabiners: the main outcropping, Indian Rock, is a practice site for rock climbers.

8 *Homage to Alice Waters* 6:30 p.m.

Scoring a reservation at **Chez Panisse** (1517 Shattuck Avenue; 510-548-5525; chezpanisse.com; $$$$), the renowned restaurant created by the groundbreaking chef Alice Waters in 1971, can be a labor-intensive project. A creative, casual alternative is **Gather** (2200 Oxford Street; 510-809-0400; gatherrestaurant.com; $$), very much built on the Waters tradition but heading down its own contemporary organic/local ingredients/eco-chic path. The stated aim is to please both vegetarians and omnivores, and even the pizzas, nicely blistered and chewy, shed

light on the concept. How about morel pizza topped with fontinella, stinging nettles, and braised leeks?

9 *Berkeley Roots* 8 p.m.

Berkeley may be the perfect town for roots music. The genre of the '60s is not forgotten, although there's no objection to some updating. Shows at **Freight and Salvage Coffeehouse** (2020 Addison Street; 510-644-2020; freightandsalvage.org) feature nationally known musicians performing folk, bluegrass, and modern takes on traditional music like jazz folk and Celtic jazz. Be warned. There's no alcohol. It really is a coffeehouse.

SUNDAY

10 *Fourth and Long* 11 a.m.

Fourth Street is not far from Telegraph, but it's miles away in style. This trendy shopping district

has become a chic, open-air mall with funky home décor, local art, and designer fashions. One of the most interesting of the shops and galleries is the **Stained Glass Garden** (1800 Fourth Street; 510-841-2200; stainedglassgarden.com), which carries elegantly curved glassware, dangly jewelry that resembles Calder mobiles, and kaleidoscope-like lampshades.

OPPOSITE ABOVE Sather Gate, leading into the central campus of the University of California.

OPPOSITE BELOW The Pacific Film Archive.

ABOVE California hills from Tilden Park.

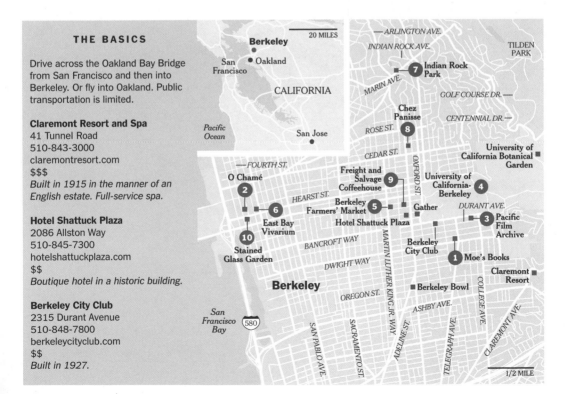

THE BASICS

Drive across the Oakland Bay Bridge from San Francisco and then into Berkeley. Or fly into Oakland. Public transportation is limited.

Claremont Resort and Spa
41 Tunnel Road
510-843-3000
claremontresort.com
$$$
Built in 1915 in the manner of an English estate. Full-service spa.

Hotel Shattuck Plaza
2086 Allston Way
510-845-7300
hotelshattuckplaza.com
$$
Boutique hotel in a historic building.

Berkeley City Club
2315 Durant Avenue
510-848-7800
berkeleycityclub.com
$$
Built in 1927.

Napa Valley

If you don't know where to look, the Napa Valley of California can seem uninspiring: big, Disney-ish wineries, lines four deep at the tasting rooms, and one too many tour buses. But nudge just a little off the tourist track, and you're instantly back in the rolling, bucolic paradise that first beckoned wine growers decades ago — quirky little vineyards, tiny towns, and a genuinely slower pace, despite the massive industry all around. In the bright days of summer and the misty moodiness of winter, this 30-mile-long region hums with life — and invites an air of reflection perfectly suited to those big California reds. — BY CHRIS COLIN

FRIDAY

1 *Vintage Cycling* 3 p.m.

Rent a bicycle at the **Calistoga Bike Shop** (1318 Lincoln Avenue, Calistoga; 707-942-9687; calistogabikeshop.com) and do some exploring. Some of the prettiest roads are found around Calistoga, a funky and unstuffy town on the northwest tip of the valley — a bit of whiskey before the pinot. For your first taste of Napa Valley wine, pedal two miles to the Michael Graves-designed **Clos Pegase Winery** (1060 Dunaweal Lane, Calistoga; 707-942-4981; clospegase.com) and feel the terroir under your tires.

2 *The Food Is Local, Too* 7 p.m.

Stay in Calistoga for dinner at **JoLe Farm to Table** (1457 Lincoln Avenue; 707-942-5938; jolerestaurant. com; $$), which aims to live up to its name with seasonal cuisine made from organic locally farmed ingredients. Selections change frequently, but you might find scallops with leeks, mushrooms, and pancetta or chicken fried quail with Cobb salad. The wine list, naturally, also leans local.

3 *Bring Your Earplugs* 10 p.m.

Beer in Napa? It might sound like blasphemy, but the **Calistoga Inn Restaurant & Brewery** (1250 Lincoln Avenue, Calistoga; 707-942-4101; calistogainn.com) makes a mean Pilsener, along with various ales and stouts. There's live music every night at this wood-paneled watering hole — and who wants to drink merlot while dancing to rock? Besides, there will be plenty of other wines this weekend.

SATURDAY

4 *Sling Some Mud* 9 a.m.

Calistoga's name has been mud, or at least synonymous with it, ever since the Gold Rush pioneer Sam Brannan dipped into the Wappo tribe's ancient mud baths. Some claim the volcanic ash and geothermally heated water rejuvenate the pores; others find relief from aches and pains. At a minimum, it's fun and weird to float in hot goop with cucumbers on your eyes. With a manicured lawn and white cottages, the **Indian Springs Resort and Spa** (1712 Lincoln Avenue; 707-942-4913; indianspringscalistoga.com) resembles a colonial hill town under the British Raj and claims the title of the oldest continually operating spa in California.

5 *Sizing Up the Grapes* 11 a.m.

Time to hit the vineyards. With hundreds to choose from in this valley, there's no perfect lineup. But some stand out for personality, memorable wines, or both. Stop first at **Casa Nuestra** (3451 Silverado Trail North, St. Helena; 707-963-5783; casanuestra.com; appointments required). This is a small family winery, and with your sips of chenin blanc or tinto you can expect a taste of old California informality — just ask the goats out front that clamor for snacks, emboldened by having a blend named after them (Two Goats Red). From there it's a short drive to the **Culinary Institute**

OPPOSITE Ballooning over the Napa Valley, an exhilarating adventure for a Sunday morning.

RIGHT Grapes on the vine at a Napa vineyard.

of America at **Greystone** (2555 Main Street, St. Helena; 707-967-1010; ciachef.edu/california), the California campus of the chef-training school in Hyde Park, New York. It's not a winery, but it occupies a picturesque century-old stone building that was originally the Christian Brothers' Greystone Cellars, and its shop and the campus are worth a look around.

6 *Main Street Retail* Noon
You could have lunch at the Culinary Institute's restaurant, but you'll want to stop anyway in the precious town of St. Helena, a shopaholic's delight. Have an avocado and papaya salad or a burger with house-made pickles at **Cindy's Backstreet Kitchen** (1327 Railroad Avenue; 707-963-1200;

cindysbackstreetkitchen.com; $$). Then shop Main Street. **Footcandy** (No. 1239; 877-517-4606; footcandyshoes.com) carries Jimmy Choos and Manolo Blahniks with heels as high as stemware. **Woodhouse Chocolate** (No. 1367; 707-963-8413; woodhousechocolate.com) sells handmade artisanal chocolates in an elegant space that looks more like a jewelry shop. And the local interior designer Erin Martin has bronze sculptures, porcelain lamps, and other housewares at her shop, **Martin Showroom** (No. 1350; 707-967-8787; martinshowroom.com).

7 *Back to the Grapes* 2 p.m.
Large wineries often suffer in the character department, but not **Quintessa** (1601 Silverado Trail; Rutherford; 707-967-1601; quintessa.com). From the graceful crescent facade to the fascinating tours of its production facilities, this 280-acre estate makes a great stop — and it produces wonderful Bordeaux-style wines. For drop-dead gorgeous scenery, swing

ABOVE The misty moodiness of the Napa Valley in December.

LEFT Cycling the quiet roads near Calistoga, the unstuffy town on the valley's northwest tip.

OPPOSITE Mustard, a winter crop growing amid the rows of leafless vines.

by **Frog's Leap** (8815 Conn Creek Road, Rutherford; 707-963-4704; frogsleap.com) and its five acres of lush gardens, orchards, beehives, chickens, photovoltaic cells, and everything else that puts this among Napa's more forward-thinking operations. And for unforgettable architecture, visit **Quixote Winery** (6126 Silverado Trail, Napa; 707-944-2659; quixotewinery.com). Its turreted, multicolored, cartoonlike building was designed by Friedensreich Hundertwasser, Vienna's late 20th-century answer to Antoni Gaudí. Appointments are required at each of these vineyards, and all have tasting fees.

8 *Riverfront Dining* 8 p.m.

For memorable fare and setting, go to **Angèle** in the city of Napa (540 Main Street; 707-252-8115; angelerestaurant.com; $$$), a converted boathouse on the Napa River where locals and tourists come to get away from the tourists. French brasserie classics like braised rabbit and cassoulet are served under a

beamed ceiling and warm lighting. Regulars can be spotted ordering the off-menu burger with blue cheese. Needless to say, the wine list is varied and extensive.

9 *Make It Swing* 9:30 p.m.

The city of Napa rolls up its sidewalks after dark, but **Uva** (1040 Clinton Street; 707-255-6646; uvatrattoria.com) makes an exception for free live jazz every Saturday until midnight. Photos of old jazz greats crowd the walls, and you can tap along from the swanky dining room or the crowded bar.

SUNDAY

10 *The Overview* 6 a.m.

By this time, you've noticed that the Napa Valley is beautiful country, with corduroy-pattern vineyards carpeting its rolling golden hills and the Napa River easing its way from north to south. There's no better way to see it than from a slow-floating hot-air balloon.

Several companies will take you up and away for $200 to $300 per person; one standby is **Napa Valley Balloons** (1 California Drive, Yountville; 707-944-0228; napavalleyballoons.com). After a ride lasting about an hour, you will be served a Champagne brunch. The balloons leave early in the morning to catch favorable air currents.

11 *Art of Winemaking* 11 a.m.

For a nontipsy perspective on wine, drive up the winding, woodsy road to the ivy-covered **Hess**

Collection (4411 Redwood Road, Napa; 707-255-1144; hesscollection.com), the winery and contemporary art museum built by the Swiss multimillionaire Donald Hess. Tours of the bright gallery, which are self-guided and free, take you past works by Frank Stella, Robert Motherwell, and Francis Bacon. At one point, a window provides a view of the fermentation tanks — the suggestion that wine equals art is not lost. Judge for yourself: the tasting room, just off the lobby, specializes in mountain cabernets.

ABOVE Dining at the Calistoga Inn Restaurant & Brewery, an outpost of beer in the wine country.

OPPOSITE Oak barrels in a cave at Quintessa. Stop in to see how its Bordeaux-style wines are made.

THE BASICS

The Napa Valley is about 50 miles north of San Francisco, just over an hour's drive. Make someone in your group the designated driver.

Indian Springs Resort and Spa
1712 Lincoln Avenue, Calistoga
707-942-4913
indianspringscalistoga.com
$$$
Retro glamour in an authentic, century-old spa. Olympic-size mineral springs pool.

River Terrace Inn
1600 Soscol Avenue
707-320-9000
riverterraceinn.com
$$$
Well-appointed rooms; close to riverside walks.

Auberge du Soleil
180 Rutherford Hill Road, Rutherford
707-963-1211
aubergedusoleil.com
$$$$
Spa, pool, tennis court, and terraces with valley views.

128 **Calistoga**
Clos Pegase Winery
Casa Nuestra 5
DUNA WEAL LN.
Cindy's Backstreet Kitchen/ Woodhouse Chocolate/ Martin Showroom
6
Culinary Institute of America at Greystone
Indian Springs Resort and Spa 4
JoLe Farm to Table
2 — LINCOLN AVE.
Footcandy
St. Helena
Auberge du Soleil
L. Hennessey
Quintessa 7
Frog's Leap
— CONN CREEK RD.
1 Calistoga Bike Shop
Rutherford
3 Calistoga Inn Restaurant & Brewery
NAPA VALLEY
Napa Valley Balloons 10
Quixote Winery
Yountville
SOSCOL AVE.
River Terrace Inn
CALIFORNIA 29
— CLINTON ST.
9
Uva
MAIN ST.
Hess Collection 11
REDWOOD RD.
Napa R.
SILVERADO TRAIL
Napa
8
Angèle
SONOMA NAPA
5 MILES

CALIF.
Napa NEV.
San Francisco
Pacific Ocean
Los Angeles

Sonoma County

If you're looking for a chocolate pinot noir sauce, keep driving. The rustic region of Sonoma County, California, may be a wine lovers' playground, but it lacks many of the touristy trappings of its more upscale and better-known neighbor, Napa. Not that Sonomans are complaining. Bumper stickers carry messages like "Kill Your TV" and "Subvert the Dominant Paradigm," and people here mean it. The freethinking tradition is being nurtured by a new generation of oenophiles who appreciate Sonoma's low-key charms, filling its beautiful historic towns with upscale boutiques, art galleries, and Old World-style restaurants. — BY KABIR CHIBBER

FRIDAY

1 *Young Blood* 4 p.m.
Wineries in Sonoma still tend to be small, young, and family-owned. One of the youngest is **Scribe Winery** (2300 Napa Road, Sonoma; 707-939-1858; scribewinery.com), started by Andrew Mariani and his family in 2007 on an estate of almost 200 acres that used to be a turkey farm. The winery, with its dusty driveway and artfully rundown hacienda, is so new the first wines from these vineyards, a pinot noir and chardonnay, could not be released until 2011. Early visitors to the winery tasted blends made from grapes grown nearby.

2 *Tragedy Loves Company* 7 p.m.
The hills of Sonoma come alive with music in the summer and fall. The town of **Cloverdale** has free evening concerts in its main square, next to the farmers' market (cloverdaleartsalliance.org). For a dose of high culture, the **Sonoma City Opera** (484 East Napa Street, Sonoma; 707-939-8288; sonomaopera.org) holds concerts, and the **Sonoma County Repertory Theater** (104 North Main Street, Sebastopol; 707-823-0177; the-rep.com) produces plays from Shakespeare to contemporary fare.

3 *La Bella Sonoma* 9 p.m.
Sondra Bernstein's first restaurant, the Girl and the Fig, is an institution. In 2008 she opened another, **Estate** (400 West Spain Street, Sonoma; 707-933-3663; thegirlandthefig.com; $$-$$$), in a historic home, serving regional Italian cuisine using Northern Californian ingredients. Sit outside and start with the prosecco spritzer and the burrata with homemade olive oil. Some favorite past entrees have been porchetta with polenta served in pork jus and Pacific rock cod with wood-fire roasted Yukon golds.

SATURDAY

4 *Farmer's Choice* 10 a.m.
A bit too early to be an oenophile? Luckily, there's much more to Sonoma than wine. The local food movement is long-established here, and Sonomans are as passionate about what they eat as what they drink. Sample the locally produced cheeses and kefirs using goat's milk at **Redwood Hill Farm** (2064 Highway 116 North, Sebastopol; 707-823-8250; redwoodhill.com) and organic wildflower honey from **Quivira Vineyards & Winery** (4900 West Dry Creek Road, Healdsburg; 707-431-8333; quivirawine.com). And **La Michoacana** (18495 Highway 12, Sonoma; 707-938-1773) makes soft, creamy ice creams with flavors like caramel and mango, just like those found in Tocumba, Mexico, where the owner, Teresita Carr, grew up.

OPPOSITE Sonoma, a wine region of low-key charms.

BELOW Estate, a restaurant in the former home of a daughter of Mariano Vallejo, a governor in Mexican California.

5 *Canvases and Fans* 12:30 p.m.

Healdsburg, one of Sonoma's main towns, is full of boutiques and second homes of the San Francisco Bay Area's beautiful and wealthy, but it retains a youthful vibe. It also has a sizable collection of modern art. The **Healdsburg Center for the Arts** (130 Plaza Street; 707-431-1970; healdsburgcenterforthearts.com) features a rotating cast of local and regional artists, while **Hawley Tasting Room and Gallery** (36 North Street; 707-473-9500; hawleywine.com) displays the landscape paintings of Dana Hawley, who is the wife of the respected local winemaker John Hawley. The Capture gallery (105 Plaza Street; 707-431-7030; capturefineart.com) has high-end photography of the Sonoma terrain. And don't leave without checking out the **Hand Fan Museum** (219 Healdsburg Avenue; 707-431-2500; handfanmuseum.com), the first in the country dedicated to the once popular accessory.

6 *The Padrino (of Wine)* 2:30 p.m.

Around here, Francis Ford Coppola is known more as a winemaker than as an Oscar-winning director, having been a vintner for decades at the Rubicon Estate in Napa. In 2010 Coppola opened the **Francis Ford Coppola Winery** in Sonoma (300 Via Archimedes, Geyserville; 707-857-1471; franciscoppolawinery.com). The 88-acre estate has a restaurant called Rustic featuring some of Coppola's favorite dishes, two outdoor swimming pools to keep things child-friendly, and Hollywood memorabilia like Vito Corleone's desk from *The Godfather*. Best of all, some tastings of standard wines are free—a rarity in California.

7 *Bubble Bath* 5:30 p.m.

Sonoma has its fair share of high-end resorts for feeling sequestered from the world. But it's better to take advantage of the excellent day spas in the area that let you pop in and out at your leisure. **A Simple Touch Spa** (239C Center Street, Healdsburg; 707-433-6856; asimpletouchspa.com) lets you lie in a bath of sparkling wine, mustard, or fango mud and then enjoy a half-hour massage. The stylish spa at **Hotel Healdsburg** (25 Matheson Street, Healdsburg; 800-889-7188; hotelhealdsburg.com) has a reviving body wrap using wine and local honey.

8 *Polished Classics* 7 p.m.

In 2004, when the French chef Bruno Tison took over the restaurant **Santé** at the historic **Fairmont Sonoma Mission Inn and Spa** (100 Boyes Boulevard, Sonoma; 707-938-9000; fairmont.com/sonoma; $$$), he set his sights high, with a creative menu that paired French flavors with American favorites. The gamble seems to have paid off: the restaurant received a Michelin star in 2009—one of only four in Sonoma County to be awarded the distinction. Expect dishes like macaroni and cheese with Maine lobster and black truffles, or roasted duck breast in a "dirty rice" of mushrooms and foie gras, accompanied by a duck confit. There's an extensive selection of regional wines.

9 *Cocktail Tasting* 10 p.m.

Wine country is not renowned for its night life, but that doesn't mean you can't have fun. The cocktail bar at the sleek and minimalist **El Dorado Hotel** (405 First Street West, Sonoma; 707-996-3220;

ABOVE At the Francis Ford Coppola Winery, taste the vintages made by the renowned film director. Then pop into the Movie Gallery for a look at props like the Godfather's desk and this Tucker car.

eldoradosonoma.com) exudes an effortless glamour and gets particularly lively during the Sonoma Jazz Festival. Try the peach jalapeño, a mix of peppers and peach vodka. The town of Santa Rosa is also filled with bars, though many can feel fratty. An exception is **Christy's on the Square** (96 Old Courthouse Square, Santa Rosa; 707-528-8565; christysonthesquare.com), which draws an older, sophisticated clientele.

SUNDAY

10 *Salt Air* 9 a.m.

Leave the vineyards behind and head to the coast, about an hour away at Bodega Bay. **Campbell Cove**, by the Bodega Head, is a secluded beach that feels as though it was made just for you and the seagulls. Spend some time on the sand and chill.

Then take a little time to drive up a few miles along the rugged Sonoma coast.

11 *Yeast Notes* Noon

Tired of pondering the finer points of merlot versus pinot noir? Well, get ready to debate the terroir of malted barley and hops — Sonoma has a fine collection of microbreweries. **Dempsey's** (50 East Washington Street, Petaluma; 707-765-9694; dempseys.com) has a stout called Ugly Dog — because the annual World's Ugliest Dog Contest is held in town. **Bear Republic Brewing Co.** (345 Healdsburg Avenue, Healdsburg; 707-433-2337; bearrepublic.com) serves special brews available only on draft, including the ultra-creamy Black Raven Porter and a pale ale called Crazy Ivan that's been mixed with a yeast used by Trappist monks.

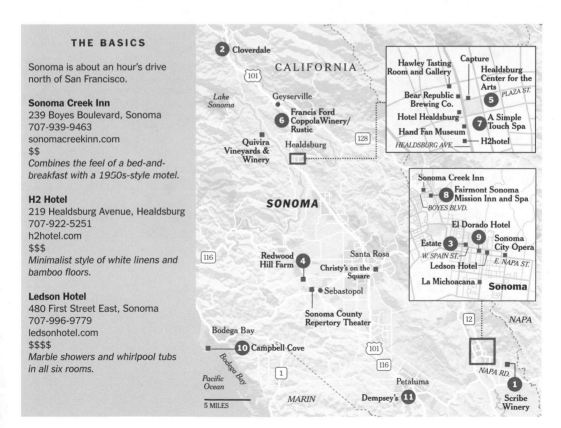

THE BASICS

Sonoma is about an hour's drive north of San Francisco.

Sonoma Creek Inn
239 Boyes Boulevard, Sonoma
707-939-9463
sonomacreekinn.com
$$
Combines the feel of a bed-and-breakfast with a 1950s-style motel.

H2 Hotel
219 Healdsburg Avenue, Healdsburg
707-922-5251
h2hotel.com
$$$
Minimalist style of white linens and bamboo floors.

Ledson Hotel
480 First Street East, Sonoma
707-996-9779
ledsonhotel.com
$$$$
Marble showers and whirlpool tubs in all six rooms.

Sacramento

California's governors and legislators may argue aggressively at its center, but the rest of Sacramento, California's capital city, has a gentle, small-town charm. Situated at the confluence of the Sacramento and American Rivers, it grew into a city as the gateway to the California Gold Rush and prospered as the home of railroad barons. What visitors will notice today is a strong theater tradition, delightful restaurants, a vibrant art scene, and a wealth of greenery — residents proudly claim that Sacramento has more trees per capita than any city in the world besides Paris. — BY BETH GREENFIELD

FRIDAY

1 *What Could Go Wrong?* 4 p.m.

Who says California's capital is prone to disarray? A stroll through the **California State Capitol** (10th and L Streets; 916-324-0333; capitolmuseum.ca.gov) — a neo-Classical confection of Corinthian and other classic columns, parget plasterwork, and mosaic floors — conveys the feeling that everything is in grand order. Painstakingly restored in the 1970s, the interior is graced with numerous artworks, including presidential portraits, WPA murals, and a stunning marble statue of Columbus and Queen Isabella by Larkin Goldsmith Mead. Outside, there's a lush park. A 250-pound bronze statue of a grizzly bear was brought by Arnold Schwarzenegger to guard the door to the governor's office. Wander at a leisurely pace while government employees rush by.

2 *Farm to Table* 6:30 p.m.

To dine in modern elegance, head a few blocks to the **Ella Dining Room and Bar** (1131 K Street; 916-443-3772; elladiningroomandbar.com; $$), which is draped with dramatic scrims of white linen. The restaurant emphasizes local produce, a sensible choice given that Sacramento sits amid some of the world's richest farmland. The menu includes dishes like pappardelle with poached egg and prosciutto in preserved lemon butter sauce or Sonoma duck

breast with lentils and roasted pears. You could also have a soothing elderflower gimlet and a chocolate-rich dessert.

3 *Act Three* 8 p.m.

Sacramento has a healthy theater scene, judging by the well-chosen plays at the intimate **B Street Theatre** (2711 B Street; 916-443-5300; bstreettheatre.org). Past productions have included *The Maintenance Man*, a comedy about divorce by Richard Harris, a prolific British playwright, and *Entertaining Mr. Sloane*, a tale of seduction and sibling rivalry by Joe Orton. Draw out the drama with a nightcap at **Harlow's** (2708 J Street; 916-441-4693; harlows.com), where you'll find live rock or jazz downstairs and purple backlighting and plush and inviting seats in the Momo Lounge upstairs.

SATURDAY

4 *Mimosa Brunch* 10 a.m.

The **Tower Cafe** (1518 Broadway; 916-441-0222; towercafe.com; $$) sits across the street from the original (and, sadly, defunct) Tower Records. Get there early, and you'll have a better chance of snagging an outdoor table under the shady mimosa tree. But you could also do a lot worse than sitting indoors — where you'll be surrounded by an eclectic collection of objets d'art including African beaded belts, Mexican Day of the Dead sculptures, and 1930s travel posters. Dive into toothsome specialties like the Mexican scramble, blueberry cornmeal pancakes, or chorizo burrito.

OPPOSITE The California State Railroad Museum.

RIGHT Bond with the American River by riding along the 32-mile Jedediah Smith Memorial Bike Trail.

5 *Buffet of Art* 11:30 a.m.

The **Crocker Art Museum** (216 O Street; 916-808-7000; crockerartmuseum.org) is the perfect museum for a weekend getaway: compact yet diverse, including works from prehistoric to modern times. Oswald Achenbach's painting *Festival and Fireworks by Moonlight*, circa 1855, has a fiery luminescence so true that you expect to feel heat rising off the canvas.

ABOVE The rotunda in the California State Capitol, both working center of government and restored landmark.

BELOW Dry hills and green oaks on the bike trail.

In the contemporary gallery, the Mexican artist Rufino Tamayo's *Laughing Woman*, from 1950, is dark and whimsical. The original building, an 1872 Victorian Italianate mansion, is absolutely grand, and a 2010 addition that tripled the museum's size works in tasteful counterpoint.

6 *Boats and Trains* 1:30 p.m.

Old Sacramento (oldsacramento.com), a historic district with costumed cowboys and Old West facades, is a hokey, tourist-mobbed scene. But two spots stand out: the **Pilothouse Restaurant** (1000 Front Street; 916-441-4440; deltaking.com; $$) and the **California State Railroad Museum** (Second and I Streets; 916-445-6645; californiastaterailroadmuseum.org). The restaurant is on the *Delta King*, a 1920s riverboat-turned-floating-hotel, and offers dishes like a Shrimp Louie salad or fish and chips. The museum contains restored locomotives and railroad cars that you can climb aboard, including a 1937 stainless-steel dining car with white linen, fancy china, and a vintage menu offering a "lamb chop, extra thick" for 80 cents.

7 *Shop Midtown* 4 p.m.

Midtown, the area bordered roughly by 17th and 29th Streets and H and P Streets, is Sacramento's hippest district. Stop into boutiques like **Dragatomi** (2317 J Street; 916-706-0535; dragatomi.com) for designer collectibles like Kidrobot. Midtown is also

home to art galleries, so if you're not in town for a Second Saturdays Art Walk, pop into a few, including **b. sakata garo** (923 20th Street; 916-447-4276; bsakatagaro.com) or the **Center for Contemporary Art Sacramento** (1519 19th Street; 916-498-9811; ccasac.org).

8 *Capital Cuisine* 6:30 p.m.

For a taste of Sacramento's new culinary scene, make reservations at **Grange** (926 J Street; 916-492-4450; grangesacramento.com; $$$), an airy restaurant in the Citizen Hotel. Michael Tuohy uses local ingredients to make seasonal dishes like risotto with morels and fava beans, grilled sturgeon with polenta and shiitake mushrooms, or slow-smoked pork shoulder with turnips.

9 *Closer to Wine* 8:30 p.m.

If the art gods are on your side, you'll be in town for a **Second Saturdays Art Walk**, when galleries stay open until 10 p.m. with live music, food vendors,

and, of course, vino. Though most of the action is in Midtown, around K Street, galleries in other neighborhoods get involved, too; it's best to check in with the art walk's map, on its Web site (2nd-sat.com). Any other Saturday, remind yourself how close you are to California wine country with a trip to **Revolution Wines** (2831 S Street; 916-444-7711; revolution-wines.com), a tiny industrial-chic winery with free tastings, or **L Wine Lounge and Urban Kitchen** (1801 L Street; 916-443-6970; lwinelounge.com), which has at least 20 wines by the glass.

ABOVE A gallery at the Crocker Art Museum.

BELOW Old Sacramento, a historic district with touristy shops behind Old West facades.

10 *Paint the Town Green* 10 p.m.

Sacramento isn't known for night life, but there are a few surprises. One is the glossy and upscale **Lounge on 20** (1050 20th Street; 916-443-6620; loungeon20.com), where a seat on the patio, glass of emerald absinthe in hand, conjures up South Beach — without the limos, celebrities, and models. Across the street is **Faces** (2000 K Street; 916-448-0706; faces.net), one of five gay clubs clustered near K and 20th Streets.

SUNDAY

11 *Bike the River* 10 a.m.

Bond with the American River by riding along the **Jedediah Smith Memorial Bike Trail**, a 32-mile loop that snakes along the water and through a series of parks featuring sand dunes, oak groves, picnic areas, and fishing nooks. **Practical Cycle** (114 J Street; 916-706-0077; practicalcycle.com), in Old Sacramento, has rentals.

ABOVE An indoor-outdoor view of passersby and reflected diners at the Grange restaurant in the Citizen Hotel.

OPPOSITE The skyline and the Sacramento River.

THE BASICS

Fly into Sacramento International Airport or drive about 80 miles from San Francisco. Drive or ride a bicycle on the smooth, flat streets.

The Citizen Hotel
926 J Street
916-447-2700
citizenhotel.com
$$
Designer boutique hotel in California's Joie de Vivre collection, site of popular Grange restaurant and Scandal bar.

Inn & Spa at Parkside
2116 6th Street
916-658-1818
innatparkside.com
$$$
Eleven elegant rooms and a spa in a 1936 mansion.

Delta King
1000 Front Street
800-825-5464
deltaking.com
$$
Hotel aboard a riverboat in Old Sacramento.

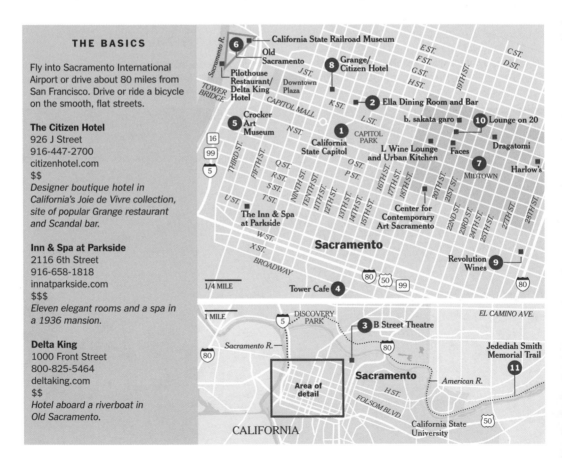

Lake
Tahoe

Politics and religion aside, 200,000 people can't be wrong. According to the California Tahoe Conservancy, that's the estimated crowd at Lake Tahoe on a busy summer weekend. That's enough people to make you rethink your vacation plans, but Tahoe never feels too frantic. Maybe it's the enormous mountain lake standing center, proudly straddling California and Nevada, that lets you know right away who's in charge, but the weekenders who flood the 72 miles of shoreline instinctively bow to nature's pace. And there's that other little fact, too—far less provable, but widely asserted: There's nothing quite like a weekend spent circling Tahoe. The endless activities of summer are standard enough, but they're set to a Sierra backdrop of soaring evergreens and crystalline water worthy of a thousand poets. Throw in the late-night siren call of the Nevada casinos, and it's a tough act to follow.
— BY CINDY PRICE

FRIDAY

1 *Deeper Shades of Blue* 3 p.m.
　Wordsmiths have beat themselves silly trying to capture the true color of Lake Tahoe, so take your pick—cobalt, azure, electric, sapphire. Suffice it to say that it's pretty darn blue. And cold. Even in late summer, the water averages 65 to 70 degrees, given the many mountain streams that slither into it. Judge for yourself on a guided kayak trip out of Sand Harbor, Nevada, with the **Tahoe Adventure Company** (530-913-9212; tahoeadventurccompany.com), which offers individual tours that are part geology lesson and part history lesson. Paddle out past the children cannonballing off the rocks, and learn about the lake's underlying fault lines—and the tsunami that may have burst forth there sometime in the last 10,000 years.

2 *Drama on the Sand* 7 p.m.
　Shake yourself dry, slip on your flip-flops, and head up the beach to the **Lake Tahoe Shakespeare Festival**

OPPOSITE Set high in the Sierra Nevada, Lake Tahoe is the largest alpine lake in North America.

RIGHT The lake straddles California and Nevada. At the Cal Neva Resort, the border divides a fireplace chimney.

(Sand Harbor State Park, Nevada; 800-747-4697; laketahoeshakespeare.com). Patrons pile up on the inclined sand banks, carrying towels, wine, and fat dinner spreads. You can bring your own, or check out the food court and beer garden. The plays are staged at dusk, the lake deftly employed as a silent witness to the unfolding action. If you miss the play, you don't have to miss the beautiful park.

SATURDAY

3 *Frank's Joint* 10 a.m.
　Frank Sinatra owned what is now the **Cal Neva Resort, Spa, and Casino** (2 Stateline Road, Crystal Bay, Nevada; 800-233-5551; calnevaresort.com) for three short years (from 1960 to 1963), but he left a wealth of scandal in his wake. The resort, called the Cal-Neva Lodge when Sinatra owned it, rests on the state line, and the property is marked down the center. Poke your head into the old Celebrity Showroom, where Frank and his buddies performed. Marilyn Monroe often sat up front, and members of the hotel staff say she overdosed on sleeping pills here two weeks before her death, amid a swirl of rumors of sex and foul play. Find the Indian Room yet? Secret passages run below it that lead to the closets of Cabin 3 (Marilyn's) and Cabin 5 (Frank's). The Chicago mobster Sam Giancana is said to have used the tunnels to conduct business.

4 *High Noon* 12 p.m.
　It's noon on the lake, and you're 6,225 feet above sea level. A cheeseburger washed down with an

ice-cold Anchor Steam is not only agreeable; it's mandatory. You're now in California, coming down the west side of the lake. Find your way through Tahoe City and take a right just past Fanny Bridge (called "rump row" for the line of backsides that forms as people lean over the railing to stare at the Truckee River and its fish). **Bridgetender Tavern and Grill** (65 West Lake Boulevard, Tahoe City; 530-583-3342; $) is home to one of the juiciest cheeseburgers on the lake as well as a generous outdoor patio that winds along the Truckee.

5 *Just Drift Away* 2 p.m.

Follow the hoots of laughter across Fanny Bridge and arrive at the **Truckee River Raft Company** (185 River Road, Tahoe City; 530-584-0123; truckeeriverraft.com) for a lazy afternoon on the river. You can paddle, but the ride is best enjoyed as one long floating party. Families drift alongside groups of friends with tubes lashed together as they bask and pass each other beer. A little more than halfway, you might find a shallow, standing-room-only party complete with makeshift stickball games (the paddles double as bats).

6 *Cocktail of the Brave* 7 p.m.

South Lake Tahoe isn't known as a gastronomic hotbed, but a seat at the sushi bar at the **Naked Fish** (3940 Lake Tahoe Boulevard, South Lake Tahoe; 530-541-3474; thenakedfish.com; $$) offers up ace rolls and a frisky pre-casino crowd. Kick your night off with an appetizer of barbecued albacore and the surprisingly tasty house drink, the Money Shot, which involves a bolt of hot sake, a drizzle of ponzu sauce, fish eggs, a Japanese mountain potato, and a few other nerve-racking ingredients.

7 *Poker Faces, Old and New* 10 p.m.

Itching for the dull tumble of dice on felt, or the shudder and snap of a fresh deck of cards being shuffled? You'll have no trouble finding it. South Tahoe's casinos are snugged up against each other

along the border of Stateline, Nevada. Refurbishing has made them sexier. Witness the vampy **MontBleu Resort Casino & Spa** (55 Highway 50; 775-588-3515; montbleuresort.com), a k a the old Caesar's sporting a slap of paint and a fresh attitude, or the swank bar at **Harveys Resort Casino** (18 Lake Tahoe Boulevard; 775-588-2411; harveystahoe.com). Still, old-timers and hipsters might enjoy the old-school ambience and low-limit tables at the **Lakeside Inn and Casino** (168 Highway 50, 800-624-7980; lakesideinn.com).

SUNDAY

8 *Now That's Venti* 10 a.m.

Ride the touristy but must-do **Heavenly Gondola** (Heavenly Mountain Resort; 4080 Lake Tahoe Boulevard, South Lake Tahoe; 775-586-7000; skiheavenly.com), a ski lift that doubles as a sightseeing excursion in summer. Hop on board when it opens and cruise 2.4 miles up the mountain to the observation deck. Grab a very decent mocha at the cafe and soak in the stunning views of the Carson Valley and the Desolation Wilderness — not to mention that big blue thing in the center.

BELOW Warming up at the Bridgetender Tavern and Grill. In the winter, Tahoe turns into ski country.

9 *Pesto Bread, Just Like Mom's* Noon

There's an art to gathering beach provisions, and Tahoe regulars know there's good one-stop shopping at the **PDQ Market** (6890 West Lake Boulevard, Tahoma, California; 530-525-7411; $), where customers can secure not only the usual Coke and sun block, but also one of the tastiest sandwiches in town. Press through the store, and you'll find a little homegrown operation pushing out delicious sandwiches on fresh-baked breads like jalapeño or pesto. The half-size sandwich, loaded high with shaved meats like pastrami or turkey, is a steal.

10 *Decisions, Decisions* 2 p.m.

Trying to pick the right Tahoe beach is a bit like plucking a date off the Internet. Zephyr Cove is young and likes to party. Meeks Bay is into poetry and likes long walks on the beach. The good news is that each is better looking than the next. For

those given to fits of polarity, try **D. L. Bliss State Park** (Highway 89, South Lake Tahoe; 530-525-7277; parks.ca.gov), a camping ground with sheltered coves for swimming and lazing, as well as a few bracing hikes for the restless. The pristine beaches make it hard to resist the former, though. Imagine you've found the turquoise waters of Vieques in the middle of the Black Forest of Germany. Until you dip your hand in, of course.

OPPOSITE ABOVE Learning about the lake on a kayaking tour with Tahoe Adventure Company.

ABOVE A ski lift does summer duty ferrying sightseers.

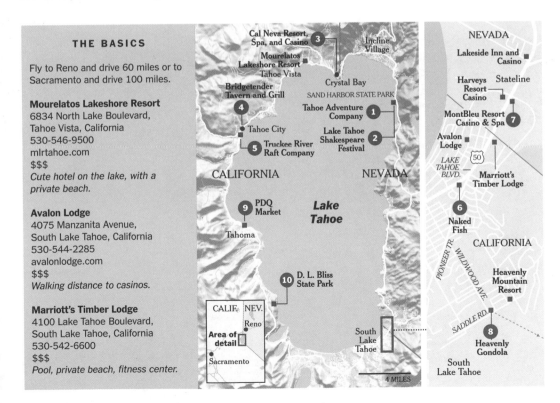

THE BASICS

Fly to Reno and drive 60 miles or to Sacramento and drive 100 miles.

Mourelatos Lakeshore Resort
6834 North Lake Boulevard, Tahoe Vista, California
530-546-9500
mlrtahoe.com
$$$
Cute hotel on the lake, with a private beach.

Avalon Lodge
4075 Manzanita Avenue, South Lake Tahoe, California
530-544-2285
avalonlodge.com
$$$
Walking distance to casinos.

Marriott's Timber Lodge
4100 Lake Tahoe Boulevard, South Lake Tahoe, California
530-542-6600
$$$
Pool, private beach, fitness center.

The Oregon Coast

You could drive down the southern third of the Oregon coast in a couple of hours, and you'd think, How beautiful! Highway 101, the Oregon Coast Highway, hugs the shoreline enough to give you views of the sand and windblown trees, rocks and crashing waves that give this stretch its fame. But to instill memories that will make these gorgeous seascapes your own, plan a leisurely weekend of detours and side trips with plenty of time to stop at the beaches and lighthouses, gulp the salt air, and kick back in the harbor towns.
— BY DAVID LASKIN

FRIDAY

1 *Park Land* 1 p.m.

In North Bend, leave Highway 101 to pick up Route 540 and head south as it leaves city streets behind to become the **Cape Arago Highway**. You'll descend quickly into Charleston, a tiny place with a working harbor, a fish-and-chips shack, and tidal shallows raked by whitecaps on windy days. The road—despite its "highway" designation, it's only a few miles long—leads from there to a series of three adjoining oceanside state parks (oregonstateparks.org). Stop at the first, **Sunset Bay**, for beachcombing and your first photo ops, but don't be tempted to stay too long. You'll need time at the next one, **Shore Acres**, to sniff the luxe ivory Elina roses in the well-kept garden of a former private estate perched atop a forbidding cliff.

2 *Cape Arago* 3 p.m.

The last stop on the road, before it loops around to point you back toward Charleston, is **Cape Arago State Park**, where you'll find the rocky headland, topped by a lighthouse, that all of this has been leading to. Hike on one of the cove trails down to the beach and look for seals and tide pools. When you've seen enough, drive back to Charleston and pick up Seven Devils Road, which will lead you to West Beaver Hill Road to complete the loop back to Highway 101.

OPPOSITE Highway 101 winds close to the water's edge along rocky coast south of Cape Sebastian State Park.

RIGHT Surf fishing in Port Orford, a town where every street seems to end in a view of the sea.

3 *Old Town Wine List* 4 p.m.

Find a little West Coast slice of Nantucket in **Bandon**, a town of 3,100 people with terrific beaches to the west and the silvery estuary of the Coquille River to the north and east. Check out the shops and galleries in the compact Old Town before heading to dinner at the **Alloro Wine Bar** (375 Second Street Southeast; 541-347-1850; allorowinebar.com; $$-$$$). It serves superb dishes like feather-light lasagna, sautéed local snapper, and fresh fava beans. Relax over a Walla Walla cabernet or another of the Northwest vintages on its wine list.

SATURDAY

4 *Sea Stacks* 10 a.m.

Take the lightly trafficked **Beach Loop Road** south of town. It parallels the coast for four and a half miles, and although there are a few too many cottages and motels, you forget all about them when you stop to wander on the beach amid fantastically carved sea stacks and watch colorful kites slashing against the sky. After the loop rejoins Highway 101, follow it as it leaves the coast for an inland stretch past ranches and cranberry bogs. When you come to Route 250, the Cape Blanco Road, turn right and drive through rolling sheep pastures reminiscent of Cornwall. It's not far to the sea.

5 *Blown Away* 11 a.m.

State parks are strung along this coast, and you can't hit them all. But **Cape Blanco** is a must-stop—the farthest west point on the Oregon coast, the state's oldest lighthouse, one of the windiest spots in the United States. Be prepared for that wind as you walk toward the stark circa-1870 lighthouse. The view at the headland is worth it, so stand and stare as long as you can withstand the blast.

6 *On the Edge* 1 p.m.

Imagine the shabby picturesque waterfront of an outer Maine island fused onto the topographic drama of Big Sur: that's **Port Orford**. Mountains covered with Douglas firs plunge down toward the ocean, and you feel how truly you are at the continent's edge. The town itself has a salty, dreamy, small-town vibe; every street ends in blue sea framed by huge dark green humps of land. Look around and then find lunch. **Griff's on the Dock** (490 Dock Road; 541-332-8985; $$) and the **Crazy Norwegian's** (259 Sixth Street; 541-332-8601; $$) are good bets for fish and chips.

7 *End of the Rogue* 3 p.m.

The Rogue River, known for the whitewater along its 200-mile journey from the Cascades, looks wide, tame, and placid as it meets the sea in **Gold Beach**. The bridge that carries Highway 101 over it is a beauty, multiple-arched, elegant, and vaguely Deco. The city isn't particularly inviting—utilitarian motels hunkering along the strand, a drab dune obstructing views of the ocean. But don't miss the well-stocked **Gold Beach Books** (29707 Ellensburg Avenue; 541-247-2495; oregoncoastbooks.com), which in addition to covering every literary genre has an art gallery and coffee

ABOVE The harbor in Crescent City, a town just south of the Oregon state line in California.

RIGHT Driftwood piled up by the surf at a beach along Beach Loop Drive in Bandon, Oregon.

house. **Jerry's Rogue River Museum** (29880 Harbor Way; 541-247-4571; roguejets.com/museum.php) is worth a look around and has an unusual feature—you can book a jetboat trip on the Rogue there. There's also good hiking just outside town at **Cape Sebastian State Park**, with miles of trails and views down the coast to California.

8 *Gold Beach Dining* 7 p.m.

If you can get a reservation, head out of town for dinner at the **Tu Tu' Tun Lodge** (96550 North Bank Rogue River Road; 541-247-6664; tututun.com; $$$), a fishing resort a few miles upstream on the Rogue. If you're staying in town, **Spinner's Seafood Steak and Chophouse** (29430 Ellensburg Avenue; 541-247-5160; $$$) features hefty portions of entrees like grilled duck breast, Alaska halibut, and ribeye steak.

SUNDAY

9 *More and More Scenic* 9 a.m.

Have a filling breakfast at the **Indian Creek Café** (94682 Jerry's Flat Road; 541-247-0680) and get back on the road. From here on it just keeps getting better. About 14 miles south of Gold Beach you will enter **Samuel H. Boardman Scenic Corridor**, a nine-mile roadside corridor along Highway 101 with turnouts overlooking natural stone arches rising from the waves, trailheads accessing the Oregon Coast Trail, and paths winding down to hidden beaches and tide pools. The scenic summa may be **Whaleshead Beach**, a cove with the mystical beauty of a Japanese scroll—spray blowing off the crest of a wave, massive

sea rocks dazzled in the westering sun, and maybe a kid or two making tracks in the sand.

10 *Tsunami Zone* 11 a.m.

Glance around in **Brookings**, by far the toastiest town on the Oregon coast. Its curious microclimate — winter temperatures in the 80s are not unheard of — is a point of pride, as is its park devoted to preserving native wild azaleas. Then push on south into California to **Crescent City**, a place distinguished by its unfortunate history. In 1964 it was struck by a tsunami that destroyed 300 buildings and killed 11 residents. The vulnerability remains in this region of the Pacific coast. In 2011, the harbors in both Brookings and Crescent City were

severely damaged by the tsunami that swept away cities in coastal Japan. You're tantalizingly close to California's towering redwoods here, so turn a few miles inland and make a final stop at **Jedediah Smith Redwoods State Park**, where you can wander among 200-foot-tall trees. Their majesty matches that of the rocky windswept coast you've just left behind.

ABOVE The Patterson Bridge in Gold Beach.

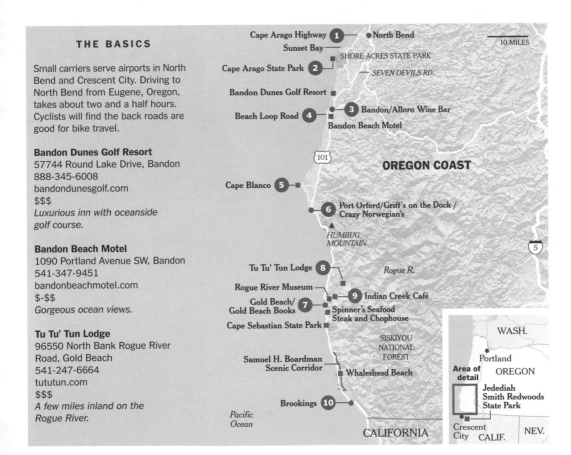

THE BASICS

Small carriers serve airports in North Bend and Crescent City. Driving to North Bend from Eugene, Oregon, takes about two and a half hours. Cyclists will find the back roads are good for bike travel.

Bandon Dunes Golf Resort
57744 Round Lake Drive, Bandon
888-345-6008
bandondunesgolf.com
$$$
Luxurious inn with oceanside golf course.

Bandon Beach Motel
1090 Portland Avenue SW, Bandon
541-347-9451
bandonbeachmotel.com
$-$$
Gorgeous ocean views.

Tu Tu' Tun Lodge
96550 North Bank Rogue River Road, Gold Beach
541-247-6664
tututun.com
$$$
A few miles inland on the Rogue River.

Cape Arago Highway **1** — ● North Bend
Sunset Bay
SHORE ACRES STATE PARK
10 MILES
Cape Arago State Park **2** — SEVEN DEVILS RD.

Bandon Dunes Golf Resort ■
3 Bandon/Alloro Wine Bar
Beach Loop Road **4**
Bandon Beach Motel

101
OREGON COAST

Cape Blanco **5** ■

6 Port Orford/Griff's on the Dock / Crazy Norwegian's

HUMBUG MOUNTAIN
5

Tu Tu' Tun Lodge **8**
Rogue R.
Rogue River Museum
9 Indian Creek Café
Gold Beach/ **7**
Gold Beach Books
Spinner's Seafood Steak and Chophouse
Cape Sebastian State Park ■

SISKIYOU NATIONAL FOREST

WASH.

Samuel H. Boardman Scenic Corridor
Whaleshead Beach

Portland
Area of detail OREGON
Jedediah Smith Redwoods State Park

Brookings **10** ●
Pacific Ocean

CALIFORNIA

Crescent City CALIF.
NEV.

Portland
Oregon

"Nice" is an adjective that Portland, Oregon, can't seem to shake. But below the fleece-clad and Teva-wearing exterior lurks a cool and refreshingly unneurotic city that marches to its own cosmopolitan beat. Truth is, Portland doesn't want to be Seattle, its highly caffeinated neighbor to the north. With less traffic, better public transportation, and Mount Hood in its backyard, this self-styled City of Roses doesn't stand in anybody's shadow. Its vibrant downtown overflows with urban pleasures like chic restaurants, funky nightclubs, and sprightly neighborhoods crackling with youthful energy, but nobody's boasting. That's another nice thing about Portland.
— BY DAVID LASKIN

FRIDAY

1 *Fresh Orientation* 6 p.m.

The pastel roses peak in the late spring at the **International Rose Test Garden** (850 SW Rose Garden Way; 503-227-7033; rosegardenstore.org), but the blooms last for months and the view from this hillside terraced garden is fantastic year-round. Even if clouds keep you from seeing Mount Hood, you still get a bird's-eye view of colorful wood-frame houses surrounding a tidy grove of skyscrapers. Breathe in the pine-scented air and stretch your legs on the hillside paths of this precipitous chunk of green, five minutes from downtown by car, or 15 minutes on the efficient MAX Light Rail.

2 *Bright Brasserie* 7:30 p.m.

The trendy Pearl neighborhood has evolved rapidly from a raw industrial zone to a neighborhood of galleries, parks, and condos. Take in the district's new maturity at the French restaurant **Fenouil** (900 NW 11th Avenue; 503-525-2225; fenouilinthepearl.com; $$$). A sleek, soaring space, Fenouil makes the most of its location overlooking Jamison Park with big windows that roll up like garage doors in nice weather. Local and regional ingredients come with a French touch in dishes like

OPPOSITE There's a vista at the International Rose Test Garden even when the roses aren't in bloom.

RIGHT Portland's skyline from the outskirts.

Sonoma foie gras or duck breast with rillette, beets, and onions.

3 *Downtown Jazz* 9:30 p.m.

Portland's nightlife scene offers plenty of choices, from torchy lounges to high-decibel indie hang-outs. A much-loved institution is **Jimmy Mak's** (221 NW 10th Avenue; 503-295-6542; jimmymaks.com), an intimate jazz club with a national profile. You'll see high-quality local musicians or jazz stars like Joey DeFrancesco or Louis Hayes. Reserve if you want a table.

SATURDAY

4 *Market to Teahouse* 10 a.m.

Even if you can't stand handcrafted soaps, dangly earrings, gauzy scarves, chunky ceramics, fancy pet bowls, messy street food, and the people who make them, the **Portland Saturday Market** is worth visiting (portlandsaturdaymarket.com). Tucked under the Burnside Bridge, the market is a perfect starting point for a leisurely walk amid the cast-iron buildings of Old Town and into Chinatown. Drop in at stores like **Seven Planet** (412 NW Couch Street; 503-575-9455; sevenplanet.com), a good match for green Portland with its bamboo pashminas and cutlery made of recycled plastic, or **Floating World Comics** (20 NW 5th Avenue; 503-241-0227; floatingworldcomics.com), a shop that approaches comic books as an art form. Wend your way to the serene **Lan Su Chinese Garden** (239 NW Everett Street; 503-228-8131; portlandchinesegarden.org), where you can refuel with a cup of tea in the ornate teahouse beside Zither Lake.

5 *Walk to Lunch* Noon

Downtown Portland has about five neighborhoods, each with its own mood and flavor, but it isn't very big. In 20 minutes, you can walk from Chinatown in the northwest to the cultural district in the southwest. Which brings you to lunch. At **Southpark Seafood Grill & Wine Bar** (901 SW Salmon Street; 503-326-1300; southparkseafood.com; $$), you can plunk down at the bar for a quick meal and ask for sightseeing suggestions from the young downtown crowd. Seafood holds center stage; check the menu for bouillabaisse or fried calamari with spicy aioli.

6 *How Nice* 1 p.m.

South Park takes you to the **Portland Art Museum** (1219 SW Park Avenue; 503-226-2811; portlandartmuseum.org), which has an impressive collection of photographs. They run the gamut from 19th-century daguerreotypes to contemporary landscapes. Another strong point in the permanent collection is Japanese scrolls from the Edo period. If you'd like to buy art objects to take home as well as look at them, proceed to the nearby **Russian Art Gallery** (518 SW Yamhill Street; 503-224-5070; russiangalleryportland.com), which carries religious

icons for several hundred to several thousand dollars, along with nesting dolls and Gzhel pottery, all imported from Russia.

7 *Roll Out of Town* 3 p.m.

Stash your stuff, don your Spandex and rent a bicycle at **Waterfront Bicycles** (10 SW Ash Street No. 100; 503-227-1719; waterfrontbikes.com) for a ride along the Willamette River. If you're feeling mellow, ride the three-mile loop that goes north on the Waterfront Bike Trail in **Tom McCall Waterfront Park**, across the river via the Steel Bridge to the **Vera Katz East Bank Esplanade**, and back across on the Hawthorne Bridge. For a tougher workout, stay on the East Bank Esplanade and continue south on the **Springwater Corridor** for an 18-mile ride through the city's semirural outskirts. The trail terminates at the town of Boring (its slogan: "An Exciting Place to Live").

8 *Hot Reservation* 8 p.m.

Serious foodies head to **Park Kitchen** (422 NW Eighth Avenue; 503-223-7275; parkkitchen.com; $$$). In a former garage, the restaurant has a warren of dark and cozy rooms that faces an open kitchen. The chef and owner, Scott Dolich, combines elements of French, Italian, and Northwestern cooking in an imaginative fusion all his own. The menu changes with the season, but the tastes are always superb.

ABOVE The Portland Saturday Market in full swing. Portland's vibrant downtown overflows with youthful energy.

9 *Hang Out, Rock On* 10:30 p.m.

Check out the latest indie bands at **Doug Fir Lounge** (830 East Burnside Street; 503-231-9663; dougfirlounge.com), connected to the trendy Jupiter Hotel. It is Portland's primo spot to hang out, drink good local beer, rub shoulders with the young and pierced, and catch emerging groups from all over the country. The room is surprisingly modern and woodsy for a dance club, with gold-toned lighting, a fire pit, and walls clad in Douglas fir logs.

SUNDAY

10 *Petit Dejeuner* 10 a.m.

For a taste of Paris, pop over to **St. Honoré Boulangerie** (2335 NW Thurman Street; 503-445-4342; sainthonorebakery.com; $-$$), a French-style bakery where Dominique Geulin bakes almond croissants, apricot tarts, and Normandy apple toast, a mix of

French toast, brioche and custard. The cafe is airy, with huge windows and lots of wicker. Equally important, the coffee is among the city's finest.

11 *City of Books* 11 a.m.

It says a lot about Portland that **Powell's City of Books** (1005 West Burnside; 503-228-4651; powells.com) is one of the city's prime attractions—a store so big that it provides maps. The dusty, well-lighted store is larger than many libraries, with 68,000 square feet of new and used books. Plan to stay a while.

ABOVE Comb the shelves at Powell's City of Books.

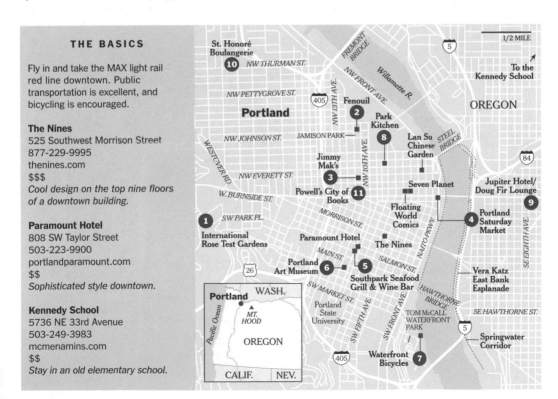

THE BASICS

Fly in and take the MAX light rail red line downtown. Public transportation is excellent, and bicycling is encouraged.

The Nines
525 Southwest Morrison Street
877-229-9995
thenines.com
$$$
Cool design on the top nine floors of a downtown building.

Paramount Hotel
808 SW Taylor Street
503-223-9900
portlandparamount.com
$$
Sophisticated style downtown.

Kennedy School
5736 NE 33rd Avenue
503-249-3983
mcmenamins.com
$$
Stay in an old elementary school.

St. Honoré Boulangerie
10 NW THURMAN ST.

NW PETTYGROVE ST.

NW JOHNSON ST.

Portland

NW EVERETT ST.

W. BURNSIDE ST.

SW PARK PL.

International Rose Test Gardens

FREMONT BRIDGE

Willamette R.

NW FRONT AVE.

405

Fenouil **2**

Park Kitchen

JAMISON PARK

Lan Su Chinese Garden **8**

Jimmy Mak's

3

Powell's City of Books **11**

Floating World Comics

Seven Planet

MORRISON ST.

Paramount Hotel

The Nines

Portland Art Museum **6**

5

Southpark Seafood Grill & Wine Bar

MAIN ST.

SALMON ST.

SW MARKET ST.

Portland State University

SW FIFTH AVE.

SW FRONT AVE.

405

Waterfront Bicycles **7**

TOM McCALL WATERFRONT PARK

HAWTHORNE BRIDGE

STEEL BRIDGE

1/2 MILE

5

To the Kennedy School

OREGON

84

Jupiter Hotel/ Doug Fir Lounge **9**

4 Portland Saturday Market

SE EIGHTH AVE.

Vera Katz East Bank Esplanade

SE HAWTHORNE ST.

5

Springwater Corridor

WESTOVER RD.

NAITO PKWY.

26

1

Portland
MT. HOOD
OREGON

Pacific Ocean

WASH.

CALIF.　NEV.

Seattle

Seemingly overnight, whole swatches of downtown Seattle, Washington, and close-in neighborhoods — notably South Lake Union and the Pike-Pine Corridor — have transformed themselves into vibrant enclaves of restaurants, bars, and galleries. With so many converted and repurposed buildings, Seattle's cityscape is starting to look as layered as the wardrobes of its inhabitants. The tarry pitch of this old timber port city has never disappeared; it was just plastered over with grunge flannel, tech money, yuppie coffee, Pacific Rim flavors, and more recently the backyard chickens and chard of urban pioneers. Don't let one of Seattle's famous rainshowers keep you from entering the mix. This is one of the rare American cities where you can be outdoors year-round without either shivering or sweating. — BY DAVID LASKIN

FRIDAY

1 *Park Tower View* 4 p.m.

Volunteer Park (1247 15th Avenue East; 206-684-4075; seattle.gov/parks), a 10-minute cab or bus ride from downtown at the north end of Capitol Hill, has gardens designed a century ago by the Olmsted Brothers, a conservatory bursting with plants from regions around the world, and a squat brick water tower that you can ascend for terrific views of the city below and the mountains and sea beyond. Rain or shine, it's the ideal place for orientation. If hunger strikes, stroll a couple of blocks east through one of Seattle's oldest and prettiest neighborhoods for a slice of lemon Bundt cake and a Stumptown coffee at the cozy, humming **Volunteer Park Cafe** (1501 17th Avenue East; 206-328-3155; alwaysfreshgoodness.com; $$).

2 *Coolest Corridor* 6 p.m.

The Pike-Pine Corridor is Seattle's happiest urban makeover: from a warren of shabby flats and greasy spoons to an arty but not oppressively gentrified hamlet just across the freeway from downtown. When the locally revered **Elliott Bay Book Company** (1521 10th Avenue; 206-624-6600; elliottbaybook.com)

OPPOSITE A streetcar rolls along Westlake Avenue in the South Lake Union area, a thriving urban village.

abandoned Pioneer Square downtown to relocate here, the literati gasped — but now it looks like a perfect neighborhood fit, what with the inviting communal tables at **Oddfellows** (1525 10th Avenue; 206-325-0807; oddfellowscafe.com; $$) two doors down, and a full spectrum of restaurants, vintage clothing shops, and home décor stores in the surrounding blocks. When it's time for a predinner drink, amble over to **Licorous** (928 12th Avenue; 206-325-6947; licorous.com). Behind the shack-like facade is a soaring, spare, just dark and loud enough watering hole that serves creative cocktails (Bound for Glory, with Bacardi, allspice, lime juice, and Jamaican bitters) and bar snacks like a salumi plate.

3 *Fresh and Local* 7:30 p.m.

One of the most talked-about restaurants in town, **Sitka & Spruce** (1531 Melrose Avenue East; 206-324-0662; sitkaandspruce.com; $$), looks like a classy college dining room with a long refectory table surrounded by a few smaller tables, concrete floors, exposed brick, and duct work. But there's nothing sophomoric about the food. The chef and owner, Matt Dillon, who moved the restaurant to the Pike-Pine Corridor in 2010, follows his flawless intuition in transforming humble local ingredients (smelt, nettles, celery root, black trumpet mushrooms, turnips, pumpkin) into complexly layered, many-textured but never fussy creations like beer-fried smelt with aioli, spiced pumpkin crepe with herbed labneh, and salmon with stinging nettles. Heed your server's advice that entrees are meant to be shared — you will have just enough room for dessert (try warm dates, pistachios, and rose-water ice cream), and you will be pleasantly surprised by the bill.

SATURDAY

4 *Art and Water* 9 a.m.

There used to be two complaints about downtown Seattle: it offered no inspiring parks and no waterfront access worthy of the scenery. The **Olympic Sculpture Park** (2901 Western Avenue; 206-654-3100; seattleartmuseum.org), opened four years ago by the Seattle Art Museum, took care of both problems in one stroke. Masterpieces in steel, granite, fiberglass, and bronze by nationally renowned artists have

wedded beautifully with maturing native trees, shrubs, ferns, and wildflowers. Wander the zigzagging paths and ramps past the massive weathered steel hulls of Richard Serra's *Wake* and Alexander Calder's soaring painted steel *Eagle* until you reach the harborside promenade. From there continue north to a pocket beach and into the adjoining grassy fields of waterfront **Myrtle Edwards Park**. It's all free.

5 *Urban Village* 10:30 a.m.

The development of South Lake Union into a thriving urban village, brainchild of the Microsoft tycoon Paul Allen, is finally alive and kicking. This former industrial no man's land now houses the city's best galleries, an ever increasing collection

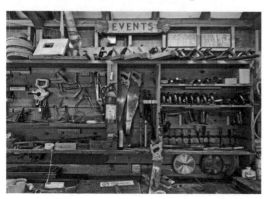

of dining spots, some nifty shops, and the spanking new Amazon campus. Use the South Lake Union Streetcar to hop from **Gordon Woodside/John Braseth Gallery** (2101 Ninth Avenue; 206-622-7243; woodsidebrasethgallery.com), which specializes in Northwest landscapes, to **Honeychurch Antiques** (411 Westlake Avenue North; 206-622-1225; honeychurch.com), with museum-quality Asian art and artifacts, and on to the **Center for Wooden Boats** (1010 Valley Street; 206-382-2628; cwb.org), where you can admire the old varnished beauties or rent a rowboat or sailboat for a spin around Seattle's in-city lake. Need a (really rich) snack? The newly renamed **Marie & Frères Chocolate** (2122 Westlake Avenue; 206-859-3534; claudiocorallochocolate.com) has some of the most exquisite chocolate macaroons ever confected.

6 *Lunch beside the Chief* 1 p.m.

Tilikum Place, with its imposing fountain statue of the city's namesake, Chief Sealth, is Seattle's closest thing to a piazza, and the **Tilikum Place Café** (407 Cedar Street; 206-282-4830; $$) supplied the one

ABOVE AND LEFT A dock and a tool shop at the Center for Wooden Boats, where you can admire classic boats or rent a rowboat or sailboat for a spin around Lake Union, Seattle's in-city lake. The center also offers boatbuilding workshops and other woodworking classes.

missing element—a classy informal restaurant—when it opened. Understated elegance is the byword here, whether in the delicate purée of butternut squash soup with bits of tart apple, the beet salad with arugula and blue cheese, or the light and piquant mushroom and leek tart.

7 *Walk on Water* 4 p.m.

You don't have to leave the city limits to immerse yourself in the region's stunning natural beauty. Drive or take a bus 15 minutes from downtown to the parking lot of the **Museum of History and Industry** (2700 24th Avenue East; 206-324-1126; seattlehistory.org) and pick up the milelong **Arboretum Waterfront Trail**. A network of well-maintained paths and boardwalks takes you through thickets of alder, willow, and elderberry into marshy islands alive with the trills of red-winged blackbirds and marsh wrens, and over shallows where kayakers prowl amid the rushes and the concrete pillars of the freeway overhead. If the sun is out, you'll want to prolong the outing with a stroll through the flowering fruit trees in the adjoining **Washington Park Arboretum** (depts.washington.edu/uwbg).

8 *La Dolce Vita* 8 p.m.

Maybe it's the stylish Italian vibe or the pretty people basking in the soft glow of dripping candles, or maybe it's the sumptuous, creatively classic food—whatever the secret ingredient, **Barolo**

Ristorante (1940 Westlake Avenue; 206-770-9000; baroloseattle.com; $$$) always feels like a party. The pastas would do a Roman mother proud— gnocchi sauced with braised pheasant, leg of lamb ragù spooned over rigatoni. The rack of lamb with Amarone-infused cherries is sinfully rich, and the seared branzino (sea bass) exhales the essence of the Mediterranean. Don't leave without at least a nibble of cannoli or tiramisù.

TOP The beach at Myrtle Edwards Park next to the Olympic Sculpture Park in downtown Seattle.

ABOVE Sitka & Spruce looks like a classy college dining room, but there's nothing sophomoric about the food.

9 *The Beat Goes On* Midnight

At **See Sound Lounge** (115 Blanchard Street; 206-374-3733; seesoundlounge.com) young and not so young Seattle join forces to party to house music spun by a revolving cast of D.J.'s. There's a small dance floor — but the compensation is lots of booths and sofas to crash on. The scene outside can get

ABOVE See Sound Lounge, where Saturday night house music goes into Sunday morning.

OPPOSITE A stroll near Alexander Calder's steel sculpture, *Eagle*, at the Olympic Sculpture Park.

rowdy in the wee hours, but inside the beat and liquor flow smoothly.

SUNDAY

10 *Bayou Brunch* 10:30 a.m.

Lake Pontchartrain meets Puget Sound at **Toulouse Petit** (601 Queen Anne Avenue North; 206-432-9069; toulousepetit.com; $$), a funky bistro-style spot near the Seattle Center in Lower Queen Anne. Grab a booth and settle in with a basket of hot, crispy beignets; then indulge in something truly decadent, like pork cheeks confit hash topped with a couple of fried eggs or eggs Benedict with crab and fines herbes. You can cleanse your system afterward with a brisk walk up the hill to **Kerry Park** (211 West Highland Drive) for a magnificent farewell view.

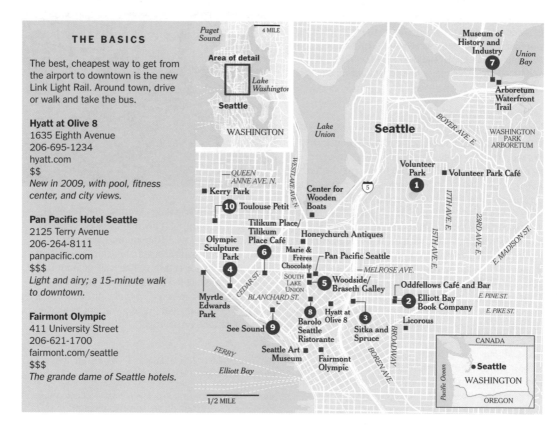

THE BASICS

The best, cheapest way to get from the airport to downtown is the new Link Light Rail. Around town, drive or walk and take the bus.

Hyatt at Olive 8
1635 Eighth Avenue
206-695-1234
hyatt.com
$$
New in 2009, with pool, fitness center, and city views.

Pan Pacific Hotel Seattle
2125 Terry Avenue
206-264-8111
panpacific.com
$$$
Light and airy; a 15-minute walk to downtown.

Fairmont Olympic
411 University Street
206-621-1700
fairmont.com/seattle
$$$
The grande dame of Seattle hotels.

Northwest
Seattle

Long ago the expanding city of Seattle swallowed up two of its neighbors, and neither of them has ever forgotten. Fremont and Ballard, once cities in their own right, are now Seattle neighborhoods of a particularly independent-minded kind. They're close together, though not contiguous, and still have unique character that resists complete assimilation — arty and free-spirited in Fremont; Nordic and proudly maritime in Ballard. Each is undergoing a kind of 21st-century renaissance, with shops and restaurants moving in, and a new, often young crowd arriving to live or just to play. But in either one, you can still lose yourself so thoroughly that you will barely even remember you're in the same town as the Space Needle.
— BY DAN WHITE

FRIDAY

1 *Welcome to Fremont* 3 p.m.

As they cross the orange-and-blue Fremont Bridge on their way from downtown Seattle, drivers are met by a neon Rapunzel, a sign proclaiming Fremont the Center of the Universe, and instructions to set their watches back five minutes. From there on, it's a cross between a family-friendly bohemian enclave and a larger-than-life-size hipster sculpture garden. Don't be surprised if the cast-aluminum commuters standing near the bridge, waiting for a train that has not run for years, are wearing flamboyant clothes and headgear. Ever since *Waiting for the Interurban* was installed in 1979, whimsical Fremonters have clad them in continually changing costumes. (During the Abu Ghraib scandal someone put hoods over their heads, but it's not usually that political.) A block to the southeast, beneath the busy Aurora Bridge, the two-ton **Fremont Troll** crouches beneath a support wall, staring with his one eye and squashing a Volkswagen Bug in his left hand. Children sometimes crawl up his forearms and wedge their hands into his nostrils while parents take pictures.

2 *Scrap Art* 3:30 p.m.

You'll see a variety of outdoor art around Fremont — clown statues, dinosaur topiaries, a street sign pointing to Atlantis — but don't miss two more high spots. The seven-ton bronze **statue of Lenin** (Evanston

Avenue North and North 36th Street), rescued from an Eastern European scrapyard after the Soviet collapse, loses some of its symbolic power when adorned with lights at Christmas or dressed in drag during Gay Pride Week. Another must-see is the **Fremont Rocket** (601 North 35th Street), a reborn piece of cold war junk pointing 53 feet into the sky. Some Fremontians, still pining for their lost independence, claim that it is aimed at Seattle's City Hall.

3 *Retail Trail* 4 p.m.

Do some exploring on foot. Beneath the rocket, check out **Burnt Sugar and Frankie** (206-545-0699; burntsugarfrankie.com), selling handbags, books, and more. Walk west on 35th Street to **Theo Chocolate** (3400 Phinney Avenue North; 206-632-5100; theochocolate.com), a chocolate factory that offers tours and has a retail shop. A bit farther south, find the entrance to the **Burke-Gilman Trail** near where Phinney Avenue intersects with North Canal Street and walk southeast along the Lake Washington Ship Canal amid the joggers and cyclists. Just before you reach the Fremont Bridge, head back north on Fremont Avenue to find shops like **Jive Time Records** (3506 Fremont Avenue North; 206-632-5483; jivetimerecords.com), **Ophelia's Books** (3504 Fremont Avenue North; 206-632-3759; opheliasbooks.com)

OPPOSITE Autumn shopping at the Farmers Market in Ballard, a Seattle neighborhood with an independent streak.

BELOW Cocoa beans at Theo Chocolate in Fremont, another part of town with its own quirky identity.

and **Show Pony** (702 North 35th Street; 206-706-4188; showponyseattle.com), a clothing boutique.

4 *Fremont Fodder* 7:30 p.m.

Assess your mood and choose a place for dinner. **The Red Door** (3401 Evanston Avenue North; 206-547-7521; reddoorseattle.com; $) has outdoor patio dining year-round (think burgers and salads) and a wide selection of craft brews. Or go upscale at the **35th Street Bistro** (709 North 35th Street; 206-547-9850; 35bistro.com; $$-$$), where you can sip a martini made with seasonal ingredients and order wine pairings with entrees like chicken confit or herb-crusted trout.

SATURDAY

5 *Eggs of the Universe* 9 a.m.

Start the day at **Silence-Heart-Nest** (3508 Fremont Place North; 206-633-5169; silenceheartnest.com; $), a vegetarian cafe. It's a total-immersion experience in itself, with sari-clad wait staff asking diners to ponder business cards printed with inspirational verses while serving up sesame waffles and Center of the Universe scrambled eggs. After breakfast, it's time to leave Fremont. Drive northwest on Leary

ABOVE The bar at King's Hardware on Ballard Avenue.

Way, which becomes Northwest 36th Street, and into Ballard, where neighborhood assertion goes in a different direction.

6 *Nordic Pride* 10:30 a.m.

Follow the mazelike layout of the surprisingly beguiling **Nordic Heritage Museum** (3014 Northwest 67th Street; 206-789-5707; nordicmuseum.org) as it snakes through three floors of a former schoolhouse, guiding you past a centuries-old fishing boat and a life-sized replica of an Icelandic sod house. Seafaring Scandinavians were the heart of old Ballard, and although ethnicities are mixed up now, the neighborhood still celebrates Norwegian Constitution Day every May 17 with a parade and much flag-waving. It was water that persuaded reluctant Ballardites to accept annexation in 1907 by a narrow margin—they needed access to Seattle's freshwater supply. Not everyone is reconciled to it even now. On the 100th anniversary, some people wore black armbands.

7 *Cohos on the Move* Noon

The nearly century-old **Hiram M. Chittenden Locks** (3015 Northwest 54th Street; 206-783-7059) help keep the salt water of Puget Sound from despoiling freshwater Lake Washington. They also lift boats from sea level to the lake's 26-foot elevation. Watch yachts and fishing boats steadily rise as the locks fill like a giant bathtub—a sight that can seem surreal.

But the irresistible flourish is the glass-lined tunnel that, if you're here in salmon spawning season, lets you spy on cohos and chinooks as they make their way up the fish ladder, a series of ascending weirs. You can press your face a few millimeters away from the fat fish, which clunk into each other, form traffic jams, and sometimes turn their vacant expressions on the humans.

8 *The Sound of Lunch* 1:30 p.m.

Ballard's southern boundary is the Washington Lake Ship Canal, its western boundary is Puget Sound, and **Ray's Cafe**, at Ray's Boathouse Restaurant (6049 Seaview Avenue Northwest; 206-789-3770; rays.com) sits right about where they meet. Grab a table on the outdoor deck and order fish for lunch.

9 *Dunes in the City* 3 p.m.

The maritime spirit feels alive at **Golden Gardens Park** (8498 Seaview Place Northwest; 206-684-4075),

arguably the loveliest picnic spot in all of Seattle, with sand dunes, a lagoon, secluded benches, occasional sightings of bald eagles, and heart-stopping views of the distant Olympic Mountains at sunset. Walk the paths, find a spot for relaxing, and chill.

10 *Hometown Ravioli* 8 p.m.

Combine Northwestern with Italian in a dinner at **Volterra** (5411 Ballard Avenue Northwest;

ABOVE Underwater windows let curious humans spy on salmon at the Hiram M. Chittenden Locks.

BELOW The Fremont Troll peers out from under the Aurora Bridge. His left hand is squashing a Volkswagen Bug.

206-789-5100; volterrarestaurant.com; $$), where the Dungeness Crab ravioli is made using house-made pasta. Then finish out the evening with drinks in the area around Ballard Avenue Northwest. One choice is **King's Hardware** (No. 5225). Another is **Hattie's Hat** (No. 5231). Students, fishermen, professionals, and laborers gather at its hand-carved

ABOVE Music at Ballard Sunday Farmers Market, which is open year-round.

OPPOSITE Golden Gardens Park, one of the loveliest places for an afternoon escape in all of Seattle.

bar. "Everyone comes here," Brian Plonsky, the bartender, said. "This has been a bar for 100 years."

SUNDAY

11 *Sunday Shoppers* 11 a.m.

Ballard's eastern edge feels more contemporary, with dining, shopping, and a lively social scene. Year-round, the **Ballard Sunday Farmers Market** (Ballard Avenue between Vernon Place and 22nd Avenue; ballardfarmersmarket.wordpress.com) brings out vendors and shoppers in a scene that some Ballardites insist surpasses Seattle's well-known Pike Place Market. Spend some time people watching and checking out the quintessentially Pacific Northwestern products on offer: giant radishes, tiny potatoes called spud nuts, jugs of homemade cider, milk from purebred Boer goats, and spiced blackberry wine.

THE BASICS

Fremont and Ballard are easily reachable from downtown. Drive a car and park to walk.

Watertown Hotel
4242 Roosevelt Way Northeast
206-826-4242
watertownseattle.com
$$
Lodging is scarce in both Fremont and Ballard; this stylish alternative is nearby in the University district.

University Inn
4140 Roosevelt Way Northeast
206-632-5055
universityinnseattle.com
$$
Another University District option.

Courtyard Seattle Downtown/Lake Union
925 Westlake Avenue North
206-213-0100
marriott.com
$$
Reliable chain hotel nearby.

The San Juan Islands

You could spend years getting to know the more than 170 San Juan Islands of Washington, but it's easy to become acquainted with three of the biggest. Lopez, Orcas, and San Juan are jewels of the Pacific Northwest, great for sailing, kayaking, hiking, biking, diving, or just relaxing. Visit, and you'll find out how a quarrel over the killing of a farm animal in the 19th century nearly led to war, spot wildlife in a way you've probably never done before, and find yourself drifting onto island time. — BY BOB MACKIN

FRIDAY

1 *To Lopez for Dinner* 6 p.m.

After the pleasant 40-minute passage by car ferry (206-464-6400, wsdot.wa.gov/ferries) from Anacortes, Washington, to quiet Lopez Island, take a quick drive to Lopez Village for dinner. The view is fantastic from a window seat at the **Bay Café** (9 Old Post Road; 360-468-3700; bay-cafe.com; $$), and so is the food. Look out on the bay and the islands beyond as you dig into fresh local fish or locally raised beef or lamb. Make a reservation in advance. Residents of other islands make the trip to Lopez just to dine.

2 *To Orcas for Dessert* 7:30 p.m.

After dinner, head back to the ferry landing. The timetable is often more theoretical than actual, so your boat to Orcas Island is likely to be late. But after 30 minutes across the water and a 25-minute drive, you'll be at the **Rosario Resort & Spa** (1400 Rosario Road, Eastsound; 360-376-2222; rosarioresort.com). The waterside resort is built around the Moran mansion, which was completed in 1909 by a ship-building magnate and former mayor of Seattle. Order dessert in the lounge — selections change often, but one day's standout was a marionberry cobbler. A special treat is the music room, where the musician and mansion curator, Christopher Peacock, offers tours and demonstrates the 1,972-pipe organ.

SATURDAY

3 *Sea to Summit* 10 a.m.

At 2,409 feet, Mount Constitution on Orcas Island is the highest point in the San Juans. The 15-minute drive to the top is full of hairpin turns on a narrow road. But if the weather cooperates, you'll be rewarded with breathtaking views as far as Vancouver, British Columbia; the Cascade and Olympic ranges; and the islands and ships in Puget Sound. Mount Constitution is part of **Moran State Park** (3572 Olga Road, Olga; parks.wa.gov), granted to Washington in 1921 by Robert Moran, whose mansion you visited last night. He built that house when doctors told him to retire early, but he wound up living to 86, thanks, it is said, to the serene beauty of Orcas.

4 *Pig War* Noon

Take the boat to San Juan Island to hear the strange tale of the Pig War. In 1859, an American settler killed a Hudson's Bay Company pig. Within two months, more than 400 American troops, dispatched to protect the settler from arrest, faced off against some 2,000 British soldiers, sailors, and marines. But no shots were fired, and small detachments from each nation remained until 1872, when Kaiser Wilhelm I, acting as arbitrator, awarded the islands to the United States, not British Canada. Today, the British and American camps make up the **San Juan Island**

OPPOSITE The view from the highest vantage point in the San Juans, Mount Constitution on Orcas Island.

BELOW Boats docked near Eastsound on Orcas Island.

National Historical Park (360-378-2902; nps.gov/sajh). During summer, it comes alive as local history buffs don period costumes for historical recreations.

5 *Whale Watch, Minus Boat* 1 p.m.

Pack a picnic, keep binoculars handy, be patient. That's the three-pronged strategy for enjoying your time at **Lime Kiln Point State Park** (1567 Westside Road, Friday Harbor; 360-378-2044; parks.wa.gov). The 36-acre park has Douglas fir, arbutus and even cactuses along its forest trails. But from late spring to early fall, it may be the world's best place to see orca whales from land. Park your car in the lot and hike the lighthouse trail to the rocky outcrop in the shadow of the Lime Kiln Point lighthouse. Set up your picnic on the rocks and watch for the shiny black and white orcas. If you're lucky, they'll come close enough that they can also see you. If you miss a pod on parade, you're still likely to see seals and eagles. The lighthouse, built in 1919, is now a whale behavior research center. In summer, park staff members are often available to provide information on the whales and also offer evening tours of the lighthouse; day tours can be arranged.

6 *Purple Pleasure* 4 p.m.

Lavender farming has made its way to the San Juans, so ask if there's lavender oil available when you choose hot stone massage, Swedish massage, reiki, or all three at **Lavendera Day Spa** (440 Spring Street, Friday Harbor; 360-378-3637; lavenderadayspa.com), ideal after a spell of hiking and sitting on rocks. When you've achieved blissful relaxation, make a visit to the **Pelindaba Lavender Farm** (33 Hawthorne Lane, off Wold Road; 360-378-4248; pelindabalavender.com), where you're welcome to tour the rippling purple in flowering season.

7 *San Juan Locavore* 6 p.m.

This is Washington, and salmon should be on the menu. Expect it at **Coho Restaurant** (120 Nichols Street, Friday Harbor; 360-378-6330; cohorestaurant.com; $$$), along with shellfish from the Straits of Juan de Fuca, meat from a Lopez Island farm, and local produce from several island growers. The desserts are house-made, and the wine list is filled with vintages from Washington, Oregon, and California.

8 *Sculptured Trail* 8 p.m.

A visit to the **IMA Sculpture Park** (Roche Harbor Road, Roche Harbor, overlooking Westcott Bay), a location of the **San Juan Islands Museum of Art & Sculpture** (360-370-5050; sjima.org), is a great way to spend the late, late afternoon. Scattered along the trails are more than 100 sculptures (by artists from the Pacific Northwest and beyond) looking magical in their open-air setting as the light fades.

SUNDAY

9 *Whale Talk* 10 a.m.

A modest two-story building, the former Odd Fellows Hall in Friday Harbor, is the home of the **Whale Museum** (62 First Street North; 360-378-4710; whale-museum.org), a remarkable collection of whale photographs, skeletons, and even some brains. Take a few minutes to listen to the library of whale vocalizations in a phone booth.

10 *A Drink of Lavender* 11 a.m.

The proprietors of the lavender farm you visited yesterday have cleverly opened the **Pelindaba Lavender shop** in downtown Friday Harbor near the ferry terminal (First Street; 360-378-4248; pelindabalavender.com). The lavender-infused lemonade is the perfect drink to quaff on a summer day's cruise among the San Juans as you return to the mainland.

OPPOSITE Sunset and serenity in the San Juans.

ABOVE A busy ferry system, carrying passengers and cars, keeps the islands connected and tied to the mainland.

THE BASICS

Take the Washington State Ferries from Anacortes, about 80 miles north of Seattle.

Hop from island to island by car ferry, and drive.

Inn on Orcas Island
114 Channel Road, Deer Harbor
360-376-5227
theinnonorcasisland.com
$$$
Eight artfully decorated rooms, cottages, and suites, all facing a bay. Breakfast is included.

Tucker House Inn
275 C Street, Friday Harbor
360-378-2783
tuckerhouse.com
$$$
Rooms, cottages, and suites in century-old buildings.

Rosario Resort and Spa
1400 Rosario Road, Eastsound
rosarioresort.com
$$
Tastefully decorated rooms with sweeping water views.

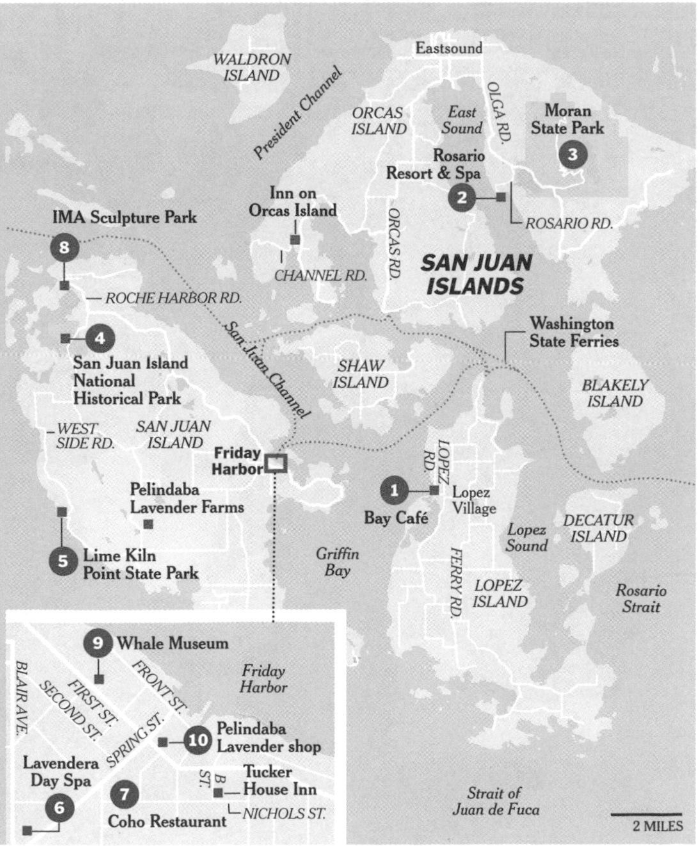
WALDRON ISLAND
Eastsound
President Channel
ORCAS ISLAND
East Sound
OLGA RD.
Moran State Park
3
Rosario Resort & Spa
2
ROSARIO RD.
Inn on Orcas Island
IMA Sculpture Park
8
ORCAS RD.
CHANNEL RD.
SAN JUAN ISLANDS
ROCHE HARBOR RD.
4
San Juan Channel
Washington State Ferries
San Juan Island National Historical Park
SHAW ISLAND
BLAKELY ISLAND
WEST SIDE RD.
SAN JUAN ISLAND
Friday Harbor
LOPEZ RD.
1
Lopez Village
Bay Café
Pelindaba Lavender Farms
DECATUR ISLAND
Lopez Sound
5
Lime Kiln Point State Park
Griffin Bay
FERRY RD.
LOPEZ ISLAND
Rosario Strait
9
Whale Museum
FRONT ST.
Friday Harbor
BLAIR AVE.
SECOND ST.
FIRST ST.
SPRING ST.
10
Pelindaba Lavender shop
Lavendera Day Spa
B ST.
Tucker House Inn
6
7
Coho Restaurant
NICHOLS ST.
Strait of Juan de Fuca
2 MILES

Vancouver

Vancouver, British Columbia, is often heralded as
one of the world's most livable cities. It is blessed
with a snowcapped mountain backdrop and
crystal blue harbors. It is a gateway to the Inside
Passage — the marvelous maze of glacier-carved
fjords and forested islands that are a cruise lover's
delight. In the city itself and close by, outdoor lovers
will find miles of scenic hiking and biking trails.
But what really sets Vancouver apart is its urban
density. With sprawl kept in check by geography,
the city thinks vertically. Neighborhoods overlap,
apartments rise. That seems to heighten the city's
international mix. — BY DENNY LEE

FRIDAY

1 *Assembly Point* 4 p.m.

Blame the great outdoors, but Vancouver lacks
a central square where citizens turn inward and
visitors feel they have arrived. A quirky stand-in is
the **Mount Pleasant** district, which is becoming cooler
by the minute. Scattered among dingy bingo parlors
are trendy boutiques like **Lark** (2315 Main Street;
604-879-5275; lark.me), which carries Chimala jeans
from Japan, and **Jewellerbau** (2408 Main Street;
604-872-7759; jewellerbau.blogspot.com), with modern
industrial jewelry. The local designer Hajnalka
Mandula spins lacy and brooding finery for *Twilight*
goths at **Mandula** (206 Carall Street; 604-568-9211;
mandula.com). An anchor is the artist-run **Western
Front** (303 East Eighth Avenue; 604-876-9343;
front.bc.ca), which has galleries, stages, and arch
architecture. Look up while you're there: those are
the North Shore Mountains looming over the
faux cornice.

2 *Pigging Out* 7:30 p.m.

With salmon-rich waters out front and heritage
pig farms out back, locavore eating is a way of life
in Vancouver. The barn-to-bistro ethos is buoyed by

Refuel (1944 West Fourth Avenue; 604-288-7905;
refuelrestaurant.com; $$), a casual restaurant in the
affluent Kitsilano district. Start with an irresistible
bowl of spiced pork ribs and offal, rubbed with
cayenne, citric acid, paprika, and other spices and then
deep-fried to crunchy bliss. Your cardiologist won't
understand. For the main course, a recent favorite
included salmon (wild and local, of course), grilled
and served in a pool of fragrant leeks and clams.

3 *Club Corner* 10 p.m.

Vancouver isn't known for nighttime debauchery,
thanks partly to tough liquor laws. If you insist on
getting dolled up, a party train of 20-somethings forms
along Granville Street, a still-seedy strip with a cluster
of velvet-roped bars like **Granville Room** (957 Granville
Street; 604-633-0056; granvilleroom.ca), which has a
handsome interior of brick walls and chandeliers. A
skip away is Davie Street, the city's gay strip, with
plenty of night spots to choose from.

SATURDAY

4 *Granola Island* 10 a.m.

Take a water taxi across False Creek to the
tiny peninsula known as **Granville Island**
(granvilleisland.com), which has a popular food market
brimming with farmers, butchers, and fishmongers.

OPPOSITE Outdoor lunch on Granville Island, with a
metropolitan view across False Creek.

RIGHT Fresh merchandise at Lobster Man, a vendor at the
popular food market on Granville Island. The market brims
with farmers, butchers, fish sellers, and artisans.

It also has a hippie side—from yoga and crafts studios to a pottery gallery and theater. Grab a multigrain loaf at **Terra Breads** (terrabreads.com) and stroll through the island's jam-packed aisles and alleys. Look for the **Lobster Man** (1807 Mast Tower Road; 604-687-4531; lobsterman.com), with its tanks of kayak-size lobsters, and the **Artisan Sake Maker** (1339 Railspur Alley; 604-685-7253; artisansakemaker.com), which makes small batches of junmai sake on the premises and, for a couple of dollars, will let you taste.

5 *Creative Curries* 12:30 p.m.

Mark Bittman, the *New York Times* columnist and longtime food writer, once called **Vij's** (1480 West 11th Avenue; 604-736-6664; vijsrestaurant.ca; $$$), which serves regional interpretations of familiar Indian foods, "among the finest Indian restaurants in the world." But for lunch, pop in next door to its colorful sister, **Vij's Rangoli** (1488 West 11th Avenue; 604-736-5711; vijsrangoli.ca; $$), which looks like a takeout diner. Memorable combinations included a goat meat and jackfruit curry with a coconut cabbage salad.

6 *Photoconceptualism* 2 p.m.

Before Vancouver's film industry was nicknamed Hollywood North, the city's cultural high point may have been the Vancouver School of post-conceptual photography, led by artists like Jeff Wall and Roy Arden, who blurred the line between documentation and artifice. The school lives on at a pair of galleries in the South Granville district. **Monte Clark Gallery** (2339 Granville Street; 604-730-5000; monteclarkgallery.com) represents Arden, Stephen Waddell, and others. Down the block is the **Equinox Gallery** (2321 Granville Street; 604-736-2405; equinoxgallery.com), where you're likely to see Fred Herzog's vintage mid-20th-century photographs, reprinted using color-saturated inkjets.

7 *Where Olympians Trod* 4 p.m.

Before hosting the Winter Olympics in 2010, Vancouver built a billion-dollar waterfront Olympic Village to house the athletes. Afterward, it reinvented the jumble of elegant towers as **Millennium Water**, a new residential district clustered around a central square. The recession and housing bust hurt sales, but the neighborhood is beating with a bohemian pulse. Have an uber-healthy snack at **OrganicLives** (1829 Quebec Street; 778-588-7777; organiclives.org; $), where you may hear customers raving about the macaroons. Then drop in at the **Beaumont** (316 West Fifth Avenue; 604-733-3783; thebeaumontstudios.com), a 7,000-square-foot, two-story collective of studios

ABOVE The seawall path at Stanley Park, a favorite spot for strolling, running, and biking.

in a former denture manufacturing plant, to watch the artists work and see what's for sale.

8 *Neo-Fusion* 8 p.m.

From Tokyo-style izakayas to banh mi cafes, the flavors of Asia are well represented in Vancouver. The large Asian population has also raised the bar on fusion. For haute interpretations of humble Thai dishes, **Maenam** (1938 West Fourth Avenue; 604-730-5579; maenam.ca; $$) has drawn comparisons to the Michelin-starred Nahm in London, where its chef and owner apprenticed. The pink-and-bamboo spot draws a foodie set with playful dishes like spicy braised duck with sweet longans, confit potatoes, and cucumber relish. Another option is **Bao Bei** (163 Keefer Street; 604-688-0876; bao-bei.ca; $$), an upscale Chinese brasserie in Chinatown.

9 *Drink Sets* 10:30 p.m.

A smattering of high-concept watering holes — the kind serving wine and beer flights — have opened in Gastown. Popular with the Hollywood North set is the **Alibi Room** (157 Alexander Street; 604-623-3383; alibi.ca), a loft-like space with wooden

ABOVE Make your way to Maenam for haute interpretations of humble Thai dishes.

BELOW Its setting on the calm waters of the Burrard Inlet, a long coastal fjord, made Vancouver a prosperous port.

tables and a long list of bottled and draft beers. Wine imbibers head to the **Salt Tasting Room** (45 Blood Alley; 604-633-1912; salttastingroom.com), a cellar-like bar with a large chalkboard menu that lists eclectic wines, cheeses, and exotic cured meats.

SUNDAY

10 *The Rainforest* 10 a.m.

To experience one of the largest and most diverse urban parks in North America — and be reminded that this area is naturally a temperate rain forest — spend a few hours at **Stanley Park**

(vancouver.ca/parks/parks/stanley), a gloriously green peninsula. A six-mile walking and cycling bicycle path on a sea wall rings the park's 1,000 acres of gardens and majestic cedar, hemlock, and fir trees, tracing much of the seafront. Bicycle rentals are close by at several shops, including **Denman Bike Shop** (710 Denman Street; 604-685-9755; denmanbikeshop.com) and **Bayshore Bike Rental** (745 Denman Street; 604-688-2453; bayshorebikerentals.com). Don't miss the totem pole display at Brockton Point, which according to the park's Web site is the most visited tourist attraction in British Columbia.

ABOVE Vij's Rangoli, the more colorful, affordable sister restaurant of the acclaimed Vij's next door.

OPPOSITE Western Front, a gallery and performance space in the gentrifying bohemian Mount Pleasant district.

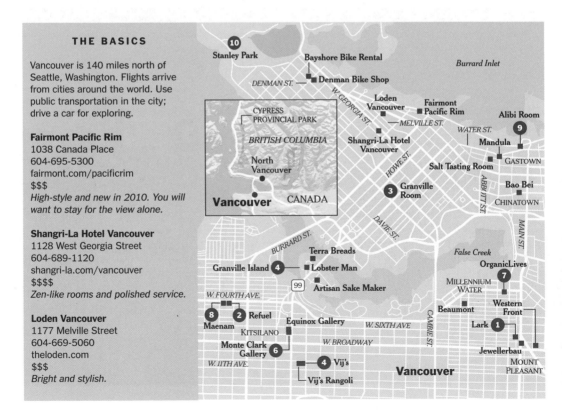

THE BASICS

Vancouver is 140 miles north of Seattle, Washington. Flights arrive from cities around the world. Use public transportation in the city; drive a car for exploring.

Fairmont Pacific Rim
1038 Canada Place
604-695-5300
fairmont.com/pacificrim
$$$
High-style and new in 2010. You will want to stay for the view alone.

Shangri-La Hotel Vancouver
1128 West Georgia Street
604-689-1120
shangri-la.com/vancouver
$$$$
Zen-like rooms and polished service.

Loden Vancouver
1177 Melville Street
604-669-5060
theloden.com
$$$
Bright and stylish.

Whistler

Whistler, British Columbia, North America's biggest ski resort, invites a listing of statistics. A mile of vertical drop, 37 lifts, 8,100 skiable acres, 200 runs spread across its two mountains, Whistler and Blackcomb. In 2010, the Winter Olympics, lured by all that snow, brought skiers to town from around the planet. But this steep mountain valley is home to a diversity that has nothing to do with international competitions. Walk down the main promenade and see everyone from rich urban castaways and old-school hippies to stylish French-speaking Québécois and weathered dropouts shouldering skis the size of ironing boards. It makes Whistler feel worldly and cosmopolitan, even when gold medals aren't being handed out. — BY CHRISTOPHER SOLOMON

FRIDAY

1 *Cultural Powder* 4 p.m.

Before you hit the snow, pay homage to the ground underneath: for thousands of years, Whistler Valley was the hunting and berry-picking grounds of the Squamish and Lil'wat First Nations. Explore the rich history of the land you'll be skiing at the **Squamish Lil'wat Cultural Center** (4584 Blackcomb Way; 866-441-7522; slcc.ca). While the hand-carved canoes, baskets, and smoked-salmon bannocks (kind of a local panini) are diverting, what really makes this 30,000-square-foot museum shine are the friendly aboriginal "youth ambassadors," who welcome visitors with native songs and totem-carving exhibitions.

2 *Carbo Load* 8 p.m.

It's easy to spend money in Whistler. Those watching their loonies should follow the local ski bums to **Pasta Lupino** (4368 Main Street, Whistler Village North; 604-905-0400; pastalupino.com; $$). Tucked near a 7-Eleven at the edge of the resort, the small, cheery restaurant serves fantastic fresh pastas with homemade Bolognese and Alfredo sauces. And the budget-friendly prices for pastas, soup or salad, and freshly baked focaccia make it easy to indulge.

3 *Pre-Ski Cocktails* 10 p.m.

Maybe it's all the snow, but Whistler doesn't skimp when it comes to watering holes. They run the spectrum from hockey sports bars to "ice" bars where you can chill your drink between sips. For the latter, head to the august **Bearfoot Bistro** (4121 Village Green; 604-932-3433; bearfootbistro.com; $$$$). There you can have your flute of B.C. bubbly with a side of tinkling piano music and appetizers by Melissa Craig, an award-winning chef. For a more boisterous setting, stomp your Sorel boots over to **Crystal Lounge** (4154 Village Green; 604-938-1081), a basement bar in the village center festooned with TVs and hockey sweaters. It's packed with local skiers and boarders eating chicken wings and drinking pitchers of Granville Island English Bay Pale Ale.

SATURDAY

4 *Where to Schuss* 8 a.m.

Which mountain, Whistler or Blackcomb? Skiers used to have to pick one, but thanks to the **Peak 2 Peak Gondola**, this whole behemoth resort is now within easy reach. If the snow is good, Whistler will be packed, so here's a plan. In the morning, avoid the crowded Village Gondola at Whistler and go to

OPPOSITE The Peak 2 Peak Gondola links Whistler and Blackcomb Mountains, the two peaks whose 8,100 skiable acres make Whistler North America's largest ski area.

BELOW Quattro at Whistler, a spot for Italian cuisine.

Blackcomb's base area to ride the Wizard Express and Solar Coaster Express lifts. The lines are shorter, and they get you right up Blackcomb Mountain. Warm up on the gentle Jersey Cream run and check the lighted boards to see which mountaintop lifts are open. When you reach the top, take your pick of ego powder runs like Showcase or the mettle-testing Couloir Extreme. When you're ready, swoop across to Whistler on the Peak 2 Peak, which is an event in itself: the cabins, which fit 28 passengers, dangle up to 1,427 feet high over a span of almost three miles.

5 *Belgian Waffles and BBQ* Noon

Come lunchtime, the huge lodges can feel like rush hour. So seek out the lesser-known on-

mountain restaurants. On Blackcomb, the **Crystal Hut** (whistlerblackcomb.com/todo/MountainDining) is a small log cabin near the top of the Crystal Chair that serves Belgian waffles all day and lunch specialties from a wood-burning oven. On Whistler, the **Chic Pea** near the top of the Garbanzo Express lift serves toasted sandwiches, pizza, and barbecue on its outdoor deck.

6 *Heaven on Skis* 2 p.m.

If the sun is smiling, head over to Blackcomb's **7th Heaven** area, which has great views and is warmed by the afternoon's rays. It also has something for everyone: long, bumpy runs like Sunburn and Angel Dust, harder-to-reach powder stashes like Lakeside Bowl, and lingering intermediate groomers like Hugh's Heaven and Cloud Nine, which seem to meander to the valley floor.

7 *Boards at the Source* 4 p.m.

Independent ski and snowboard makers like Igneous Skis and Never Summer Snowboards have sprung up all over in recent years. One of the oldest is **Prior Snowboards and Skis** (104-1410 Alpha Lake

ABOVE The new timber-and-stone Nita Lake Lodge.

LEFT The shooting range for biathletes at Whistler Olympic Park, a sprawling Nordic playground.

Road; 604-935-1923; priorskis.com), founded 20 years ago in Whistler. Every Wednesday at 5 p.m. and Saturday at 4 p.m., the company offers free one-hour tours of the factory floor. See how fiberglass layers are glued with epoxy and pressed together under enormous heat and pressure to create a springy, responsive snow toy.

8 *Playtime for All* 6:30 p.m.

A ski resort can be tricky for parents. At day's end the kids are still wound up, but the adults are ready for a cocktail. Before you push off for a good pour, drop the kids off for more vertical fun at the **Core** (4010 Whistler Conference Centre; 604-905-7625; whistlercore.com), a climbing gym and fitness center in the middle of the village with an indoor wall. Try the nightly Climb & Dine program for kids—three hours of supervised rock climbing and a pizza dinner. Reservations required.

9 *Dinner for Grownups* 7 p.m.

Yes, you had Italian last night, but this is different. The snug and romantic **Quattro at Whistler** (Pinnacle International Hotel, 4319 Main Street; 604-905-4844; quattrorestaurants.com; $$$) serves entrees like glazed wild salmon with orange, honey, pickled fennel, and baby arugula. And yes, there

ABOVE Nordic skiing maneuvers on the biathlon course at Whistler Olympic Park.

BELOW At Prior Snowboards and Skis, see how fiberglass layers are bonded together under enormous heat and pressure to create a springy, responsive snow toy.

is pasta. One example: ravioli made with smoked pork cheek and ricotta, served with parsnip chips.

10 *What Wipeout?* 9:30 p.m.

Everyone from weary locals to visiting ski-film royalty (sometimes just returned from nearby backcountry heli-skiing) ends up at the **Garibaldi Lift Company,** fondly known as GLC (4165 Springs Lane; 604-905-2220). The crowd is big and rowdy, favoring beer by the pitcher. Count on a band or D.J. playing, a fire roaring, and hockey on the flat screen. With its floor-to-ceiling windows overlooking the slopes, the GLC is the kind of place to embellish the day's stories and make outsize promises for tomorrow.

SUNDAY

11 *Nordic Dreams* 11 a.m.

Yesterday you barreled down Whistler Mountain pretending to be Lindsey Vonn. Now go for the Walter Mitty experience. About 12 miles southwest of the resort, in the Callaghan Valley, is the **Whistler Olympic Park** (5 Callaghan Valley Road; 877-764-2455; whistlerolympicpark.com), a sprawling Nordic playground. Strap on a pair of cross-country skis, toss a firearm over your shoulder, and become a biathlete for an hour. On the open trails and snow fields among towering, moss-draped hemlocks, there's plenty of room to fulfill your Nordic gold-medal fantasies.

ABOVE A bright day on Blackcomb Mountain.

OPPOSITE Drop the kids off at the Core, a new climbing gym and fitness center that has a rock-climbing wall.

THE BASICS

Most visitors fly to Vancouver and take a shuttle 70 miles north. A car isn't needed; free buses circulate the resort.

Nita Lake Lodge
2131 Lake Placid Road
604-966-5700
nitalakelodge.com
$$$$
Timber-and-stone lodge with views of Nita Lake.

Aava Whistler Hotel
4005 Whistler Way
604-932-2522
aavawhistlerhotel.com
$$
Next to Whistler village and a five-minute walk to the lifts.

Listel Hotel
4121 Village Green
604-932-1133
listelhotel.com
$$
Serviceable and well located.

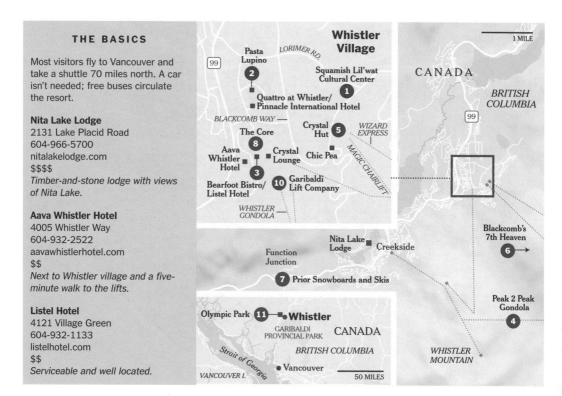

The Okanagan Valley

Glacier-formed and fertile, the Okanagan Valley is the British Columbia of popular imagination, all steep-walled mountain valleys and spectacular snow-fed lakes. But there's a bonus — it's also a wine region, with more than 100 wineries and counting, striving to hold its own with the famous California valleys to the south. Part old-fashioned summer lake resort, part cycling center, and traditionally fruit-growing country, the valley is changing fast as cherry orchards and nut farms lose ground to the vineyards and as tourism grows along with the grapes. — BY BONNIE TSUI

FRIDAY

1 *A Sheet of Blue* 2 p.m.

Kelowna, the Okanagan Valley's gateway city, combines a pedestrian-friendly waterfront and mountain views with tracts of gas stations and big-box stores. Head straight for Lake Okanagan, a sheet of blue that is the defining signature of this region, and rent a kayak from the marina at the **Hotel Eldorado** (500 Cook Road, Kelowna; 250-763-3625; hoteleldoradokelowna.com). Sailboats and canoes skim the water as you paddle, while back at the marina, margarita drinkers from the hotel bar watch the buzzing watercraft leaving the slips. As you near the middle of the lake, the steep walls of the valley rise up dramatically on either side, one shade of green fusing subtly into the next. Look for the telltale corduroy of the vineyards.

2 *Go to the Grapes* 4 p.m.

A wine tour of the 120-mile-long Okanagan Valley satisfies many tastes. The southern end delivers big reds like merlots and cabernet sauvignons that are robust and jammy, with soft, pleasing finishes. In the north, near Kelowna, crisp, fresh whites have fruity characteristics reminiscent of the orchards they are displacing. Drive a few miles out of town to the **Cedar Creek Estate Winery** (5445 Lakeshore Road; 250-764 8866; cedarcreek.bc.ca), where you'll find vines producing pinot noir, pinot gris, chardonnay,

OPPOSITE Mission Hill, the valley's largest winery.

RIGHT Fruit for sale along Highway 97. Before wine took center stage in the Okanagan Valley, orchards were supreme.

gewürztraminer, ehrenfelser, riesling, and merlot grapes. The tasting room and a terrace restaurant occupy a Mediterranean-style building, and as a tourist experience, the winery has a polished, yet intimate air, with service that puts it on a par with most wineries of northern California.

3 *Where It Came From* 7 p.m.

Long before the current bloom of wineries, the Okanagan Valley was known for its produce, and in recent years small vegetable farmers have begun supplying discriminating buyers from lovingly tended plots. **RauDZ Regional Table** (1560 Water Street, Kelowna; 250-868-8805; raudz.com; $$$) takes advantage of this local bounty, as well as meats and fish raised or caught nearby, in cuisine featuring regional and seasonal ingredients. Its ever-changing menu lists the origin of the main ingredient in each dish — salmon from the Fraser River, ling cod from Queen Charlotte's Sound north of Vancouver Island, lamb tenderloins from Okanagan, wild boar from nearby Enderby.

SATURDAY

4 *Shoreline Drive* 9 a.m.

Start early to cross the bridge across Lake Okanagan in Kelowna and drive 40 miles south on its western shore to **Penticton**. You'll have lake and winery views and a good perspective on Okanagan Mountain, a giant rock rising dramatically out of the water. At Penticton, scones, pastries, eggs, and coffee await at the **Bench Artisan Food Market** (368 Vancouver Avenue, Penticton; 250-492-2222;

thebenchmarket.com; $$). You have come to the end of Lake Okanagan, but not the end of the valley, which stretches south along two smaller lakes. You have also reached the fertile Naramata Bench, just north of town on the lake's east side.

5 *Fruit Basket* 11 a.m.

As you drive north toward **Naramata**, the center of the Okanagan wine region, every visible square mile of land you see seems to be growing, blooming, bearing fruit. Tucked away among the wineries, at the ends of dirt roads, are small specialty producers: a blueberry farm here, a fruit orchard there. Taste the two themes combined at **Elephant Island Orchard Wines** (2730 Aikins Loop, Naramata; 250-496-5522; elephantislandwine.com), which specializes in fruit wines: cherry, crabapple, pear, raspberry. Some are for dessert, but others are dry dinner wines. Next make your way to **Lake Breeze Winery** (Sammet Road, Naramata; 250-496-5659; lakebreeze.ca) for a taste of icy whites. And in the town of Naramata, stop at the **Naramata General Store** (225 Robinson Avenue,

ABOVE The lights of Kelowna glow on Lake Okanagan.

BELOW The Naramata Heritage Inn.

OPPOSITE The Lake Okanagan view at Quails' Gate Estate Winery, which specializes in pinot noir and chardonnay.

Naramata; 250-496-5450) for a deli sandwich or an ice cream cone and a choice of many local wines for sale.

6 *The Pioneer* 1 p.m.

There is no road around the lake. That mountain —in Okanagan Mountain Provincial Park, and happy home for mountain goats—is in the way. So drive back to Penticton and then repeat your morning drive in the reverse direction. There are plenty of wineries along the way. You may want to visit one of the oldest in the valley, **Sumac Ridge Estate Winery** (17403 Highway 97 North, Summerland; 250-494-0451; sumacridge.com), which released its first vintage in 1980 and was the first to introduce blends with traditional Bordeaux varietals.

7 *The Biggest* 3 p.m

A few miles shy of the lake bridge, you'll come to the valley's largest winery, **Mission Hill Family Estates** (1730 Mission Hill Road, Kelowna; 800-957-9911; missionhillwinery.com), which has big buildings, a big and thriving business, and a breathtaking setting. This is a temple to wine, with manicured grounds, a concert amphitheater, a reception room with a Chagall tapestry, a terrace restaurant set high above the valley, and a state-of-the-art tasting room. Tours are offered at several different prices and levels of access.

8 *Vinotherapy* 5 p.m

Feeling a bit weary from all the driving and tasting? Revitalize at **Beyond Wrapture** (in the Coast Capri Hotel, 1171 Harvey Avenue Richter Street, Kelowna; 250-860-6060; kelownaspa.ca), a day spa next to a shopping center. Its vinotherapy massages take advantage of antioxidants found in local grapes, using seeds, skins, wine, and honey.

9 *Dine by the Lake* 7 p.m.

Cross the bridge again for the short drive to **Quails' Gate Estate Winery** (3303 Boucherie Road, Kelowna; 250-769-4451; quailsgate.com). It was a valley pioneer and specializes in chardonnays and

pinot noir. More to the point tonight, it is the home of the lakefront **Old Vines Restaurant** ($$$), where the menu offers multiple excellent choices. And of course, wines will be recommended to complement your roasted sirloin with saffron pearl couscous, black olive sauce, and pomegranate reduction, or Yukon Arctic char with vegetables and citrus-mustard cream.

SUNDAY

10 *Cycle B.C.* 9 a.m.

Breakfast on a spinach and cheddar omelet or a BC Benedict, with sockeye salmon, at the **Bohemian Cafe & Catering Company** (524 Bernard Avenue, Kelowna; 250-862-3517; bohemiancater.com/cafe;

$$). Then meet up with **Monashee Adventure Tours** (1591 Highland Drive North, Kelowna; 888-762-9253; monasheeadventuretours.com; reserve in advance) for a bicycle tour. Biking is big in the Okanagan; extensive trail networks crisscross the hills and mountains above the valley. A challenging 108-mile trail follows an abandoned section of the Kettle Valley Railway through terraced slopes (you can also hike the trail). Laid-back cruiser routes wind through provincial parks around the lakeshore. Choose your preference and pedal away.

THE BASICS

Fly into Kelowna International Airport or drive four hours from Vancouver.

A car is essential for your wine tour.

Hotel Eldorado
500 Cook Road, Kelowna
250-763-7500
hoteleldoradokelowna.com
$$
On the lake, with private boardwalk and marina.

Naramata Heritage Inn
3625 First Street, Naramata
866-617-1188
naramatainn.com
$$$
Polished wood floors, antique furnishings, and a spa.

Cove Lakeside Resort
4205 Gellatly Road, West Kelowna
877-762-2683
covelakeside.com
$$$$
On the lake's edge, with a pool and boat or kayak rentals.

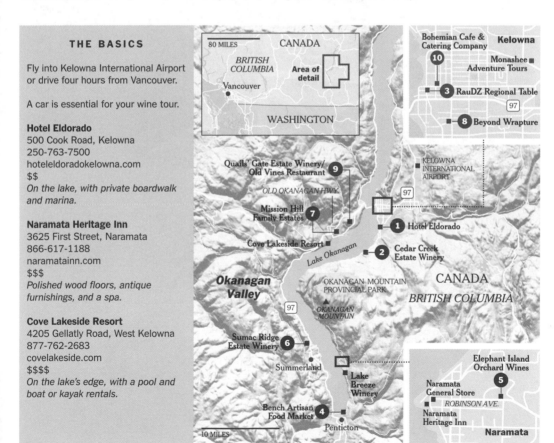

Juneau

Residents of Juneau, Alaska, brag that their town is the most beautiful state capital city in America, and they have a strong argument. Juneau is inside the Tongass National Forest, part of the world's largest temperate rain forest. Old-growth groves and glaciers lie within the municipal limits, snow-capped mountains loom overhead, and whales and other marine wildlife are a short boat ride away. The town itself is a working state capital with a utilitarian feel, but gold rush-era buildings, art galleries, quality regional theater, and fresh seafood make for pleasant companions to Juneau's stunning surroundings. — BY CORNELIA DEAN

FRIDAY

1 *Back to the Ice Age* 3 p.m.

Nature beckons. But some preparations are required. On your way into town, stop at **Western Auto-Marine** (5165 Glacier Highway; 907-780-4909; westernautojuneau.com) for a pair of brown rubber, calf-high Xtra Tuf Boots, a must-have item in any Alaskan's wardrobe. A good place to start your trek is the entrance to the **Switzer Creek and Richard Marriott Trails** (midway on Sunset Street). On the hillside, evergreens in even ranks give way to a hodge-podge of trees of different species, sizes, and shapes. This change marks the boundary between second-growth timber, on land logged decades ago, and an old-growth forest, untouched since the end of the last ice age. Hike up the trail — it's not too strenuous — and discover for yourself why environmentalists are so keen to save these ancient woods, home to an amazingly rich variety of plant and animal life. (Keep to the wooden planks at the base of the trail, and be glad you have your boots. The bog, or muskeg, is plenty wet.)

2 *Fish Don't Get Fresher* 6:30 p.m.

Locals say Juneau is not much of a restaurant town because so many people dine on fish they catch themselves. But when they want fish prepared for them, they head to the **Hangar on the Wharf Pub & Grill** (2

Marine Way; 907-586-5018; hangaronthewharf.com; $$-$$$). The building's exterior of plain blue clapboard isn't designed to impress, but the harborside location offers dazzling views of the Gastineau Channel and the mountains of Douglas Island west of downtown. There's halibut on the menu, of course, and salmon (guaranteed wild-caught) and king crab.

3 *Indoor Drama* 8 p.m.

Take in a play at the **Perseverance Theatre**, a nonprofit repertory company across the Gastineau Channel on Douglas Island (914 Third Street, Douglas; 907-364-2421; perseverancetheatre.org). A pillar of Juneau's cultural life for more than 30 years, it stages high-quality classic and contemporary plays, and the prices are low.

SATURDAY

4 *Seeing Sea Life* 9 a.m.

What better way to start your Saturday than with some close-up views of Juneau's wildlife? A number of companies offer whale-watching trips from Auke Bay, a short car (or bus) ride north of downtown. Find one offering a trip up the Lynn Canal to **Berners Bay**, and you are sure to see Steller sea lions basking on a rocky haul-out, harbor seals bobbing in the water, and harrier hawks, geese, and ducks. Also watch for eagles nesting along the shores. Most companies guarantee you will see whales; chances of spotting humpbacks are best in late spring when the herring-like fish called eulakon ("hooligan" in a local native language) are running.

OPPOSITE A navigational buoy near Juneau makes a convenient perch for Steller sea lions and a bald eagle.

RIGHT Cruise ships turn their sterns toward town at the end of daylong stops in Juneau's harbor.

5 *Up North, Down South* Noon

Back in town, enjoy a taste of old Juneau at the **Triangle Club** (251 Front Street; 907-586-3140; triangleclubbar.com; $). Order a hot dog and some Alaskan Amber — one of the local beers brewed and bottled right in town. If the Triangle looks a bit louche for your tastes, try **El Sombrero** around the corner (157 South Franklin Street; 907-586-6770; $$), a Juneau institution. The modest place has been dishing out generous helpings of Mexican standards since the oil boom began in the 1970s.

6 *They Came First* 1:30 p.m.

For some historical perspective, visit the **Alaska State Museum** (395 Whittier Street; 907-465-2901; museums.state.ak.us), which houses a collection covering the Athabascans, Aleuts, and other Alaska natives, the state's history as a Russian colony, and the 1880s gold rush that helped create Juneau. The museum's store stocks native crafts including baskets, prints, and dolls. Keep walking farther from the port and you'll come upon what is probably Juneau's least-known gem: the lichen-covered tombstones in **Evergreen Cemetery** (601 Seater Street; 907-364-2828). Joseph Juneau and Richard Harris, the prospectors who founded the city, are buried there, and the cemetery was also the site of the funeral pyre of Chief Cowee, the Auk who led them to Juneau's gold.

7 *Arts and Crafts* 3 p.m.

When cruise ships are in town, the locals say they stay out of "waddling distance" of the piers. And with good reason: most of the shops that line the streets of downtown are filled with mass-produced "native" items for the tourist trade. But not all. The **Juneau Artists Gallery** (175 South Franklin Street; 907-586-9891; juneauartistsgallery.net), a co-operative shop, sells jewelry, prints, pottery, drawings, and other work. Be sure to chat with the gallery staff — each is an artist and a member of the co-op. For apparel a little more exotic than the ubiquitous Alaska-themed sweatshirt, try **Shoefly & Hudsons** (109 Seward Street; 907-586-1055; shoeflyalaska.com), which offers unusual designs in footwear, handbags, and accessories. (People in Juneau say it was one of Sarah Palin's favorite shops when she was the governor.) But the city's most unusual retail outlet is **William Spear Design** (174 South Franklin Street; 907-586-2209; wmspear.com), a purveyor of tiny enamel pins, zipper pulls, and other items — many with edgy political messages.

8 *On the Page* 4:30 p.m.

If your shopping interests are geared more toward the written word, you are in luck: Juneau is friendly to independent bookstores. One in downtown is the **Observatory** (299 North Franklin Street; 907-586-9676; observatorybooks.com), perched up the hill from the harbor. From a tiny blue house not much younger than the town itself, the shop's proprietor, Dee Longenbaugh, offers an extensive stock of books on Alaska, particularly the southeast region. She prides herself on her collection of maps and charts as well as works on regional plants, animals, and geology.

9 *Alaskan Mediterranean* 7 p.m.

With its high ceiling and wood floors, **Zephyr** (200 Seward Street; 907-780-2221; $$$) is Juneau's most elegant restaurant. It serves fish, of course,

ABOVE AND BELOW Spectacular scenery courtesy of Juneau's in-town glacier, the Mendenhall Glacier. Downstream, Nugget Falls cascades from the glacial melt, while upstream the glacier itself holds onto its frozen grandeur.

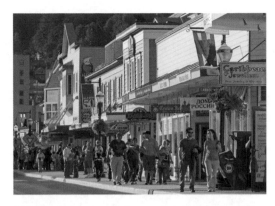

but Mediterranean style, for example the halibut provençale, with tomatoes and olives. Nonseafood options include the mushroom risotto. The crème brûlée and other desserts are rich, so save some appetite. After dinner, you can get back into the gold rush mood with a game of pool and an Alaskan pale ale in the bar of the **Alaskan Hotel** (167 South Franklin Street; 907-586-1000; thealaskanhotel.com).

SUNDAY

10 *Coffee and a View* 9 a.m.

Grab a coffee and a pastry at the downtown location of the **Heritage Coffee Company** chain (174 South Franklin Street; 907-586-1087; heritagecoffee.com) before donning your boots and heading out to Juneau's in-town glacier, the **Mendenhall Glacier**, off Glacier

Spur Road. Dress warmly—cool air flows constantly off the 12-mile stream of ice, and it is typically 5 or 10 degrees cooler there than in town. In part because of global warming, the glacier is retreating perhaps as much as 100 feet a year. Even from the visitor center (8510 Mendenhall Loop Road; 907-789-0097), you can see the kinds of rock and soil it deposited as it moved inland. But if you are feeling energetic, try the Moraine Trail for a first-hand look at what glaciers leave behind.

ABOVE Tourists cruise South Franklin Street.

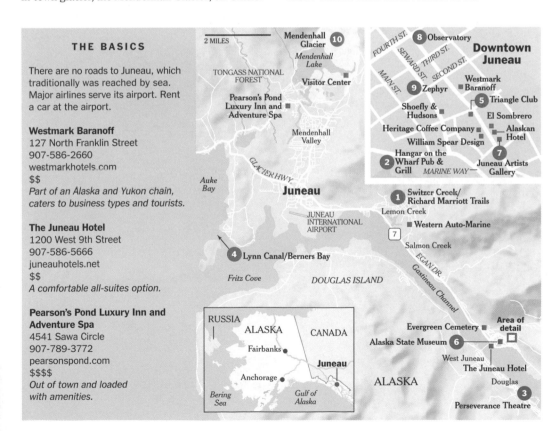

THE BASICS

There are no roads to Juneau, which traditionally was reached by sea. Major airlines serve its airport. Rent a car at the airport.

Westmark Baranoff
127 North Franklin Street
907-586-2660
westmarkhotels.com
$$
Part of an Alaska and Yukon chain, caters to business types and tourists.

The Juneau Hotel
1200 West 9th Street
907-586-5666
juneauhotels.net
$$
A comfortable all-suites option.

Pearson's Pond Luxury Inn and Adventure Spa
4541 Sawa Circle
907-789-3772
pearsonspond.com
$$$$
Out of town and loaded with amenities.

Homer

As you round the final bend on the Sterling Highway in Alaska and reach the town of Homer, the view of Kachemak Bay stops you dead. Across the water, jagged mountains cut by fjords lead right to the rocky coastline, and forests lead to alpine tundra, then glaciers that glint in the sunlight. On the Homer side of the bay, fields full of purple lupine, white yarrow, and goldenrod lead to beaches; snow-capped volcanoes across a nearby inlet come into view. Homer is called the End of the Road, the Halibut Fishing Capital of the World, or the Cosmic Hamlet by the Sea, depending on whom you happen to ask. Located on the Kenai Peninsula, a 220-mile drive south of Anchorage, Homer is a small town of homesteaders and artists, fishermen and ex-hippies, with a sprinkling of outlaws and seers. These categories frequently overlap, creating a funky, dynamic community that is a bit eccentric even by Alaskan standards. — BY MARIA FINN

FRIDAY

1 *Across the Water* 4:30 p.m.

The road on the Homer Spit, a four-mile-long sliver of land jutting into the bay, leads to the boat harbor and **Kachemak Bay Ferry** (907-399-2683; halibut-cove-alaska.com/ferry.htm). Catch the ferry, the *Danny J*, for a ride across Kachemak Bay to **Halibut Cove**, a small community that has no roads, only wooden boardwalks. The *Danny J* has a wildlife tour to Halibut Cove at noon and a 5 p.m. service that takes people there for the evening. Before dinner, stroll the boardwalks and drop in at the **Halibut Cove Experience Fine Art Gallery** (907-296-2215; halibutcoveexperience.com), which showcases the works of Halibut Cove artists. Many of them also fish commercially, a way of life reflected in the salmon mosaics and drawings and the occasional halibut or herring painting.

2 *Taste of the Bay* 6:30 p.m.

The **Saltry** restaurant in Halibut Cove (907-399-2683; halibut-cove-alaska.com; $$$) serves

locally caught seafood and vegetables grown in a patch out back. There is seating indoors or outside on a covered deck that overlooks the moored boats. The Saltry has a brief list of wines to go with its main event, the seafood. Try a huge appetizer platter of tart pickled salmon or mildly spiced halibut ceviche, and an entree of grilled pesto halibut or Korean barbecued salmon.

3 *Beer on the Spit* 9 p.m.

To while away a few hours in an atmosphere of conviviality (if not urbanity), drop in at the **Salty Dawg Saloon** (4380 Homer Spit Road; 907-235-6718; saltydawgsaloon.com), a dive bar and Alaska institution. It's the place where tourists and locals drink, sing, and get silly together.

SATURDAY

4 *Tempting Aromas* 8 a.m.

Anyone cutting back on carbs should avoid **Two Sisters Bakery** (233 East Bunnell Avenue; 907-235-2280; twosistersbakery.net) in Homer's Old Town near Bishop's Beach. But the salty ocean air carrying wafts of pecan sticky buns, savory Danishes, and fresh-brewed coffee makes this place hard to resist.

5 *Natural Alaska* 10 a.m.

Get into the forest on a guided hike at the **Wynn Nature Center** (East Skyline Road; 907-235-6667; akcoastalstudies.org/wynn-nature-center.html; $7), part of the nonprofit Center for Alaskan Coastal Studies, established in 1982. The bears and moose may be elusive, but the wildflowers and trees stay in place, ready for your guide's interpretation. (The coastal studies center also offers full-day, $120 nature tours from its Peterson Bay Field Station, leaving from Homer Harbor and including a forest hike, talks about indigenous people and fantastical rock formations, and a glimpse of the sea life exposed at low tide.)

6 *Lunch and a Book* Noon

You'll be back in town in time for lunch at the cozy **Mermaid Cafe** (3487 Main Street; 907-235-7649; mermaidcafe.net; $$), where specialties include quiche

and Thai chowder. After your meal, browse next door at the **Old Inlet Bookshop** (oldinletbookshop.com), located at the same address.

7 *Paddling Tour* 2 p.m.

From the Homer harbor, take a water taxi ride across the bay to **Yukon Island**, where you can launch a kayak into the smooth waters of Kachemak Bay. There, translucent jellyfish pulse below the sea's surface and bald eagles perch on rocky balustrades. On clear days the volcanoes Iliamna and Augustine can be seen. Alison O'Hara, owner of **True North Kayak Adventures** (5 Cannery Row Boardwalk, Homer Spit Road; 907-235-0708) and a longtime guide in Kachemak Bay, teaches how to approach the sea otters resting in kelp beds and identifies the seabirds. You may see porpoises, whales, and seals. The half-day tour is about $100. (There are also full-day and three-quarter-day options.)

8 *The Homestead* 8 p.m.

Locals describe the **Homestead Restaurant** (at the 8.2-mile marker on East End Road; 907-235-8723; homesteadrestaurant.net; $$$) as the best in the state. Menus change weekly, but expect a variety of local seafood: perfect oysters, clams, Alaska scallops, Alaskan king crab. Another specialty is halibut, Homer's favorite fish. Dishes are nicely presented, and the wine list is extensive.

SUNDAY

9 *Cosmic Cuisine* 7:30 a.m.

Brother Asaiah Bates, a follower of South Asian mysticism, arrived in Homer in 1955 from California. He and others with him vowed not to wear shoes or cut their hair until world peace had been achieved and world hunger eradicated. They were called Barefooters. Although the group broke up, Brother Asaiah stayed on, becoming a local sage. He dubbed Homer "the Cosmic Hamlet by the Sea," and although he died in 2000, a small cafe, the **Cosmic Kitchen** (510 Pioneer Avenue; 907-235-6355; cosmickitchenalaska.com; $), shows that his legacy lives on in many forms, even in the breakfast burrito. A homemade salsa bar offers condiments

ABOVE The beach at Kachemak Bay. In the bay, translucent jellyfish pulse below the sea's surface. On rocky overlooks, bald eagles find perches.

LEFT A fresh catch of halibut is prepared for market on a dock along the Homer Spit.

OPPOSITE Catch the ferry to Halibut Cove, a community that has boardwalks instead of roads but offers visitors a good restaurant and a gallery of works by local artists.

for the breakfasts of burritos with chorizo or huge plates of huevos rancheros accompanied by fresh hash browns.

10 *Head of the Bay* 8:30 a.m.

Just about the only way to get to the head of Kachemak Bay is on horseback, and it's worth it for the trip. **Trails End Horse Adventures** (53435 East End Road; 907-235-6393) takes visitors down a steep switchback that leads to the beach, and then past the Russian Orthodox village of Kachemak Selo. The tour continues on to the Fox River Flats. Turning toward the Homer Hills, the horses follow a narrow path flanked by elderberry bushes that open into a breathtaking site that was a Barefooters

homestead in the 1950s and is now abandoned. Bald eagle chicks peer down from cottonwood trees and clusters of wildflowers dot the open fields. It feels like timeless Alaska.

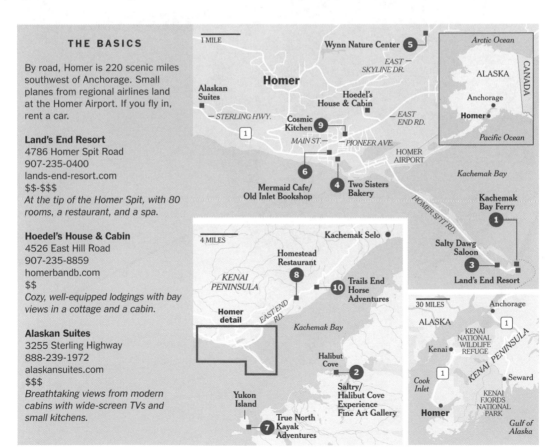

THE BASICS

By road, Homer is 220 scenic miles southwest of Anchorage. Small planes from regional airlines land at the Homer Airport. If you fly in, rent a car.

Land's End Resort
4786 Homer Spit Road
907-235-0400
lands-end-resort.com
$$-$$$
At the tip of the Homer Spit, with 80 rooms, a restaurant, and a spa.

Hoedel's House & Cabin
4526 East Hill Road
907-235-8859
homerbandb.com
$$
Cozy, well-equipped lodgings with bay views in a cottage and a cabin.

Alaskan Suites
3255 Sterling Highway
888-239-1972
alaskansuites.com
$$$
Breathtaking views from modern cabins with wide-screen TVs and small kitchens.

Whitehorse

In his poem "The Spell of the Yukon," Klondike bard Robert W. Service wrote of the beauty and serenity of the "great, big, broad land 'way up yonder." Spend a winter weekend in Whitehorse (population: 26,000), and you'll find that the spell is truly contagious. Whitehorse, the capital of Canada's Yukon Territory, got its name when gold rush stampeders found that rapids in the Yukon River reminded them of the flowing manes of stallions. Whitehorse is sub-Arctic, so winter is obviously cold, with temperatures often down around zero degrees Fahrenheit (pack very warm clothes). But dark it is not. You could enjoy more rays on an abbreviated February day than in an entire week down south in the Pacific Northwest. The clear nights are often highlighted by the symphony of color produced by the Northern Lights (don't visit during a full moon if you want the best chance of seeing them). The people? Friendly—and hardy indeed.

— BY BOB MACKIN

FRIDAY

1 *Fire on the Lake* 1 p.m.

Arrive in the Great White North and be whisked from your hotel (call ahead to arrange for an early check-in) to ice fishing at Fish Lake, just outside town, by **Up North Adventures** (103 Strickland Street; 867-667-7035; upnorthadventures.com; expect to pay about $150 to $200 in either U.S. or Canadian currency). Hop on a snowmobile and skim across the frozen waters of a lake you've surely seen on many a TV commercial, then onto shore and up a trail to a log cabin built for *The Last Trapper*, a 2004 French film, for a quick hot drink. From there, return to the lake and drill a hole with an auger. Drop your line and hope to hook arctic grayling or lake trout. Your guide will build a fire on the ice to keep everyone warm and serve as a makeshift cookout for your catch. Worry not: with the chilly temps and thick ice, the flames will do little damage.

2 *Mediterranean Thaw* 7 p.m.

Should the big one get away at Fish Lake, take your hunger to **Giorgio's Cuccina** (206 Jarvis Street;

OPPOSITE Drop a line through the ice at Fish Lake.

867-668-4050; giorgioscuccina.com; $$), a corner of the Mediterranean in the North. The Italian- and Greek-inflected menu includes seafood fettuccine, lamb souvlaki, and penne with asparagus. Most of the bottles on the wine list have made the long trip here from the Southern Hemisphere.

3 *The Lights Fantastic* 9:30 p.m.

Fill a flask with something hot and get out of town. A scant five minutes up the Alaska Highway, and you're beyond Whitehorse's lights. Bundle up, gaze heavenward, and if the conditions are right, you'll see the undulating ribbons of the Northern Lights, caused when clouds of ions from the sun strike the atmosphere. For about $125 to $150, you can pursue the lights more comfortably on a Northern Lights tour with **Aurora Borealis & Northern Lights Tours Yukon** (867-667-6054; auroraborealisyukon.com). Out in the blackness, you'll sit by a campfire and drink something warm as you watch the shimmering aurora.

SATURDAY

4 *Ride the Takhini Express* 9:30 a.m.

It would cost you plenty to shoot hoops with Michael Jordan or flip a puck to Wayne Gretzky at one of those celebrity sports camps, but it's relatively cheap to mush with a living legend of sled-dog racing, Frank Turner. From his **Muktuk Adventures** (15 miles north of Whitchorse off the Alaska Highway; 866-968-3647; muktuk.com), Mr. Turner runs a pooch-powered excursion along the frozen Takhini River. That six-mile route happens to make up part of the trail for the 1,000-mile-long premier dog-sled competition—the annual Yukon Quest International Sled Dog Race between Fairbanks, Alaska, and Whitehorse. Mr. Turner won it in record time in 1995 (10 days 16 hours 20 minutes). He'll outfit you in mushing gear and set you up with a sled and a quartet of eager dogs, then lead the way in another sled or on a snowmobile for the 90-minute-or-so jaunt.

5 *The Exotic North* Noon

The motto of the **Kebabery** (302 Wood Street; 867-393-2522; thekebabery.ca; $-$$) is "The Middle East Up North," and if the shish-kebabs, shawarma,

and falafel seem a little incongruous this close to the Arctic Circle, don't let that stop you from ordering a hearty lunch. The place feels more granola than exotic, although it has sometimes spiced things up at the dinner hour with belly dancers.

6 *Inspired by the Yukon* 1 p.m.

View the current exhibitions at **Yukon Arts Centre Public Gallery** (300 College Drive; 867-667-8575; yukonartscentre.com), which emphasizes the work of Yukon artists. Then check the schedule to see what's coming up in the arts centre's theater; performances there have ranged from Montreal ballet companies to Mongolian dancers and German experimental theater. Proceed next to **Mac's Fireweed Books** (203 Main Street; 867-668-2434; macsbooks.ca), a Yukon-centric bookstore with an extensive stock of classic and contemporary works by the North's men and women of letters. Look for Service's poetry; Jack London's novels and stories based on his time in the Yukon; and *Klondike*, an eye-opening and readable account of the Yukon Gold Rush by Whitehorse-born journalist and historian Pierre Berton.

7 *Yukon Gold* 3 p.m.

After gold was found in 1896 near Dawson City and the gold rush prospectors flooded in, order was maintained under the watchful eye of the North-West Mounted Police, that era's Mounties and the precursor of today's Royal Canadian Mounted Police. The **MacBride Museum of Yukon History** (1124 First Avenue; 867-667-2709; macbridemuseum.com) recounts that pivotal time in territory history. On the rounds are an N.W.M.P. station, Engine 51 from the White Pass & Yukon Route Railroad, and Sam

ABOVE Downtown Whitehorse. Check out the restaurants, the Public Gallery, and Mac's Fireweed Books.

RIGHT The Gold Rush exhibit at the MacBride Museum of Yukon History. After gold was found in 1896 near Dawson City, hopeful prospectors flooded into the Yukon.

McGee's original 1899 log cabin. Service invoked poetic license to use McGee's name in "The Cremation of Sam McGee."

8 *All Under One Roof* 4:30 p.m.

The **Canada Games Centre** (867-667-4386; canadagamescentre.whitehorse.ca) is the territory's largest building. It could comfortably accommodate all 30,000 Yukoners, but was built for 2007's Canada Winter Games. The center includes Olympic- and N.H.L.-size hockey rinks, indoor soccer fields, a swimming pool, a waterpark, and an elevated running track. It's all open for use by the public. The drop-in schedule varies, so call ahead.

9 *Turn by the Mountie* 6 p.m.

A cold local brew and a hot Northern meal await you in the **Deck**, the heated, enclosed bar and restaurant that adjoins the popular summertime outdoor deck at the **High Country Inn** (4051 Fourth Avenue; 867-667-4471; highcountryinn.yk.ca; $$). You'll know you're at the right place when you see the 40-foot wooden Mountie statue. Have a draft Chilkoot Lager and enjoy the Alaska halibut or arctic char.

10 *Chilled Coiffure* 7:30 p.m.

Drive out to **Takhini Hot Springs** (867-633-2706; takhinihotsprings.yk.ca), 18 miles north of Whitehorse at the end of Hot Springs Road. The experience of soaking in a naturally hot outdoor mineral pool in the midst of a snowy landscape is both exhilarating

and surreal. (The management has been known to sponsor wet hair contests. To compete, you dip your head into hot water and then emerge to let your hair freeze; the winner has the most eye-catching results.) If you missed the Northern Lights last night, you might catch them tonight while floating in the soothing pool.

SUNDAY

11 *Stop by the Woods* 9 a.m.

Have coffee and a scone or a breakfast panini at **Baked Cafe and Bakery** (108-100 Main Street; 867-633-6291; bakedcafe.ca; $) and assess your remaining time and energy level. If you're game for

one more wintry activity, drive or take the bus five minutes from downtown to **Whitehorse Cross Country Ski Club** (200-1 Sumanik Drive; 867-668-4477; xcskiwhitehorse.ca), which has more than 45 miles of wide groomed trails. Rent some skis and glide out into the quiet of the snow-covered woods.

ABOVE Dogsledding with a team from Muktuk Adventures. The frozen Takhini River makes a good roadway.

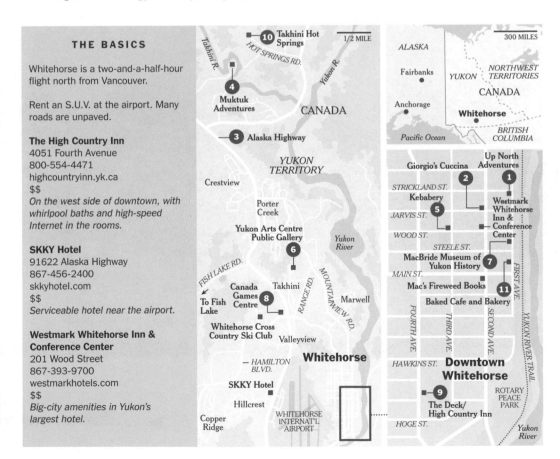

THE BASICS

Whitehorse is a two-and-a-half-hour flight north from Vancouver.

Rent an S.U.V. at the airport. Many roads are unpaved.

The High Country Inn
4051 Fourth Avenue
800-554-4471
highcountryinn.yk.ca
$$
On the west side of downtown, with whirlpool baths and high-speed Internet in the rooms.

SKKY Hotel
91622 Alaska Highway
867-456-2400
skkyhotel.com
$$
Serviceable hotel near the airport.

Westmark Whitehorse Inn & Conference Center
201 Wood Street
867-393-9700
westmarkhotels.com
$$
Big-city amenities in Yukon's largest hotel.

Honolulu

It's a cosmic irony that the longest, most grueling nonstop in the United States ends in the sweetest arrival of all. Jet-lagged, rumpled mainland travelers land in Honolulu having flown 2,500 miles from California—5,000 miles if from the East Coast. But they will have flown past Diamond Head and over the surfers and paddlers of Waikiki Beach, and their first inhalations of Hawaiian air are likely to be scented with tuberose and plumeria. Add to these timeless enchantments the ethnic restaurants and fine art galleries and hula dancers at sunset, and you have a city in full bloom. So what if you miss the mangos of summer? There are whales and surf meets in the winter, gardenias in the spring, and cultural festivals and farmers' markets year-round.
— BY JOCELYN FUJII

FRIDAY

1 *Hula and a Mai Tai* 6 p.m.

There is no better cure for jet lag than **Halekulani's House Without a Key** (2199 Kalia Road; 808-923-2311; halekulani.com), where a dancer of traditional hula (perhaps the elegant Kanoe Miller) performs at sunset, on the oceanfront and with a view of Diamond Head. Under a 125-year-old kiawe tree, as superb mai tais stream from the bar, she undulates as if dancing for the first time, and just for you.

2 *An Iron Chef Dinner* 8 p.m.

Yes, there is an act to follow. It's **Morimoto Waikiki** (1775 Ala Moana Boulevard; 808-943-5900; morimotowaikiki.com; $$$$), an indoor-outdoor aesthetic fantasy of soft greens accented with large sculptures of farmed coral and aquarium-tables of suspended moss. It's as imaginative as it is pricey, living up to the Iron Chef's reputation as a culinary wizard. Nearly drafted in Japan as a baseball catcher, Masaharu Morimoto is now in the culinary big leagues, expanding his empire with dishes like the lightly spiced organic Angry Chicken, a lunch and dinner staple, and the Wagyu beef in several

iterations (including golf-ball sized mini-burgers at lunch). Other winners: the signature sushi and raw dishes, including lamb carpaccio and several types of seafood tartare, and the always appealing chirashi, sashimi served over sushi rice. Tofu cheesecake is lighter and more delectable than it sounds.

SATURDAY

3 *From the Good Earth* 8 a.m.

Arrive early at the **Saturday Farmers' Market** at **Kapiolani Community College** (4303 Diamond Head Road; 808-848-2074; kapiolani.hawaii.edu/object/farmersmarket.html), and take your pick of lush orchids from the Big Island, fresh corn from Waimanalo, persimmons from Kula (in season), or beans and brews from coffee farms throughout Hawaii. You can have an open-air breakfast (beignets, oat cakes, omelets) and sample local agricultural products—all on the slopes of Diamond Head.

4 *The Heiress's Treasures* 11 a.m.

To glimpse the private passions of the late reclusive billionaire Doris Duke, take a peek at **Shangri La** (shangrilahawaii.org), her oceanfront estate on the other side of Diamond Head. Two-hour tours of the Islamic museum there begin and end at the **Honolulu Academy of Arts** (900 South Beretania Street; 808-532-8701; reservations required). A 15-minute shuttle ride takes you to the site, where a Mughal garden quiets the mind and 13th-century Persian tiles line the walls of the central courtyard. The 8th- to 20th-century artifacts are integrated into

OPPOSITE A paddleboarder near Diamond Head.

RIGHT Waikiki Beach, flanked by hotels and curving toward Diamond Head.

the architecture, so you can stand at a 13th-century prayer niche, called a mihrab, and then sit in the gleaming Turkish Room, where Duke, a tobacco heiress, entertained guests after dinner.

5 *Fresh Fish Daily* 1:30 p.m.

Nico's (Pier 38, 1133 North Nimitz Highway; 808-540-1377; nicospier38.com; $), at the Honolulu waterfront, is just the place for a post-museum lunch: fresh fish plucked from an auction a few feet away and served on foam plastic plates under a cheerful awning a few feet away from the boats, with live blues or Hawaiian music. There are fresh fish specials at plate-lunch prices, and a pleasing open-air atmosphere. Order a grilled ahi sandwich, fish and chips, or even beef stew while yachts and fishing boats bob nearby. At the fish auction, chefs from Honolulu's upscale restaurants stock up on the day's catch, then often head to Nico's for breakfast or lunch.

6 *Art of the Garden* 3 p.m.

The Contemporary Museum, Honolulu (2411 Makiki Heights Drive; 808-526-1322; tcmhi.org) swaddled in green and with a panoramic view, features a setting and architecture that are as much a draw as its art collection—some of which is displayed outdoors. The gardens, built by a Japanese garden master, the Rev. K. H. Inagaki, in the 1920s, encourage contemplative strolls around a gracious estate built in 1925 by Alice Cooke Spalding, founder of the Honolulu Academy of Arts. The green serenity complements George Rickey's kinetic sculptures and Deborah Butterfield's larger-than-life signature horse.

7 *Stroll and Sniff* 5 p.m.

Follow the scent of jasmine, plumeria, and tuberose to the lei stands that line Maunakea Street, where vendors sell fragrant garlands among the ethnic restaurants, Chinese herb shops, Asian grocery stores, and Vietnamese pho houses. A burgeoning arts scene has peppered the area with galleries like ARTS at Marks Garage (1159 Nuuanu Avenue; 808-521-2903; hawaiiartsalliance.org/index.php/marks), the Louis Pohl Gallery (1111 Nuuanu Avenue; 808-521-1812; louispohlgallery.com), and the Pegge Hopper Gallery (1164 Nuuanu Avenue; 808-524-1160; peggehopper.com). All over the neighborhood, ethnic shops and small plazas brim with local products and contemporary local artists display their stone and native-wood sculptures, mixed-media collages, and abstract paintings.

8 *Seafood Hong Kong Style* 7 p.m.

At the busy Little Village Noodle House (1113 Smith Street; 808-545-3008; littlevillagehawaii.com; $), the sizzling scallops have a kick and the tofu pot stickers have a following. Vegetarian choices abound, and even traditional Chinese offerings like broccoli beef and noodles, kung pao chicken, and walnut shrimp are tastier—and healthier—than the norm.

9 *Jazz with a Dragon* 9 p.m.

The Dragon Upstairs (1038 Nuuanu Avenue; 808-526-1411; thedragonupstairs.com), an intimate jazz club, is a Chinatown hotspot in a former tattoo parlor lined with red walls, dragon masks, and glass-shard sculptures by Roy Venters, the Andy Warhol of Honolulu. Affixed to the wall is a large glittery dragon, a former stage prop for opera. While the mood is friendly and upbeat, it's the music that soars:

ABOVE Hike up Diamond Head for 360-degree views.

BELOW The lights of downtown Honolulu, a metropolitan enclave in an island paradise.

some of the best jazz in town can be heard here, and because many in the audience are musicians, you can count on hearty improv and guest artists.

SUNDAY

10 *Under the Sea* 10 a.m.

Snorkeling cures all ills, particularly early in the morning before the crowds arrive, when the water is glassy at tiny **Sans Souci Beach** in front of the **New Otani Kaimana Beach Hotel** (2863 Kalakaua Avenue). To the right and left of the sandy area, butterfly fish, Picasso fish (humuhumunukunukuapuaa), and yellow tangs flit and flash among the reefs, making for surprisingly good snorkeling at the Diamond

Head end of Waikiki. Across the street, Kapiolani Park is a recreational hub, with many of its joggers, tennis players, and yoga practitioners adding a swim and snorkeling session to their regimen.

11 *Windward Walk* Noon

No trip to Honolulu is complete without a drive to the easternmost point, **Makapuu**, about 30 minutes from Waikiki. Once past the suburban towns, the Ka Iwi coastline is a marvel of steep cliffs, tidal-pool-dotted shoreline, and the treacherous bodysurfing magnet **Sandy Beach**. A new scenic lookout at Makapuu has parking and improved access to a trail that leads to the Makapuu Lighthouse and its sprawling—and breathtaking—views of the windward coast.

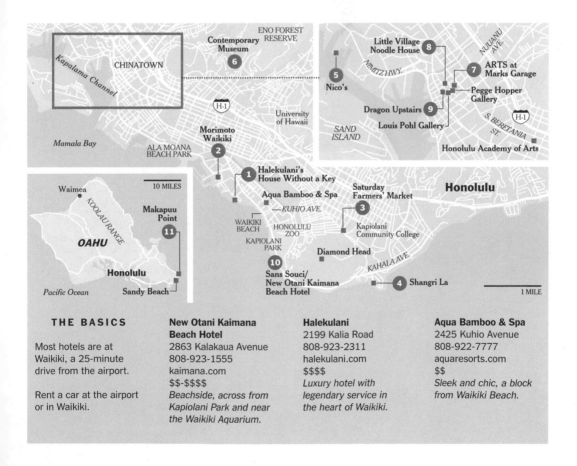

THE BASICS

Most hotels are at Waikiki, a 25-minute drive from the airport.

Rent a car at the airport or in Waikiki.

New Otani Kaimana Beach Hotel
2863 Kalakaua Avenue
808-923-1555
kaimana.com
$$-$$$$
Beachside, across from Kapiolani Park and near the Waikiki Aquarium.

Halekulani
2199 Kalia Road
808-923-2311
halekulani.com
$$$$
Luxury hotel with legendary service in the heart of Waikiki.

Aqua Bamboo & Spa
2425 Kuhio Avenue
808-922-7777
aquaresorts.com
$$
Sleek and chic, a block from Waikiki Beach.

Molokai

You've got to really want to go to Molokai, a steppingstone Hawaiian island between Oahu and Maui. Its stunning beaches and rugged jungle interior invite exploration, and the tragic tale of its leper colony, where native Hawaiians used to be summarily exiled, inspire an unavoidable curiosity. But hotel rooms are few, tourist amenities scarce, and developers actively discouraged. Yet for those who remember an older Hawaii — magical, sensuous, isolated — or for those who want to find some sense of how things were on Maui, the Big Island, and Kauai before they were drawn into the hustle and flow of Oahu, Molokai is more than worth the trouble. Its lifestyle is more traditionally Polynesian, its people reserved, but when their veneer is cracked, warm and full of an ancient joie de vivre. — BY CHARLES E. ROESSLER

FRIDAY

1 The Moccasin 1 p.m.

Pick up your rental car in the lava-rock terminal of tiny **Hoolehua Airport**, in the center of Molokai, and drive west on Highway 460 to **Maunaloa**, an old cattle ranching settlement. You won't encounter much traffic on these 10 miles of road, or anywhere on Molokai, which has 7,400 residents. The island is shaped roughly like a moccasin, 10 miles wide and 38 miles long from east to west. While eastern Molokai has a wet climate and junglelike foliage, the west end is arid with scrub vegetation. But it is rich in Hawaii's mythical history. Puu Nana, east of Maunaloa, is revered as the birthplace of the hula, which its practitioners consider to be a sacred dance, and every May dancers arrive to celebrate it. Molokai is also famous for its kahuna, powerful priests who could either provide life-giving herbal remedies or pray a healthy person to death.

2 Clear Waters 3 p.m.

Go for a swim at tiny **Dixie Maru Beach** at the lower end of a string of idyllic beaches that line the west coast. Ignore the temptation to swim at

OPPOSITE AND RIGHT Kaluapapa National Historic Park, the former leper colony that forms the core of Molokai's story of beauty and tragedy. A limited number of visitors are allowed; they arrive by mule ride or on foot.

Papohaku, two gorgeous miles of 100-yard-wide sandy beach; it harbors danger from sharp hidden coral reefs and swift, treacherous rip currents. Dixie Maru, not much more than a protected cove, is enticing in its own way: clear, deep-blue water with a calming undulation. If you take a careful walk over the lava rocks framing the left side of the bay, you may get lucky and spot a honu (a sea turtle) bobbing and weaving along the shoreline. This area was once dominated by a resort called Molokai Ranch, but it closed in 2008 after Molokai residents rejected a plan for its expansion.

3 Try the Opakapaka 6 p.m.

A bare-bones place reminiscent of a '50s diner, with old Coca-Cola decals on the wall, the **Kualapuu Cookhouse** (102 Farrington Avenue, Highway 470; 808-567-9655; $$-$$$) is a Molokai institution, serving fresh fish, beef, pork, and chicken dishes. Mahi-mahi and opakapaka (pink snapper) are local catches, subject to availability. The restaurant does not sell alcohol, but you can bring your own wine. Eat outdoors — you might share a picnic table with other customers who can tell you about life on the island. There may be live music — perhaps a ukelele and a one-string, gut-bucket bass — but be warned: the restaurant closes early.

SATURDAY

4 Island Market 10 a.m.

Saturday morning offers an opportunity to mix with the locals at the **Molokai Farmers Market**

(Alamalama Street) in what passes for a downtown in tiny Kaunakakai, the island's largest town. On a short street lined with stands, browse for papaya and poi, T-shirts, animal carvings, and shell jewelry in a convivial, relaxed atmosphere. Molokai never surrendered to tourist-first faux aloha spirit: the people here are genuine. They call Molokai the Friendly Island, but it can turn into the surly island to the outsider who ignores local protocol. The outdoor market is an opportunity to take in the local color and meet the locals on neutral ground.

5 *Fishponds and Spears* Noon

Have lunch at **Molokai Pizza** (15 Kaunakakai Place, just off Highway 460, Kaunakakai; 808-553-3288), which boasts the best pan pizza on the island, along with deli sandwiches on its own bread. Then set out to explore the south shore, driving east from Kaunakakai on Route 450, the East Kamehameha V Highway. In the first 20 miles you'll see 19th-century churches and some of the 60 ancient fishponds that dominate the southern coast. The Hawaiians who built

them seven or eight centuries ago used lava rocks to surround and trap fish attracted to underground streams. At Mile Marker 20, stop at **Murphey's Beach**, a popular snorkeling spot. Watch locals spearfishing for dinner while children frolic on the sand, shouting and laughing.

6 *Old Ways* 2 p.m.

The last seven miles of the trip to the east end rival Maui's famous Road to Hana in adventure and beauty. The pulse quickens as you drive inches away from the ocean on the one-lane road. Inland views are a window onto a traditional Hawaii. Foliage is dense, and families have their horses and goats tied close to the road. On many of their one-acre plots, gardens and fruit trees vie for space with chickens, dogs, rusted car skeletons, and modest homes. Fishing nets and hunting accouterments, including dog kennels, attest to the survival of old ways of finding food; wild pigs, goats, and deer are the hunters' prey.

7 *The Far East* 3 p.m.

The road ends at **Halawa Park** in the spectacular Halawa Valley, surrounded by mountains and ocean. The isolated beaches in the bay are good for a dip in summer and great for big-wave surfing in winter. In the verdant valley, an ancient complex of terraces and taro patches, built by the Polynesians who first settled this island, helped sustain life on Molokai

ABOVE The verdant, isolated Halawa Valley.

OPPOSITE ABOVE An ancient Molokai fishpond.

OPPOSITE BELOW A fisherman casts his net on a school of fish in Honouli Wai Bay.

from about 650 A.D. to the mid-20th century, when other job opportunities lured residents away. What remained of the taro was destroyed by a tsunami in 1946 and floods in the 1960s. You can learn about attempts to restore it — and can hike to lovely Moalua Falls — if you have some extra time and arrange a private tour (book at Hotel Molokai in Kaunakakai; about $80). On your drive back, go a half-mile or so past Kaunakakai to **Kaiowea Park** to see the **Kapuaiwa Coconut Grove**, a cluster of tall coconut palms that remain from 1,000 of their kind planted here in the 1860s by King Kamehameha V.

8 *Night Life* 7 p.m.

Find Molokai's weekend social scene at the casual **Hula Shores** restaurant in the Hotel Molokai (1300 Kamehameha V Highway, Kaunakakai; 800-535-0085; hotelmolokai.com; $$). Try a local dish like kalua pork and cabbage or hibachi chicken

and listen to live music, likely to feature ukeleles. The adjoining tiki bar, only yards away from the tranquil Pacific, conveys a feeling of timelessness as you sway in a hammock, one of three catching the slight breeze. If you're still out and about at 10, join the line at **Kanemitsu Bakery** (79 Ala Malama Avenue; 808-553-5855) waiting for hot French bread. It's what's happening Saturday night in Kaunakakai.

SUNDAY

9 *The Colony* 10 a.m.

Drive up Highway 470 to the north shore. Much of it is impenetrable, with soaring cliffs pitched

straight down 2,000 feet. In the center is **Kalaupapa National Historic Park** (nps.gov/kala), a small peninsula where native Hawaiian victims of leprosy were dropped off by ship and isolated. It was also the home of Father Damien, now St. Damien of Molokai, the 19th-century priest and Hawaiian folk hero who worked with the lepers until he contracted their disease and died. The unique community that developed there has a small-town New England feel, with tidy churches and modest homes belying past horrors. It is open to small numbers of visitors by permit; they can hike a cliff trail down or go with **Molokai Mule Ride** (800-567-7550; muleride.com; about $200) Monday through Saturday. Get a good

view from the **Kalaupapa Overlook**, 1,700 feet above the peninsula in **Palaau State Park**. If you know the story, the sight of the village below sets the mind racing with searing images of lepers being tossed overboard offshore and ordered to sink or swim to the peninsula—never to leave again.

ABOVE Ignore the temptation to swim at Papohaku, two gorgeous miles of 100-yard-wide sandy beach. It harbors danger from sharp hidden coral reefs and rip currents.

OPPOSITE The grave of Father Damien, now St. Damien of Molokai, at Kalaupapa National Historic Park. He devoted his life to the people exiled to a leper colony there.

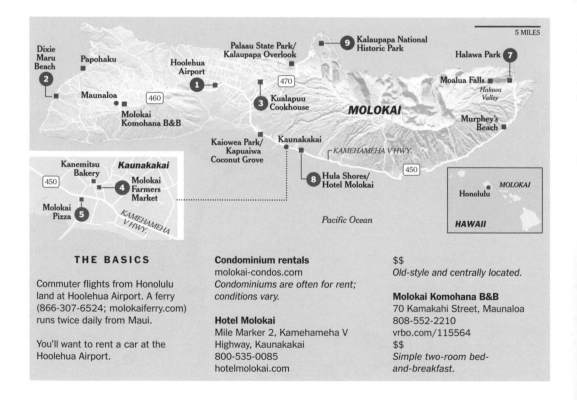

THE BASICS

Commuter flights from Honolulu land at Hoolehua Airport. A ferry (866-307-6524; molokaiferry.com) runs twice daily from Maui.

You'll want to rent a car at the Hoolehua Airport.

Condominium rentals
molokai-condos.com
Condominiums are often for rent; conditions vary.

Hotel Molokai
Mile Marker 2, Kamehameha V Highway, Kaunakakai
800-535-0085
hotelmolokai.com

$$
Old-style and centrally located.

Molokai Komohana B&B
70 Kamakahi Street, Maunaloa
808-552-2210
vrbo.com/115564
$$
Simple two-room bed-and-breakfast.

Maui

"I went to Maui to stay a week and remained five,"
wrote Mark Twain in 1866. Whether lazing on a warm
sugary beach, gazing awestruck at a Haleakala sunrise,
or snorkeling to the song of humpback whales, visitors
to Maui today would likely feel the same. And while it
is known for its sparkling coastline and fertile green
interior, Hawaii's second-largest island appeals equally
to the urbane. Resorts hugging the south and west
shores claim some of the state's finest restaurants,
shops, and spas. A thriving arts community keeps
culture and creativity in high gear. In upcountry
Maui, on the slopes of the 10,000-foot Haleakala, you
can sample just-picked fruit or walk among fields of
lavender. Mark Twain had it right: it's not an easy
island to leave. — BY JOCELYN FUJII

FRIDAY

1 *Beauty and the Beach* 2:30 p.m.
Tucked between the condo-studded town of Kihei
and the upscale resort of Wailea, the white-sand beach
of **Keawakapu** is south Maui's hidden jewel. Lined with
lavish Balinese- and plantation-style homes, this half-
mile playground has gentle waves, talcum-soft sands,
and free public parking along South Kihei Road. If it's
winter when you take a dip there, listen for the groans
and squeaks of the humpback whale, a haunting,
mystifying song.

2 *Drive-by Birding* 4 p.m.
For a glimpse of Maui's remarkable biodiversity,
take a stroll on the boardwalk at the **Kealia Pond
National Wildlife Refuge** (Milepost 6, Mokulele
Highway 311; 808-875-1582; fws.gov/kealiapond),
a 700-acre natural wetland and seabird sanctuary.
Among the birds that shelter here are endangered
Hawaiian stilts, black-crowned night herons, and
Hawaiian coots, as well as migrating birds like
ruddy turnstones.

3 *Fairway Pizza* 6 p.m.
There is no shortage of expensive restaurants
in Wailea packed with well-heeled tourists, which
makes **Matteo's Pizzeria** (100 Ike Drive, Wailea;
808-874-1234; matteospizzeria.com; $) all the more
inviting. An affordable joint that is wildly popular
with the locals, this casual restaurant is run by an

Italian couple who serve fresh thin-crust margherita
pizza, zesty penne in vodka sauce, and meaty lasagna.
After ordering at the counter, grab one of the tables
that overlook a golf course.

4 *Fine Arts* 7 p.m.
The stellar collection of contemporary art
(including Jun Kaneko, Toshiko Takaezu, and a bevy
of island superstars) at **Four Seasons Resort Maui**
at Wailea (3900 Wailea Alanui Drive; 808-874-8000;
fourseasons.com/maui) is reason enough to go there.
Add designer cocktails, live Hawaiian music, hula, and
jazz in the open-air Lobby Lounge, and it becomes a
seduction. Take the self-guided audio tour through half
of the 68-piece art collection, then settle in for martinis
and musical magic at the bar by the grand piano.
Live nightly entertainment covers a gamut of musical
tastes. (If you want a romantic view, time your visit to
catch the setting sun.)

SATURDAY

5 *Upcountry Adventures* 9 a.m.
Jump start your morning at **Grandma's Coffee
House** in the village of Keokea (9232 Highway 37, or
Kula Highway; 808-878-2140; grandmascoffee.com),
on the slopes of Haleakala volcano. On a wooden deck

OPPOSITE A windy beach on Maui, an island known for its
sparkling coastline and fertile green interior.

BELOW Kula Farm Stand sells just-picked fruit, like pineapple
and guavas, along with homemade mango bread.

with million-dollar views, you can sip Grandma's Original Organic, an espresso roasted blend from the family's fifth-generation coffee farm. Then move on to the **Kula Country Farm Stand** (Highway 37, or Kula Highway, across from Rice Park; 808-878-8381), a green-and-white produce stand selling just-picked fruit. Here's a chance to pick up fresh mangos (in season), rare pineapple guavas, and homemade mango bread before heading to lavender fields a few twists and turns away. With its view, acres of lavender, and fragrant jellies, scones, potions, and creams, **Ali'i Kula Lavender Farm** (1100 Waipoli Road; 808-878-3004; aklmaui.com), is a multisensory delight.

6 *Hot Art* Noon

Art is hot in **Makawao**, the cowboy town turned art colony that is about 1,600 feet above sea level on the slopes of Haleakala. Here you will find old wooden storefronts, mom-and-pop restaurants, chic boutiques, and hippie herb shops. At **Hot Island Glass** (3620 Baldwin Avenue; 808-572-4527; hotislandglass.com), the furnace burns hot and glass-blowing is performance art as molten glass evolves into jellyfish, bowls, and oceanic shapes. Next door, Maui artists display their work in the airy plantation-style space of **Viewpoints Gallery** (3620 Baldwin Avenue; 808-572-5979; viewpointsgallerymaui.com).

7 *Put the Top Down* 3 p.m.

The hourlong drive from Maui's hilly upcountry to Lahaina, a popular resort town on the island's west coast, provides nonstop entertainment. With the shimmering Pacific on your left and the chiseled valleys of the West Maui Mountains to the right, you will be hard-pressed to keep your eyes on the road. Once you reach **Black Rock**, a lava outcropping north of Lahaina in the resort named Kaanapali, you'll find equally compelling underwater sights.

RIGHT Jumping off the cliffs of Black Rock, a lava outcropping just north of Lahaina.

Grab a snorkel and explore this Atlantis-like world of iridescent fish, spotted eagle rays, and giant green sea turtles.

8 *Farm to Fork* 7:30 p.m.

Peter Merriman of **Merriman's Kapalua** (One Bay Club Place; 808-669-6400; merrimanshawaii.com; $$$) is a pioneer in Hawaii regional cuisine, a culinary movement blending international flavors with local ingredients. The oceanfront restaurant features jaw-dropping views of Molokai island, and the menu highlights local ingredients, whether chèvre from upcountry goats, Maui lehua taro cakes, or line-caught fish from nearby waters. Look for kalua pig ravioli or wok-charred ahi so fresh that it tastes as if it were cooked on the beach. With the opening of his newer Monkeypod Kitchen in Wailea, featuring handcrafted beers and food (housemade hamburger buns, made-from-scratch pies and juices), Merriman has both coastlines covered.

9 *Tiki Torches* 9:30 p.m.

The old Hawaii—tikis and plumeria trees around buildings without marble and bronze—is elusive in today's Hawaii, but you'll find it at **Kaanapali Beach Hotel**'s oceanfront **Tiki Courtyard**, where the **Tiki Bar** (2525 Kaanapali Parkway; 808-667-0111; kbhmaui.com) offers authentic Hawaiian entertainment nightly. Hula by Maui children, lilting Hawaiian music by local entertainers, and the outdoor setting under the stars are a winning combination, especially when warmed by genuine aloha.

SUNDAY

10 *Make It to Mala* 9 a.m.

Brunch at **Mala Ocean Tavern** (1307 Front Street, Lahaina; 808-667-9394; malaoceantavern.com; $$) is like being on the ocean without leaving land. At this casual restaurant, you're practically sitting on the water, enjoying huevos rancheros with black beans or lamb sausage Benedict while dolphins frolic in the ocean and turtles nibble at the shore. Ask for a table outdoors.

11 *Fly Like an Eagle* Noon

For an adrenaline finish, head to the heights of West Maui, where **Kapalua Adventures** (2000 Village Road; 808-665-3753; kapaluaadventures.com) offers an unusually long zip-line course. Beginners need

not fear, as the two-and-a-half-hour zip (about $150) requires virtually no athleticism. The four-hour trip (about $250) is not for the weak-kneed. The zip line takes you over bamboo forests, gulches, and ridges, with the luscious coastline in the distance.

OPPOSITE ABOVE Find a touch of the old Hawaii — tikis and plumeria trees under the stars — at Kaanapali Beach Hotel's tiki bar. The lilting Hawaiian music is genuine.

ABOVE At Black Rock, grab a snorkel. Below the surface are iridescent fish, spotted eagle rays, and giant turtles.

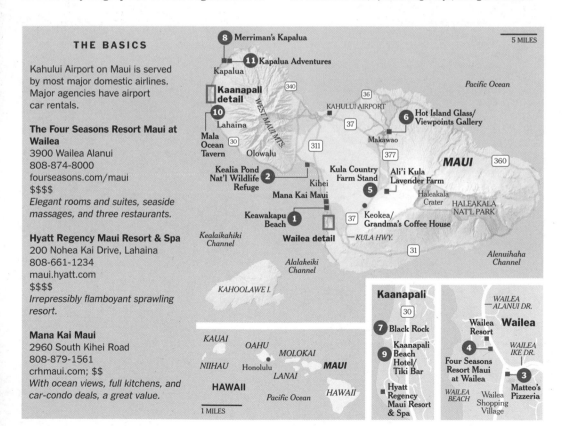

THE BASICS

Kahului Airport on Maui is served by most major domestic airlines. Major agencies have airport car rentals.

The Four Seasons Resort Maui at Wailea
3900 Wailea Alanui
808-874-8000
fourseasons.com/maui
$$$$
Elegant rooms and suites, seaside massages, and three restaurants.

Hyatt Regency Maui Resort & Spa
200 Nohea Kai Drive, Lahaina
808-661-1234
maui.hyatt.com
$$$$
Irrepressibly flamboyant sprawling resort.

Mana Kai Maui
2960 South Kihei Road
808-879-1561
crhmaui.com; $$
With ocean views, full kitchens, and car-condo deals, a great value.

8 Merriman's Kapalua

11 Kapalua Adventures

Kapalua

Kaanapali detail

340

WEST MAUI MTS.

KAHULUI AIRPORT

36

Pacific Ocean

5 MILES

10

Lahaina

Mala Ocean Tavern

30

Olowalu

311

37

Makawao

377

6 Hot Island Glass/ Viewpoints Gallery

MAUI

360

Kealia Pond Nat'l Wildlife Refuge

2

Kihei

Mana Kai Maui

Kula Country Farm Stand

Ali'i Kula Lavender Farm

5

Haleakala Crater

HALEAKALA NAT'L PARK

Keawakapu Beach **1**

Wailea detail

Kealaikahiki Channel

37

Keokea/ Grandma's Coffee House

KULA HWY.

31

Alenuihaha Channel

Alalakeiki Channel

KAHOOLAWE I.

Kaanapali

30

7 Black Rock

9 Kaanapali Beach Hotel/ Tiki Bar

■ Hyatt Regency Maui Resort & Spa

WAILEA ALANUI DR.

Wailea Resort

Wailea

4

Four Seasons Resort Maui at Wailea

WAILEA IKE DR.

3 Matteo's Pizzeria

WAILEA BEACH

Wailea Shopping Village

KAUAI

OAHU

NIIHAU

Honolulu

MOLOKAI

LANAI

MAUI

HAWAII

Pacific Ocean

HAWAII

1 MILES

Hilo

Of all the tropical postcard places in the Hawaiian Islands, Hilo, on the Big Island of Hawaii, may have the least to offer the traditional tourist. And that's exactly the reason to go. The center of power of Kamehameha the Great, the king who unified the islands in the early 19th century, Hilo combines history and raw natural power to offer a rich alternative to the resort scene. Orchids and anthuriums, fostered by the wet climate, grow amid some of the most magnificent geographic features on Earth, and the city exudes a genuine, small-town warmth and prototypical aloha spirit. No one works the tourist hustle, and the visitors don't come to vegetate. There's too much to see and do in a natural wonderland where some of the tallest mountains on Earth, as measured from sea bottom, dominate magnificent landscapes of beach and garden, rain forest and desert, with flowing lava adding more territory every day. — BY CHARLES E. ROESSLER

FRIDAY

1 *Down by the Banyans* 5 p.m.
    Cruise down **Banyan Drive**, through a cathedral of monstrous banyan trees labeled with the names of celebrities who planted them, including Babe Ruth and Amelia Earhart. Park near Queen Liliuokalani Gardens, a 30-acre formal Japanese garden with a teahouse and pond, and cross the footbridge to Coconut Island for a good late-afternoon photo op looking back at the city and bay, with Mauna Kea volcano in the background. Back on the bayfront, keep walking, passing young boys fishing with bamboo poles while elders work two or three large rods. It's O.K. to watch, but don't talk. These locals don't work for a tourist bureau; they come down here for peace and solitude—and maybe dinner. Out on the bay, you may see teams of paddlers in 45-foot outriggers. The King Kamehameha statue in **Wailoa River State Park** is similar to the famous one in Honolulu, minus the mob.

2 *Fish Worth Flying For* 8 p.m.
    Islanders sometimes fly in from Honolulu for the aholehole, or Hawaiian flagtail, a reef fish raised in ponds for the tables at the **Seaside Restaurant and Aqua Farm** (1790 Kalanianaole Avenue; 808-935-8825; seasiderestaurant.com; $$-$$$). Ask to be seated on the patio and watch the egrets roosting in a

small tree for the night. You can't go wrong with the catch of the day, which might be ahi, mahi-mahi, or opakapaka (blue snapper).

SATURDAY

3 *The Blissful Mist* 8 a.m.
    Get up early and take a five-minute ride up Waianuenue Avenue to **Rainbow Falls**, where early morning affords the best chance to catch an ethereal rainbow rising from the mist. Refreshed with negative ions, head back to town and park near the **Hilo Farmers Market** at the corner of Mamo Street and Kamehameha Avenue (hilofarmersmarket.com). You won't be early; vendors begin to arrive at 3 a.m. to set up stalls selling exotic produce like atemoya and jackfruit. Sample a suman, a Filipino sticky-rice sweet wrapped in a banana leaf and cooked in coconut milk.

4 *Another Side of Paradise* 9:30 a.m.
    Stroll Kamehameha Avenue, checking out **Sig Zane Designs** (122 Kamehameha Avenue; 808-935-7077;

OPPOSITE Hawaii Volcanoes National Park near Hilo on the island of Hawaii — the Big Island.

BELOW The statue of King Kamehameha I, the unifier of the Hawaiian islands, in Hilo. The city was the king's power base.

sigzane.com), with floral-themed contemporary Hawaiian fashions, and **Burgado's Fine Woods** (808-969-9663), with exquisite koa furniture, and the **Dreams of Paradise Gallery** (808-935-5670; dreamsofparadisegallery.com), both in the S. Hata Building (308 Kamehameha Avenue). Take a few steps to the **Pacific Tsunami Museum** (130 Kamehameha Avenue; 808-935-0926; tsunami.org), particularly poignant after the disastrous tsunami in Japan in 2011 and the Indian Ocean tragedy in 2004. The museum explains the physics of these "harbor waves" and documents tsunami devastation in Hilo in 1946 and 1960. A 25-minute video recounts the terror of the survivors, some of whom are docents at the museum.

5 *Munching the Mochi* Noon

Pick up an inexpensive two-course lunch to go, starting with a deliciously authentic bento at the **Puka Puka Kitchen** (270 Kamehameha Avenue; 808-933-2121). For dessert, walk to the **Two Ladies Kitchen** (274 Kilauea Avenue; 808-961-4766) and get the best mochi in the islands. You can see this glutinous rice sweet being made in the tiny shop as five workers scurry around with the hot mixture sticking to big ladles. All the flavors are ono (Hawaiian for delicious), but savor the strawberry, if it's available. Pack the food in the car and make the 45-minute drive southwest to **Hawaii Volcanoes National Park** (Highway 11; 808-985-6000; nps.gov/havo), where you can dine alfresco in the picnic area.

6 *Look Out for the Lava* 1 p.m.

Get information on current conditions from the visitor center at the park entrance. Though lava is likely to be flowing somewhere in the park, the 45-minute drive on Chain of Craters Road can end in frustration if Madame Pele, the temperamental Fire Goddess, isn't sending it that way. Another choice is

ABOVE Clouds of steam and gases surge into the night sky as lava from the Kilauea volcano pours into the ocean.

LEFT Shopping at Sig Zane Designs on Kamehameha Avenue for Zane's floral-themed Hawaiian clothing and textiles.

11-mile **Crater Rim Drive**, which circles the Kilauea Caldera. Stop at the park's **Thomas A. Jaggar Museum** for a refresher course in volcanology. You'll pass through desert flora, moonscapes, and rain forest and find incredible crater views. Take in the **Thurston Lava Tube**, formed as a lava flow left behind a hardened outer crust.

7 *Free-Range and Local* 7 p.m.

Find your way to the **Hilo Bay Cafe** (315 East Makaala Street; 808-935-4939; hilobaycafe.com; $$), a local favorite and locavore haven located incongruously in a strip mall — it grew out of a health food store there, the owners explain. Start with cocktails and dine on the likes of pan-seared

ABOVE A steaming volcanic cone near Hilo.

BELOW Hiking in the lava fields at the end of Chain of Craters Road in Volcanoes National Park.

scallops with crème fraîche, black truffle tomato relish, capellini in brown butter, and tobiko. Or perhaps the coconut-crusted tofu with sauteed vegetables, rice, and sweet chili sauce. The menu suggests wine pairings — or, in the case of the local free-range beef burger, a beer pairing: Guinness.

SUNDAY

8 *Back to the Garden* 9 a.m.

Drive north on Route 19 and turn onto the Scenic Route at Onomea Bay. Drive slowly past distortions of normal plants — huge Alexandra palms, king-size gingers, and hearty African tulip trees — to the **Hawaii Tropical Botanical Garden** (27-717 Old

Mamalahoa Highway; 808-964-5233; htbg.com). You're ahead of the crowd, so relish the peace in a tropical wonderland resplendent with bromeliads, heliconias, brilliant gingers, and delicate, buttery orchids. The garden holds more than 2,000 exotic species from all over the tropics.

9 *Water Rush* 11 a.m.

Akaka Falls State Park (end of Akaka Falls Road; 808-974-6200; hawaiistateparks.org) provides a final

opportunity to inhale nature's gifts on the Big Island. It's a short drive off Route 19 through the tiny former plantation town of Honomu. Take the 20-minute circular hike through bamboo groves, fern banks, and jungle flowers to view two beautiful waterfalls. The more impressive is Akaka, which tumbles 420 feet into a turbulent gorge eaten away by centuries of aquatic pounding. It's a no-frills tourist spot breathtaking in its raw simplicity—a perfect last taste of Hilo.

ABOVE Inside the Thurston Lava Tube, formed as a lava flow left behind a hardened outer crust.

OPPOSITE Hike through bamboo groves, fern banks, and jungle flowers to Akaka Falls, which tumbles 420 feet.

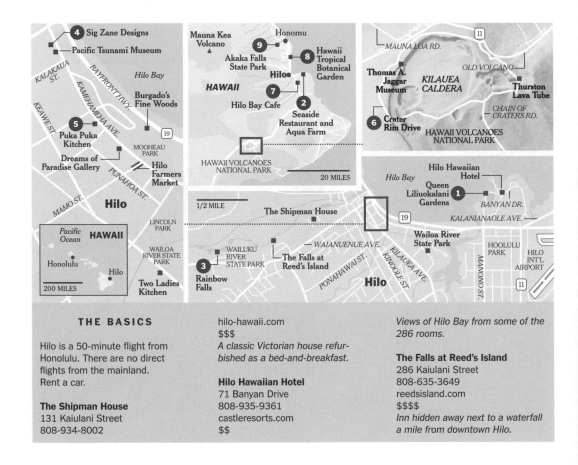

THE BASICS

Hilo is a 50-minute flight from Honolulu. There are no direct flights from the mainland. Rent a car.

The Shipman House
131 Kaiulani Street
808-934-8002

hilo-hawaii.com
$$$
A classic Victorian house refurbished as a bed-and-breakfast.

Hilo Hawaiian Hotel
71 Banyan Drive
808-935-9361
castleresorts.com
$$

Views of Hilo Bay from some of the 286 rooms.

The Falls at Reed's Island
286 Kaiulani Street
808-635-3649
reedsisland.com
$$$$
Inn hidden away next to a waterfall a mile from downtown Hilo.

Kauai

Kauai is a hot spot, and its beautiful North Shore, where majestic mountains meet the surging sea, is hottest. Two or three decades ago, when Maui was the place, Kauaians grinned and thought, "Good, we've got ours and we're going to keep it that way." Now, residents make their livings catering to tourists and pampering the movie stars and magnates who are collecting North Shore trophy homes. But with 60,000 people, this is still the least populated of the four major Hawaiian islands, and its spacious white beaches ring a lush, untrammeled interior. Kauai roads may not be marked, and numbers are rarely posted, so it helps to memorize the two most important directional words—mauka, meaning toward the mountains, and makai, for toward the ocean. When you ask directions, be ready for an answer like this: "Go a mile to the big mango tree, take a left, and head makai."
— BY CHARLES E. ROESSLER

FRIDAY

1 *Big Stretch* 5 p.m.

Your drive from the airport, north and then west on the Kuhio Highway following the curves of the coast, will take you through small towns and lush tropical countryside, with the bonus of a few coastal views, all the way to Hanalei, the last town on the North Shore. (Don't be surprised if you also see a rooster or two—wild chickens, descendants of escapees from domesticated flocks, are abundant on Kauai.) But for the best reward, stay with the highway past Hanalei, all the way until it ends at Kauai's northwest tip. On the last stretch, the road narrows, shrinking to one-lane bridges over inlets and streams, against a misty backdrop of volcanic hills and cliffs. It ends at **Haena State Park** (hawaiistateparks.org), where reef-protected Ke`e Beach offers a serene spot to take in the remains of the day. If there's time and conditions are mellow, it's a short swim out to the reef for some quality snorkeling.

2 *Feast at Sunset* 6:30 p.m.

When you enter the **St. Regis Princeville** (5520 Ka Haku Road; 808-826-9644; princeville.com) make your way straight to the **Makana Terrace** (stregisprinceville.com/dining/makana-terrace; $$$) to take in the sweeping Hanalei Bay view. Settle

in, order the signature cocktail, blending passion fruit and Champagne, and look out across the water. The mountains on the other side stood in for Bali Hai in the movie *South Pacific*. (Be sure to arrive before sunset.) You may also see some surfers if the waves are right—the North Shore is popular for surfing and all of its relatives—windsurfing, body-boarding, stand-up paddling. Stay for a buffet dinner ($$$), or move indoors in the hotel to the **Kauai Grill** ($$$), where the frequently changing menu includes entrees like soy-glazed short ribs with papaya-jalapeno puree. After dinner, walk down to the beach, spectacular under a full moon.

SATURDAY

3 *Morning by the Sea* 7:30 a.m.

Take a stroll on the Princeville walking path, paralleling the road leading into the planned community of **Princeville**, and look out over the Robert Trent Jones Jr. golf course. At this time of day there is a good chance of seeing double rainbows in the direction of the misty mountains.

OPPOSITE AND BELOW Hanalei Bay and the pier at Hanalei on a cloudy day in December. Magnates and movie stars have arrived, but Kauai is still the least populated of the four main Hawaiian islands.

4 *A Flyover* 9 a.m.

Get on board with **Sunshine Helicopters** (808-245-8881; sunshinehelicopters.com/kauai) at the tiny Princeville Airport on Highway 56 and soar

ABOVE Houses along the golf course in the North Shore planned community of Princeville.

BELOW Kauai is popular for surfing and all of its relatives — windsurfing, body-boarding, stand-up paddling.

OPPOSITE The cliffs of the Na Pali Coast, inaccessible by road. One way to see them is on a scenic helicopter ride.

into the heart of Kauai. The trip takes just 50 minutes, but you'll revisit it in dreams. You fly along the dark walls of Waialeale Crater, home to the Hawaiian gods and shoulder to the wettest spot on Earth (more than 450 inches of rain a year), Mount Waialeale (pronounced way-AH-lay-AH-lay). Among the waterfalls plunging around and below you as you sweep along the mountain faces is one that appeared in *Jurassic Park*. You soar over Waimea Canyon; knife into valleys once inhabited by the ancient Hawaiians, now home to wild pigs and goats; and glide along the dramatic Na Pali Coast. Expect to pay in the neighborhood of $300 per person.

5 *Nene Spotting* 11 a.m.

Jutting out from the North Shore, the **Kilauea Lighthouse** (end of Kilauea Lighthouse Road;

808-828-0168; fws.gov/kilaueapoint) provided a life-saving beacon for the first trans-Pacific flight from the West Coast in 1927. Now it is part of the **Kilauea Point National Wildlife Refuge** and offers both an unobstructed view of striking shoreline and a chance to spot dolphins, sea turtles, and whales. Birders who visit here check off species like the red-footed booby, the great frigatebird, and the nene, or Hawaiian goose.

6 *Saddle Up* Noon

Grab an ono (delicious) ahi wrap or other takeout lunch at **Kilauea Fish Market** (4270 Kilauea Lighthouse Road, Kilauea; 808-828-6244; $) to eat a few miles mauka as you listen to instructions for your two-hour horseback ride at the **Silver Falls Ranch** (2888 Kamookoa Road; 808-828-6718; silverfallsranch.com). Imagine what life must have been like for the cowboys who raised cattle for islanders in years past. As you meander through fern and eucalyptus toward Mount Namahana, the stately peak of an extinct volcano, listen for the small streams that trickle along, hidden by the ferns. This is the Kauai that most visitors miss and most locals love (about $100 to $125; call ahead for directions and reservations).

7 *Kauaians' Favorite Beach* 4 p.m.

Another local favorite is **Kalihiwai Beach**, at the end of Kalihiwai Road, where a wide river empties into the ocean, and joggers, boogie boarders, and dog owners share a piece of the shore. There are no amenities but you can take a dip or body surf in the shore break. And this late in the afternoon, you shouldn't need sun block if you want to stretch out and catch a few Z's or watch the seabirds work the ocean.

8 *Laid-Back Fine Dining* 7 p.m.

Postcards (5-5075 Kuhio Highway; 808-826-1191; postcardscafe.com; $$-$$$) offers mostly organic food in the picturesque town of Hanalei. Start with the taro fritters with pineapple ginger chutney, and try grilled fish with peppered pineapple sage or shrimp enchiladas. The modest portions leave room for a piece of banana and macadamia nut pie.

SUNDAY

9 *Botanicals* 9:30 a.m.

Limahuli Gardens in Haena (5-8291 Kuhio Highway; 808-826-1053; ntbg.org/gardens/limahuli.php), one of five National Tropical Botanical Gardens in the country, is in a valley where, 1,800 years ago, the first Hawaiians, with taro as their staple, developed a complex, hierarchical social system. On your self-guided tour, amid native plants like the ohia lehua tree and imports from Polynesia like breadfruit and banana trees, you can see the lava-rock terraces where taro was grown, fed by a series of

or works by Hawaii-based artists at **Aloha Images** (4-1383 Kuhio Highway; 808-821-1382). At **Mermaids Cafe** (4-1384 Kuhio Highway; 808-821-2026; mermaidskauai.com; $$), order a focaccia sandwich or a tofu coconut curry plate. Make one last stop at **Orchid Alley** (4-1383 Kuhio Highway; 808-822-0486; orchidalleykauai.com) and have some tropical flowers shipped home to meet you on the mainland.

fresh-water canals. You will also find exquisite vistas; the Polynesians chose a lovely spot. Guided tours are at 10 a.m.; reservations are required.

10 *Ship the Orchids Home* 11 a.m.

As you head back to the Lihue Airport, stop in the town of Kapaa for high-end aloha shirts and skirts at **Hula Girl the Vintage Collection** (4-1340 Kuhio Highway, 808-822-1950); glass art at **Kela's** (4-1354 Kuhio Highway; 808-822-4527; glass-art.com);

ABOVE Sunset at Ke'e Beach in Haena State Park, the last stop on the road west on the North Shore.

OPPOSITE The road to Ke'e narrows in the last stretch, shrinking to one-lane bridges over inlets and streams, against a misty backdrop of volcanic hills and cliffs.

THE BASICS

Lihue, the Kauai airport, is a 25-minute flight from Honolulu. The North Shore is a 40-minute drive north from the airport along Route 56.

Rent a car.

Princeville at Hanalei
5-3900 Kuhio Highway
808-826-9644
stregisprinceville.com
$$$$
Overlooks Hanalei Bay and has hosted many a celebrity.

Sealodge Condominiums
3700 Kamehameha Road
808-826-6751
hestara.com
$$
In Princeville, condo units with sea views.

Hanalei Bay Resort
5380 Honoiki Road
808-826-6522
tradingplaces.com/rentals
$$
156 rooms and condo units.

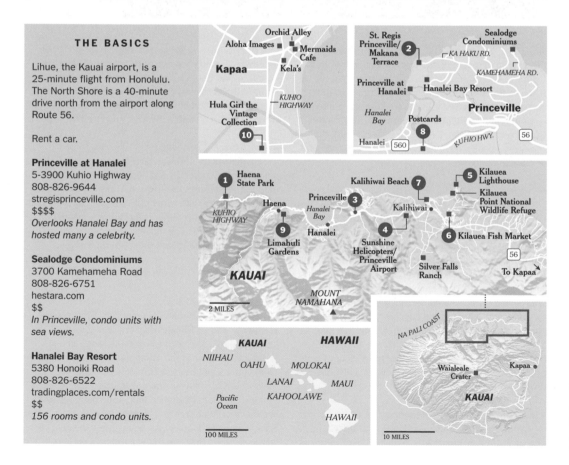

Indexes

PHOTOGRAPHERS

Acknowledgments

We would like to thank everyone at *The New York Times* and at TASCHEN who contributed to the creation of this book.

For the book project itself, special recognition must go to Nina Wiener and Eric Schwartau at TASCHEN, the dedicated editor and assistant behind the scenes; to Natasha Perkel, the *Times* artist whose clear and elegantly crafted maps make the itineraries comprehensible; to Phyllis Collazo of the *Times* staff, whose photo editing gave the book its arresting images; and to Olimpia Zagnoli, whose illustrations and illustrated maps enliven every article and each regional introduction.

Guiding the deft and artful transformation of newspaper material to book form at TASCHEN were Marco Zivny, the book's designer; Josh Baker, the art director; and Jennifer Patrick, production manager. Also at TASCHEN, David Martinez, Jessica Sappenfeld, Anna-Tina Kessler, Kirstin Plate and Janet Kim provided production assistance, and at the *Times*, Heidi Giovine helped at critical moments. Craig B. Gaines copy-edited the manuscript.

But the indebtedness goes much further back. This book grew out of the work of all of the editors, writers, photographers, and *Times* staff people whose contributions and support for the weekly "36 Hours" column built a rich archive over many years.

For this legacy, credit must go first to Stuart Emmrich, who created the column in 2002 and then refined the concept and guided its development over eight years, first as the *Times* Escapes editor and then as Travel editor. Without his vision, there would be no "36 Hours."

Great thanks must go to all of the writers and photographers whose work appears in the book, both *Times* staffers and freelancers.

And a legion of *Times* editors behind the scenes made it all happen, and still do.

Danielle Mattoon, who took over as Travel editor in 2010, has brought her steady hand to "36 Hours," and found time to be supportive of this book as well.

Suzanne MacNeille, now the column's direct editor, and her predecessors Jeff Z. Klein and Denny Lee have all superbly filled the role of finding and working with writers, choosing and assigning destinations, and assuring that the weekly product would entertain and inform readers while upholding *Times* journalistic standards. The former Escapes editors Amy Virshup and Mervyn Rothstein saw the column through many of its early years, assuring its consistent quality.

The talented *Times* photo editors who have overseen images and directed the work of the column's photographers include Lonnie Schlein, Jessica DeWitt, Gina Privitere, Darcy Eveleigh, Laura O'Neill, Chris Jones, and the late John Forbes. The newspaper column's design is the work of the *Times* art director Rodrigo Honeywell.

Among the many editors on the *Times* Travel and Escapes copy desks who have kept "36 Hours" at its best over the years, three who stand out are Florence Stickney, Steve Bailey, and Carl Sommers. Editors of the column on the *New York Times* web site have been Alice Dubois, David Allan, Miki Meek, Allison Busacca, and Danielle Belopotosky. Much of the fact-checking, that most invaluable and unsung of skills, was in the hands of Rusha Haljuci, Nick Kaye, Anna Bahney, and George Gustines.

Finally, we must offer a special acknowledgment to Benedikt Taschen, whose longtime readership and interest in the "36 Hours" column led to the partnership of our two companies to produce this book.

— BARBARA IRELAND AND ALEX WARD

Copyright © 2013 *The New York Times*. All Rights Reserved.

Editor Barbara Ireland
Project management Alex Ward
Photo editor Phyllis Collazo
Maps Natasha Perkel
Spot illustrations and region maps Olimpia Zagnoli
Editorial coordination Nina Wiener and Eric Schwartau
Art direction Marco Zivny and Josh Baker
Layout and design Marco Zivny
Production Jennifer Patrick

To stay informed about upcoming TASCHEN titles, please request our magazine at www.taschen.com/magazine or write to TASCHEN, Hohenzollernring 53, D–50672 Cologne, Germany, contact@taschen.com. We will be happy to send you a free copy of our magazine which is filled with information about all of our books.

© 2013 TASCHEN GmbH
Hohenzollernring 53, D–50672 Köln, www.taschen.com

ISBN 978-3-8365-4204-3   Printed in China

TRUST *THE NEW YORK TIMES* WITH YOUR NEXT 36 HOURS

"The ultimate weekend planner for the literate by the literate — where even Oklahoma City can be as alluring as Paris." —AMAZON READER REVIEW

AVAILABLE IN *THE NEW YORK TIMES* 36 HOURS SERIES

150 WEEKENDS IN THE USA & CANADA*

Weekends on the road. The ultimate travel guide to the USA and Canada

125 WEEKENDS IN EUROPE

(Re)discovering Europe: dream weekends with practical itineraries from Paris to Perm

* also available for iPad

USA & CANADA REGION BY REGION

NORTHEAST **SOUTHEAST** **MIDWEST & GREAT LAKES** **SOUTHWEST & ROCKY MOUNTAINS** **WEST COAST**

FOR NEWS ON UPCOMING BOOKS IN THIS SERIES, VISIT WWW.TASCHEN.COM

Whitehorse 168

VANCOUVER 144

Whistler 150

Homer 164

Juneau 160

the San Juan Islands 140

SEATTLE 128

Northwest Seattle 134

the Oregon Coast 120

PORTLAND 12

Sonoma County 106

Berkeley 96

Kauai 192

HONOLULU 172

the Mission, San Francisco 90

Silicon Valley 78

MoloKai 176

Maui 182

Hilo 186

Malibu 34

Pasadena 26

HOLLYWOOD 22

Santa Monica 30

Downtown 16